MW01093288

Account Rendered

A Dossier on my Former Self

ISBN: 978-0-9614696-4-1

Published by Plunkett Lake Press, 2016
www.plunkettlakepress.com

Also available from Plunkett Lake Press as an electronic book:
www.plunkettlakepress.com/ar

Account Rendered

A Dossier on my Former Self

by Melita Maschmann

translated from the German by Geoffrey Strachan

introduction by Helen Epstein

afterword by Marianne Schweitzer Burkenroad
with Helen Epstein

PLUNKETT LAKE PRESS

Lexington, Massachusetts

CONTENTS

Introduction by Helen Epstein   7

Author's note   13

Account Rendered (sections 1 through 18)   14

Afterword by Marianne Schweitzer Burkenroad
with Helen Epstein   276

Introduction

Why is Plunkett Lake Press republishing this memoir by a former member of the Hitler Youth 50 years after it first appeared in Germany in the spring of 1963?

The simple answer is that *Account Rendered: A Dossier on my Former Self* was highly recommended to us by a friend and veteran editor. Arthur Samuelson was a student at Hampshire College in 1971 when he designed one of the first courses on the Holocaust. "There weren't a lot of books by former Nazis in the Sixties," he said. "I found in it someone who had been overtaken by history, was struggling to make sense of what no longer made sense, and to understand why it had once done so. In other books, the Jews were an abstraction. For Maschmann, the Jews were neighbors and friends, which complicated the process of dehumanization that she participated in. The memoir seemed believable and honest in ways that other testimonies from the defeated did not."

For many readers steeped in the literature of the second world war and for descendants of Holocaust survivors like myself, any account of how an intelligent, socially-conscious, well-educated teenager became a Nazi is extremely painful to read. In Germany of 1963 as well as in England, France, Poland, Holland, and the U.S. where it was later published in translation, many perceived *Account Rendered* as a brazen attempt at justification. However, since 1933 when 15-year-old Melita Maschmann secretly joined the Hitler Youth, the world has seen teenagers from every continent drawn to murderous movements. This memoir, whose title we might now translate as Bottom Line, is relevant and necessary reading.

7

Maschmann's memoir was published in the same year as Hannah Arendt's *Eichmann in Jerusalem: A Report on the Banality of Evil.* Maschmann and Arendt corresponded briefly then, with the author explaining that it took her 10 years to "re-orient" herself and that her aim in writing *Account Rendered* was to help her former colleagues reflect on their actions and the victims of Nazism to "better understand" people like her. Arendt replied that her book is an "important document of its time" and continued, "I have the impression that you are totally sincere, otherwise I wouldn't have written back to you." (Their brief correspondence is available online).

The German publisher, mainstream Deutsche Verlags-Anstalt Stuttgart (DVA), was well aware of *Account Rendered*'s relevance as the German parliament debated the Statute of Limitations on crimes committed during Nazism. Germans were still talking about the Eichmann Trial that had been internationally televised two years before. After receiving both positive and negative reviews, Maschmann's memoir was adopted as a textbook by the North Rhine Westphalian Office of Education and became a teaching tool in Germany, reprinted seven times between 1964 and 1987.

For former Nazis and their families, the account of Maschmann's experiences as head of Press and Propaganda in the League of Girls of the Hitler Youth and as a volunteer in the Labor Service "resettling" Polish farmers was a betrayal. Some of her former colleagues never forgave her for writing it. Many thought she should have simply kept quiet.

By 1978, German cultural and historical consciousness had evolved as Germans grappled with their 20th century history at home and in public. Independent scholar Dagmar Reese points out that "in 1963, *Account Rendered* was part of the debate on Nazi guilt and German responsibility, while in 1978, when German readers got more and more interested in ordinary life in Nazi society, her book was sold as an ostensibly ordinary memoir of a former member of the Hitler Youth." In recent years,

Germans have been exploring the theme of their own victimization by Hitler.

Historians of Nazism, including Daniel Goldhagen and Claudia Koonz, utilized *Account Rendered* as a primary source; scholars from other disciplines recognized it as rare testimony by a woman perpetrator; still others as a meaty text to problematize. They questioned Maschmann's reliability as a narrator, her veracity, and her motivation in writing it at the age of 40 — years after her putative de-Nazification. They theorized about the Jewish school friend to whom the memoir is addressed. Was she a construct, a composite, or a reality?

* * *

There is little biographical information about Melita Maschmann in the public domain and what follows is from interviews of her sister-in-law, niece and nephew: Melita and her twin brother Hans-Hermann were born on January 10, 1918 in Berlin, the third and fourth children of an upper-middle class German family. Their mother Frieda was the daughter of Adam Hufnagel, "purveyor to the Court" of leather goods in Darmstadt, a small city in the western German province of Hesse. Their father, Johann, was from nearby Mainz. The Maschmanns married in 1904 and in 1908 moved to Berlin where Johann and his brother ran Thomas Cook's World Travel Agency.

The Maschmanns' eldest son Ernst was born in 1904 and continued in the family's bourgeois tradition. He studied law in Berlin and Tübingen and became an administrative judge. A second son, Helmut, was born in 1909, joined the family's leather business in Darmstadt, and took it over after his uncle's death.

While the Maschmanns were conservative and nationalist, there is no evidence that her parents encouraged Melita toward Nazism. In *Account Rendered,* she describes learning about Hitler from the house seamstress who made her clothes. Melita found the woman's ideas so compelling that she secretly joined the Hitler Youth movement in 1933 when she was 15.

Melita in 1926 with her father, Johann Maschmann, her twin brother Hans-Hermann and her mother, Frieda Hufnagel (courtesy Maschmann family)

After finishing high school, Melita worked in press and propaganda in the League of Girls. She led a Women's Labour Service camp in occupied Poland in 1941 and then was put in charge of press and propaganda for the League of Girls in Berlin between 1943 and 1945.

She was arrested by the American Army that July as part of a clandestine Nazi group manufacturing false documents, and interned first in the "Frauenlager 77" (an internment camp for German women) near Ludwigsburg, and later in Darmstadt until 1948. She was classified by the de-Nazification authorities as a "follower" (too young to be fully responsible for her actions) and was 30 years old when she returned to civilian life in Darmstadt.

Johann and Frieda Maschmann did not survive the war. After the Nazis closed the Thomas Cook Agency in 1940, they moved to Darmstadt and lived on income from the Hufnagel leather works. They were killed during one of the Allied bombings of Darmstadt that destroyed their leather works along with 70% of the city.

During Melita's time in the Hitler Youth (1933-1945), her twin brother Hans-Hermann completed high school, compulsory labor service and military service. During the war, he served as a soldier in the Wehrmacht in Austria and Russia. In 1944, Hans-

Hermann was hospitalized for tuberculosis and treated in a sanatorium. In 1947, he moved back to Darmstadt. In 1955, he married Hannelore Wilk, the daughter of an architect, and went into the travel business.

After her release from prison, Melita had, according to her sister-in-law, difficulty finding a community in post-war Germany. She attended philosophy lectures at the University of Frankfurt am Main and spent a year in France before beginning to write articles and legal columns for the *Darmstädter Echo* and *Frankfurter Rundschau,* center-left – rather than right-wing – newspapers. In her afterword to the 1978 edition of *Account Rendered,* the historian Helga Grebing emphasized Maschmann's "severe poverty" and her resistance against any form of attachment.

Melita Maschmann in the 1950s

Melita was drawn to Eastern philosophy, traveled to Afghanistan and India in 1962-63 and decided to reside in India permanently shortly thereafter. She found a guru in Sri Anandamayi Ma, a woman venerated as a "living saint," and returned to Germany only for a few weeks every two or three years. While Sri Anandamayi Ma was alive, Melita lived in ashrams connected to her teachings. After 1982, Melita lived and worked in various institutions for orphaned or abandoned children.

In addition to *Account Rendered,* Melita wrote a few novels and short stories (*Die Aschenspur, Der Dreizehnte, Das Wort hiess Liebe*) and several books about Sri Anandamayi Ma and India (*Der Tiger singt Kirtana, Indiras Schwestern, Eine ganz gewöhnliche Heilige*).

Melita Maschmann c. 1975 *(courtesy Maschmann family)*

Melita Maschmann returned to Darmstadt in 1998, at 80, suffering from Alzheimer's disease. She died on Feb 4, 2010 in a retirement home near Darmstadt. She never married and had no children.

Helen Epstein
Lexington, Massachusetts
April 2013

Author's note

The letter form was chosen for this account because it enables the facts of the past to be presented more vividly. They can be viewed in the twin perspectives of those days and our own time. But the letter is not fiction.

Some of the names which are mentioned have been altered. All other facts are as the author has remembered them.

This is my second letter to you since we last saw one another twenty-five years ago. The first one I wrote to you in 1948, soon after my release from internment. I do not know if it reached you. I sent it to your mother, from whom I had word that she was in New York.

Since then I have often continued my conversation with you, awake and in dreams, but I have never again tried to write any of it down.

Now today I feel impelled to do so. I was prompted to this by a trivial incident. A woman spoke to me in the street and the way she held her head suddenly reminded me quite strikingly of you. But what is the real reason which made me sit down and write to you as soon as I came in?

Perhaps in the intervening years I have, without being aware of it, prepared an account within me which must be presented.

What roads we have both had to travel — roads which led us through the midst of a human catastrophe — since I repaid your trust with indifference and indeed with enmity.

I have often thought about my own road during the past ten years. Wrongs once committed can never be undone by such reflection. But perhaps it enables the individual to recognize a wrong more quickly and not to be seduced by one again.

With you as a witness, I should like to try once more to go over the result of my reflections on the past. You will compel me to be much more precise than I could be if left to myself.

But will you be in any way prepared to go along with me? Am I not asking something of you that you can only feel to be an importunity?

Do not be afraid that I want to justify myself. Even the element of fate in a person's life does not dispose of individual guilt, I know that. What I hope, dare to hope, is that you might gradually be able to understand — not excuse — the wrong and even the evil steps which I took and which I must report, and that such an understanding might form the basis for a lasting dialogue.

14

~ 1 ~

January 30 1933! We both lived through this day in Berlin, although we did not yet know one another. It was not until Easter that you joined my class. I do not know what memories you may associate with the 'Day of the seizure of power'. They will be darker ones than mine.

That day our dressmaker had to alter a dress of my mother's to fit me. I dreaded the tiresome fittings but I liked the dressmaker very much. The fact that she limped and was a hunchback set her apart from all the other people around me and I felt there was a vague connection between her physical distinctiveness and what she herself called her 'socialist convictions'.

The table on which I did my homework — I was just fifteen — stood beside her sewing machine and when my mother left us alone together she often told me about her political activities. For as long as I had known her she had worn an embossed metal swastika under the lapel of her coat. That day she wore it openly for the first time and her dark eyes shone as she talked of Hitler's victory. My mother was displeased. She thought it presumptuous for uneducated people to concern themselves with politics.

But it was the very fact that this woman was one of the common people that made her attractive to me. I felt myself drawn to her for the same reason that I often inwardly took the maids' part against my mother. I realize now that my antagonism to every manifestation of bourgeois snobbery, which I acquired early in life, was nourished by a reaction against my authoritarian upbringing. My mother expected from her children the same unquestioning obedience as she required of the maids or of my father's chauffeur. This attitude drove me to a rebelliousness which went beyond the purely personal rebellion of adolescence and was directed against the bourgeois values which my parents represented.

There must be many answers to the question — what caused young people to become National Socialists at that time. For people at a certain stage of adolescence the antagonism between the generations, taken in conjunction with Hitler's seizure of power, probably often played a part in it. For me it turned the scale. I wanted to follow a different road from the conservative one prescribed for me by family tradition. In my parents' mouths the words 'social' or 'socialist' had a scornful ring. They used them when they waxed indignant over the hunchback dressmaker's desire to play an active part in politics. On January 30 1933 she announced that a time was now at hand when servants would no longer have to eat off the kitchen table. My mother always treated her servants correctly but it would have seemed absurd to her to share their company at table.

No catchword has ever fascinated me quite as much as that of the 'National Community' *(Volksgemeinschaft)*. I heard it first from the lips of this crippled and care-worn dressmaker and, spoken on the evening of January 30, it acquired a magical glow. The manner of my first encounter with it fixed its meaning for me: I felt it could only be brought into being by declaring war on the class prejudices of the social stratum from which I came and that it must, above all, give protection and justice to the weak. What held my allegiance to this idealistic fantasy was the hope that a state of affairs could be created in which people of all classes would live together like brothers and sisters.

On the evening of January 30 my parents took us children, my twin brother and myself, into the centre of the city. There we witnessed the torchlight procession with which the National Socialists celebrated their victory. Some of the uncanny feel of that night remains with me even today. The crashing tread of the feet, the sombre pomp of the red and black flags, the flickering light from the torches on the faces and the songs with melodies that were at once aggressive and sentimental.

For hours the columns marched by. Again and again amongst them we saw groups of boys and girls scarcely older than ourselves. What was I, who was only allowed to stand on the pavement and watch, feeling at my back the icy blast which emanated from my parents' reserve? Hardly more than a chance spectator, a child who was still given schoolgirl stories for Christmas. And yet I longed to hurl myself into this current, to be submerged and borne along by it.

Do you remember the agonizing intensity of your own search for a fundamental purpose at that time? Later on we shared many conversations in pursuit of it. At that age one finds a life which consists of school work, family outings and birthday invitations wretchedly and shamefully barren of significance. Nobody gives one credit for being interested in more than these derisory trivialities. Nobody says: "You are needed for something more important; come!" Where serious matters are concerned one does not yet count.

But the boys and girls in the marching columns did count. Like the adults, they carried banners on which the names of their dead were written.

At one point somebody suddenly leaped from the ranks of the marchers and struck a man who had been standing only a few paces away from us. Perhaps he had made a hostile remark. I saw him fall to the ground with blood streaming down his face and I heard him cry out. Our parents hurriedly drew us away from the scuffle, but they had not been able to stop us seeing the man bleeding. The image of him haunted me for days.

The horror it inspired in me was almost imperceptibly spiced with an intoxicating joy. 'For the flag we are ready to die', the torch-bearers had sung. It was not a matter of clothing or food or school essays, but of life and death. For whom? For me as well? I do not know if I asked myself this question at that moment, but I know I was overcome with a burning desire to belong to these people for whom it was a matter of life and death.

Whenever I probe the reasons which drew me to join the Hitler Youth, I always come up against this one: I wanted to escape from my childish, narrow life and I wanted to attach myself to something that was great and fundamental. This longing I shared with countless others of my contemporaries.

It will be more difficult to explain how this impulse carried me forward through the twelve years up to 1945. The fact that I clung to National Socialism for so long is bound up with the experiences of my early childhood. It is noteworthy that while the 'socialist' tendency expressed in the name of the movement attracted me because it strengthened me in my opposition to my conservative home, the nationalist tendency, in contrast to this, was meaningful to me just because it was in harmony with the spirit that had been drummed into me since my infancy. In order to explain how deeply nationalist thought and feeling were ingrained into my life from an early age I must go into my childhood in more detail than might seem necessary to you in connection with the question I am discussing. But my own childhood experiences corresponded to those of a whole generation, which grew up at that time in right wing middle class surroundings, and from whose ranks much of the young leadership of the National Socialist movement and the army of the Third Reich was later drawn.

My parents were avid newspaper readers. Their exchanges of opinion about political news would begin over breakfast. Even before we had mastered our multiplication tables we knew that there were right wing and left wing parties and that our parents belonged to the German National Party, for which the subscription was collected every Monday by 'the political woman'. This was the name given her by my twin brother. She was an impoverished noblewoman. This by itself made her interesting to us children. She always wore the same oldfashioned riding habit and we would hear her bewailing the loss of her East German home in a shrill voice. Almost everything our mother ever said about politics was also uttered in a tone of lament. I never sought to ask her later on if she had, in fact, made a systematic attempt to give her children a political education. There is much to suggest that she had. She loved Germany as unquestioningly as she loved her own home town or her parents. But there was nothing joyful about this love. Countless times she impressed upon us that Germany had lost the War, although no nation had braver soldiers. Her lands had been carved up on every side in a shameful dictated peace, her economy was in decline, thanks to the reparation payments demanded by the former enemy countries. Her culture was dominated by foreigners. She was poor and mortally sick.

Long before I could see the connection in all this, indeed before I understood the meaning of the word 'Germany', I loved it as something mysteriously overshadowed with grief, something infinitely dear and threatened by danger.

My brother and I were not yet at school when my mother took us with her to her home town. At that time the Rhineland was occupied by the French. We met the first coloured soldiers on the train. The sight of them filled me with dread. We fled into an empty compartment. I cannot remember what my mother said to soothe us, but I remember a feeling of horror, as if all the misery of Germany were incarnate in those black skinned men.

One night in our seventh year my brother and I were fetched out of bed by our parents and brought into the dining room where the wireless stood. It was midnight. It was at this hour that the occupying troops began to leave the Rhineland. Our parents thrust the headphones over our tousled hair. "Can you hear? Those are the bells of Cologne Cathedral. The English are going. The occupation is over. Our home is a free country once more."

The earpieces buzzed violently and alarmingly. The parents' eyes were filled with tears and the children were left with the vague feeling that this 'Germany' must be a terrible and wonderful mystery.

As ten-year-olds my brother and I stood for hours in the company of many gaily dressed people at the window of an hotel on the Unter den Linden and waited for the moment when an old man with a mighty, square, white head, which nodded dignified greetings, drove past beneath us. It was Hindenburg's eightieth birthday. We had posies of violets in our hands which we were allowed to throw at him. We heard the surge of cheering in the distance, swelling as it drew nearer. Beneath the window someone began to sing *Deutschland, Deutschland über Alles.* The old man in the car — we understood this much — was something like a father to all Germans. Many people had hopes that he would lead our nation out of poverty. The poverty was connected with the war which we had lost. It seems to me in retrospect as if there was no topic of conversation during my childhood which was discussed more frequently or with more passionate seriousness than the World War. It was the second mystery cloaked in grief and lamentation, whose significance we only gradually grasped, but the bitterness of which had soaked into our feelings and consciousness since the day the latter began to open themselves to the world.

The War was fought over Germany, and it had been lost. But what did that mean? I remember one day in the travel bureau where my father worked sitting for a long time opposite two foreigners who were talking to one another. I asked myself then if foreign people like these two men, whose language I did not understand, had meant to march into our country and make it their own. If that were true, then one must fear and hate foreigners. They had not come as far as Berlin, but the grownups were forever lamenting the fact that they had stolen parts of our country. They had killed countless Germans who were trying to stop the foreigners robbing our country. And because too many of the men of our nation had been killed we had lost the War.

These notions only gradually took on flesh and blood. When the boy next door died in hospital and never came back to play with us, one gained some idea of what it meant for men to have died in the War — brutally killed by enemy people, like the grey cat that was killed by the porter because it chased his chickens.

In the drawer where I hoarded my 'treasures' there lay for a long time a photograph taken from a war book one of my elder brothers had thrown away, which I had 'gutted'. Five soldiers stood beside a mound of earth with their heads bowed and their steel helmets in their hands. A wooden cross was planted in the mound. I can still remember the exact wording of the caption. It said: 'The second man from the left fell next day.'

"The soldiers are praying for a fallen comrade," my mother explained. "He died for Germany and they have dug him a grave."

"We've dug a grave too," said my brother, "near the summer house, for the dead swallow that was lying by the fence this morning."

It was dreadful to hold it in one's hand. Something which had been alive, now stiff and motionless as a stone. The horror of it clung to one's hand all day. But a dead person? It was something that did not bear thinking about. Your brother, for example, who was standing there beside you — dead, stiff and motionless as a stone? They would lay him in the earth; the sand would trickle into his eyes and ears...

The picture of the soldiers at prayer both fascinated and frightened me: concealed in it were the two great mysteries, God and death, combined with the other mystery — Germany.

Gradually I built up more concrete conceptions. From our parents' political conversations at the breakfast table, which were related to their newspaper reading, we learned about current issues — the outcome of an election, new decrees, or negotiations with the former enemy countries.

One of my elder brothers amused himself by teaching me the first Latin sentence which he himself had had to learn: *Inter filios agricolae semper discordia erat.* He did explain to me what the words meant and I understood, but nevertheless they somehow impressed themselves on my mind as a formula to describe the everlasting discord between the men who met in the Reichstag to direct the fortunes of the German people.

The desperate struggle to save democracy, which was then being fought out, was not recognized or appreciated by my parents. We never heard the grownups do anything but curse about the chaotic squabbling of this parliament. Ultimately one came to understand that things ran so wild there because the Germans had splintered into a senseless multiplicity of parties, which had their knives into one another quite literally. As I remember it, hardly a day seems to have passed when my mother did not read out a news item from the morning paper about some political murder.

We had every reason to be ashamed that it was so. The woman in the oldfashioned riding habit would say: "In the old days, when there was still the Kaiser, the Germans never squabbled like this. In those days you could be proud that you were a German. But now the elected representatives of the people bombard one another with inkpots."

Part of the misery about which the adults complained daily was unemployment. One could have no conception of what it meant for four, five or even six million people to have no work. Berlin had four million inhabitants. It was the largest city in Germany. Imagine all the families living in Berlin having scarcely enough dry bread to satisfy their hunger...

Although our front door had a plate fitted to it which said *No Hawkers or Beggars,* there were days on which not an hour went by without the sad concert of organ grinders or street musicians, and often enough beggars would be ringing at front doors at the same time. It was not possible to forget, even for a short while, that we had been born in a poor country.

One episode which I associate with the unemployment remains fixed in my mind. The son of some people we knew sometimes used to lie drunk in the back yard because his father refused to let him in. At this our maid would remark: "He's boozed away all his dole money in one night again." Of course his behaviour was doubtless quite untypical of the unemployed, but that is beside the point here. One day his mother was heard screaming as if she had gone out of her mind. He had opened an artery with a kitchen knife. I had met him a few hours before, walking barefoot in a tattered army greatcoat with a little dog in his arms.

It would be easy to go on recalling such experiences. You will object that I have remembered events and facts selectively. That is true. These things impressed themselves upon me because they fitted in with the picture offered me by the political bias of my home. My parents rejected the Weimar Republic. Both consciously and unconsciously they directed their children's attention towards those facts which were likely to discredit the new system. They themselves saw only the blunders and had no eyes for the desperate struggle of the men who were trying to save the Republic. Even the exceptional burgeoning of intellectual and artistic creativity in those years escaped their notice.

All the events which I have enumerated for you tended in the same direction: they prepared me for that mysterious and fascinating summons of January 30 1933, which I could not resist, although I was still a child and in no way a precocious one.

I believed the National Socialists when they promised to do away with unemployment and with it the poverty of six million people. I believed them when they said they would reunite the German nation, which had split into more than forty political parties, and overcome the consequences of the dictated peace of Versailles. And if my faith could only be based on hope in January 1933, it seemed soon enough to have deeds to point to. But these things are familiar to you. What I wanted to attempt to explain to you and your children — for perhaps you are even now beginning to discuss these questions with them — is that the rising generation of the middle class, who stood on the threshold between childhood and adolescence at the time of Hitler's seizure of power, had been fatally prepared to fall victim to his 'ideas', even when their parents were hostile to National Socialism.

You once told me that your sister came home at that time and asked to be allowed to join the Hitler Youth. Do you remember? It was only then she learned from your parents that you were Jewish.

~ 2 ~

For many years my twin brother and I had viewed the boys and
girls we saw who belonged to youth movements with envy and
admiration. Compared with these children of our own age, we
felt at an unfair disadvantage when we had to put up with the
boredom of Sunday outings with the family. I know that you
yourself never felt any inclination to join a youth group. The fact
that from an early age you were an individualist by temperament
was later the cause of many arguments between us. But the
importance your brothers and sisters attached to life in a youth
group helped you to understand my desires, even though you did
not share them.

Gradually our parents' resistance weakened and early in 1933
we were given permission to join a youth league — though only
one whose aims were compatible with the political ideas of our
family. My brother became a member of the German National
Bismarck Youth for a few months until it was forced to disband.
I teased him quite a lot because he had allowed himself to be put
among the 'Monarchists', and when the two Stormtroopers[1]
appeared at our front door to collect his uniform, I enjoyed some
malicious pleasure in handing over his green shirt and cap. I
refused to surrender his breeches and top boots because he could
use them 'for the Hitler Youth'. I was convinced that one day he
would join.

I still remember the rally at the Luna Park in Berlin, at which
the Bismarck Youth gathered its supporters and friends for the

---

[1] Members of the S.A. *(Sturmabteilung);* the National Socialist
militia. *Translator's note.*

last time before disbanding, because of an amusing incident which occurred there. I arrived late but managed to climb through the barrier, and when most of the people were already in their seats I ran up beside a man who was being greeted respectfully on all sides. His face had a startling similarity to portraits of Frederick the Great. I later learned from my parents that it was the 'German Crown Prince', in whose party I had wangled my way onto the platform without intending to. Furthermore I had insisted on going to the rally in the uniform of the *Bund Deutscher Mädel* or B.D.M., the girls' section of the Hitler Youth. On no account did I want to be confused with those who were 'loyal to the Kaiser'. My parents were amazed that I should care to be present at all. The reason for this I carefully kept to myself. I had learned that my comrades in the Hitler Youth were planning to interrupt the proceedings. There was to be 'no harm done — just a bit of a rumpus to annoy the green herrings' — this was what we called the boys of the Bismarck Youth on account of their green shirts. The rumpus was never made, much to my disappointment. Afterwards I could only boast to my brother about how we had let them off lightly. "Anyway that was your last historic appearance!"

At that time we were in the Upper Third Class. There was a senior girl in the Lower First Class who ran the 'League of Luise'[2] group. You will hardly remember now how you and I studied this girl because my parents wanted to send me to her group. Our verdict was crushing. We deemed all the girls who flocked round her to be 'wellborn daughters', arrogant, superficial and boring. They cared only for clothes, dances, social gossip and the like. They sang sentimental songs by Hermann Löns and wore bright blue uniforms because Queen Luise's favourite flower was supposed to have been the cornflower. I therefore refused to join the League of Luise, and as my parents would not allow me to become a member of the

---

[2] Queen Luise of Prussia, wife of Frederick William III and a national heroine. *Translator's note.*

Hitler Youth I joined secretly. Now began my own private 'years of struggle'. I made up for what my new comrades had achieved before 1933, when it had cost personal sacrifices to belong to the National Socialist Youth. But, if I may anticipate, what now awaited me was a bitter disappointment, the extent of which I dared not admit to myself. The evening meetings for which we met in a dark and grimy cellar were fatally lacking in interest.

The time was passed in paying subscriptions, drawing up countless lists and swotting up the words of songs, the linguistic poverty of which I was unable to ignore, although I made a great effort to do so. Discussions on political texts from, say, *Mein Kampf* quickly ended in general silence. Our group leader was an assistant at an optician's. My only noteworthy memory of her is a disagreeable one: on the way home one evening she told me she meant to commit suicide that night. For hours I did not dare to leave her alone. We wandered through the dark streets until she promised me not to put her plan into action for the time being. I do not know what became of her.

I remember with more pleasure the weekend outings, with hikes, sports, campfires and youth hostelling. Occasionally there would be 'field exercises' with neighbouring groups. If there was any rivalry between them the game often degenerated into a first class brawl. What kind of a picture these girls fighting over a flag would have presented to an outsider I prefer not to imagine.

But for me, not even the outings made up for the tedium of the remaining 'duties'. In my group I was the only girl attending a secondary school. The others were shop girls, office workers, dressmakers and servant girls. So my desire to be accepted into the community of 'working youth' had been fulfilled. The fact that this fulfilment was a bitter disappointment I explained to myself thus: these girls came from the lower middle class and regarded the 'wellborn daughters' I was trying to escape from with envy. They were not the real companions I was looking for; 'young working girls' from factories. I understood that such girls had no militant class consciousness, and I wanted to struggle to woo them away from Communism on behalf of the National

Community. I had taken an interest in 'workers' poetry' and my outlook on such matters tended to be romantic.

I soon found a way to break free from my disappointing group, but in so doing I moved in the very direction I had sought to avoid.

You and I discussed all these matters fully on the way to school together, so perhaps much of this will surface again in your memory. In the company of a friend I took the initiative of forming a group that called itself unashamedly the 'Elite Club', which was made up from a selection of girls with intellectual interests from several neighbouring groups. We resolved that we would have no leader but would form a community of equals. We had joined forces not illegally, but certainly unofficially, so we could not allow ourselves to be seen at any club room, and met by turns at the houses of the members. As far as I recall, we tried to read *Foundations of the Nineteenth Century* by Houston Stewart Chamberlain. Most of us went to secondary schools. This worried me, but I comforted myself with the fact that our Elite Club had the express aim of adopting interested members from the working class wherever possible.

The degree of my naivety in those days concerning the aims of National Socialism is apparent from the fact that I plagued you to join our group. I knew you were Jewish and the Party was against the Jews. But after all, of my group 'only half' belonged to the Hitler Youth... You refused and we argued about your 'individualism'. The fact that you probably refused because you had a keener sense of what lay before us only became clear to me many years later. The Elite Club could not survive. The news of its existence reached the ears of our area B.D.M. leader. I was summoned to the subregional office and lectured until my eyes swam and my ears buzzed — dangerous separatism, the Hitler Youth was not a discussion group for wellborn daughters, and so on. I appreciated that I had sinned against the spirit of a community whose badge expressly bore the words: National Socialist Working Youth. My remorse placated the sub-regional leader, and she proposed to me that as I clearly enjoyed reading I should take over the press section. Henceforth my duties consisted of supplying the small daily newspapers which appeared in the area with information and reports about the activity of the B.D.M., as well as collaborating in the production of a series of National Socialist Youth publications.

I was honoured by the task. I was what they called a 'March violet'[3]. My secret entry into the Hitler Youth dated from March 1 1933, and all the leading positions were occupied by the so called 'Old Guard'. I was prepared to respect and admire them without question, but in practice there were difficulties. I liked very few of them, and just because I was a March violet and a high school girl as well, they all looked down on me and made it clear to me that I was not one of them. They were sometimes painfully coarse and primitive, and corresponded — I was unhappy to observe — with the image of 'proletarians' which my mother was wont to evoke. One exception, fortunately not the only one, was afforded by Johanna, my sub-regional leader. She came from a 'humble background' and had no marked intellectual interests, a fact which naturally distressed me in my superior. But she believed in the ideal of a national renewal, which she advocated with passion, and she detested bad behaviour. Her manners were not fastidious. When we had fallen in for roll call and there was chattering in the ranks she would bawl out: "Shut your traps!" Then there was quiet at once.

Johanna's parents had a small inn which the S.A. had been using as a meeting place for years. When she and her sister, who was somewhat younger, were still children, there would often be a dozen pistols thrown under the mattresses on their beds because there was a warning of a police raid. At any rate, such were the stories told amongst the B.D.M. leaders.

The rough, noisy environment of the place had left its mark on Johanna. She would often make us march in three ranks along the

---

[3] Early in 1933 there was a big increase in the Party membership. The new members were scornfully known as 'March violets'. *Author's note.*

Kurfürstendamm and cover part of the distance at the double. When doing this we had to stamp as loudly as possible. "This is where the rich Jews live," she would say. "They need a bit of waking up from their afternoon naps."

Her opposition to the Weimar régime was bound up with the fact that her family had been driven from their West Prussian home at the end of the First World War and the government seemed to be satisfied with the frontiers drawn in 1919.

When I look back on that time from the vantage point of today, many things occur to me which should have struck me as suspicious early on, and should have led me to draw my own conclusions. For example, do you remember my telling you about the alleged murder of Schiller by Goethe?

During a conference for youth leaders we visited a 'museum of Freemasonry' which I have never heard of since. In a glass case were displayed a small bottle containing a brownish liquid and an object which resembled a knitting needle. With this instrument, so the museum attendant told us, Goethe, notorious as a sworn freemason, had treacherously murdered poor Schiller. Naturally the international tribe of freemasons had so far taken care that this crime should not become known. Nor did the Party leadership want there to be any public discussion about it, but a small, select number of particularly reliable people were to be given insight here into this sad and shameful secret. Someone brought a book to the next leaders' meeting, which bore the title *Goethe in Chains*. The wrapper showed one of the later portraits of Goethe — so far as I remember, a copy of it hung in our dining room at home. By means of a clumsy montage, arms and hands had been added to the portrait bust with heavy iron chains bound round them. Extracts were read from this book, and it contained a confirmation of the lunatic thesis that Goethe had murdered Schiller. To the same meeting I had brought the correspondence between Schiller and Goethe which I knew quite well. But my protest against the suspicion cast on Goethe went unheard. The 'Old Guard' laughed me out of court and Johanna put an end to our argument. She avoided venturing onto the thin ice of such discussions herself. In the end I withdrew angrily but I made no secret of the fact that I regarded the story of the murder as a lie.

It was then that I first consciously said to myself: Party leaders can make mistakes like everyone else; perhaps there are also rogues and charlatans amongst them who have wormed their way into office because they are hungry for power or because they want to sap the movement from within. If they dream up such shameless lies, the people who are not well enough educated to be able to judge for themselves will fall for their nonsense. Anyone who observes this should not be silent about it. But one also has no right to turn one's back on the Party on account of such disillusionments. Gradually the spirit of truth will prevail over the lies. One must hold one's ground and fight where one stood.

In later years I must often have reflected similarly — very often indeed during the war. But I found one excuse, something like this: All decent, able bodied men are in the army now; the Party has to use the sixth or seventh best to keep afloat. I incurred the displeasure of my superiors several times, and was punished, for example by loss of rank, because I was guilty of disobedience. On each occasion it was connected with one particular problem which oppressed me: Should not National Socialism rather remain the affair of a small order of leadership recruited by rigorous selection? What would it become if every German were finally admitted into the order? A monstrous company of fellow-travellers.

My tendency to work towards the formation of an élite was contrary to the Party line. I suffered as a result of the disobedience to which this tendency tempted me, but I always returned to the hope that within a few generations we should succeed in educating every German to be a decent National Socialist. I wanted to share in the task of this educational work. For this reason I stayed in the Hitler Youth. I wanted to help create the National Community in which people would live together as in one big family.

At that time, I remember, you entertained sympathies for Marxism, and, indeed, finally even went through a 'Communist phase'. Perhaps this circumstance will help you to understand how I and like minded people felt at that time. With the full naivety of youth we both aspired to an ideal of improving the world. If I had had intensive contact with Communists then instead of National Socialists, I should probably have become a Communist too. We were still unrepentant believers in progress. Your ideal and mine differed — if you will allow an admittedly gross oversimplification — in that you wanted to 'improve' the whole of mankind, while I only wanted to 'improve' the German nation. I have already written that I often had fits of scepticism, but all the same, it seemed to me not quite as Utopian to believe in the possibility of educating one nation, as in, say, the inner potential for change of the whole of mankind.

~ 3 ~

When I first resolved to write to you, I believed that a dozen pages would suffice to explain to you my political road up to the point where I now stand. Now I know that my report, which was originally planned as a rather full letter, will turn out very long indeed. Perhaps you will find it an unreasonable demand to be expected to read it.

This question keeps troubling me. Many memories rise to the surface which I reject. I desire to — and should — call your attention only to the things which are related to my political development. Personal matters which do not have any bearing on this must be omitted. But you will, in any case, still have a dim recollection of some of it; for instance the troublesome romance of my first love affair, the instalments of which you had to listen to on the way home from school almost every day for two years. When I had finally accepted the unhappy ending, there followed the period of depression and loneliness in which nothing mattered any more, neither school friends, nor family, nor Hitler Youth. Not even God. I had already broken with His official representatives while I was being confirmed, before I came under the influence of National Socialism. Perhaps you may remember: I did not go to Communion although I knew that this would provoke a serious family row. My pastor had succeeded, through his authoritarian and unimaginative manner, in turning my natural receptiveness towards religion into its opposite. Quite remarkable, don't you think: in political matters I knuckled under willingly to every authority, but where religion was concerned I would not tolerate the slightest compulsion.

One day, or more precisely one night, I surfaced from my phase of youthful melancholy. I remember returning home late through the streets of the Wilmersdorf district of Berlin. I had been to a meeting of youth leaders and heard an impressive lecture about Germans abroad, but what I experienced on the way home had no recognizable connection with this.

I stood leaning with my back against a tree, gazing into the cone of light from the nearest street lamp. Snowflakes appeared out of the darkness, slipped through the narrow strip of light and vanished into the night once more. Their noiselessness was transmitted to me as an inner stillness in which I discovered the ability to look away from myself, to cease contemplating my own unhappiness and to serve the people of my nation. I was affected by a love for which I sought no name. I felt that it would uphold me.

I was then seventeen years old. In retrospect I seem to have overcome this first crisis in a way which adults frequently adopt: I took refuge in a fanaticism for work which kept its hold on me for ten years — until the end of the Third Reich.

In doing this I had the feeling that I had taken out a kind of life insurance. The unhappy outcome of my first love affair had plunged me into a despair from which there seemed to be no escape. Now I felt: you are saved. In future you can never go through another crisis like this, because now your life has a meaning which is independent of yourself. It is not important that you should be happy, but it is important that you should work for Germany. Hitherto my parents had had every reason to complain about my laziness. Now they complained of the fact that I could no longer be parted from my books. At that time my preference was for reading philosophical works, although I only understood them in a very fragmentary way. Plato, Nietzsche and Kant piled up on my desk.

I do not need to remind you of the German and Philosophy lessons of our incomparable Dr. F. The months during which we studied the life and work of the young Goethe were the happiest of my schooldays, and this joy was doubled by the fact I could share them with you. Shortly before the end of the war I met Dr. F. once again in Berlin, and she admitted to me that it had been I who had finally reconciled her to National Socialism. My idealistic interpretations and the candour with which I had striven to bring my words into harmony with my life, had caused her to overlook much that disturbed her and to put her faith in the growing generation. When we had this conversation we were both stunned by the fear of a terrible collapse and could only recall the past with bitterness.

In enumerating the important stations of my journey there is one catchword I must not omit: Ernst Barlach. I have chiefly to thank my mother for the fact that his works made an impression on me at that time. She several times sent us, well primed, to the last exhibition of this artist's work at a private gallery. From his work I began to establish — intuitively at least — the beginnings of some objective discrimination, before 'blood and soil' art began to dominate the field. I probably owe to this last Barlach exhibition the fact that I never felt comfortable in the Munich 'House of German Art' during the next ten years. The *Peasant Venus* or *Storm Troops Attacking* bored me thoroughly. Admittedly it was only after 1945 that I really became aware of how Hitler had enslaved the driving force of German culture. I remember discussions from the period before then, in which I took the line that the inclusion of Barlach, Lehmbruck and many others amongst the 'degenerates' was a mistake which ought to be corrected.

In the Upper Second Class I began frequently to play truant from school. Working for the Hitler Youth took up more and more of my time and energy. I would often leave the house at five in the morning and only arrive at school for the second or third lesson, or I would disappear after the break for the rest of the morning.

While the lower ranks of the leaders generally disappointed me, I was always finding amongst my superiors — right up into the Reich Youth leadership — more remarkable people, to whose personal and official authority I was glad to submit.

In this I had high standards for judging people. You must know this, because you know my friendships of those years and, indeed, you know that, of all the girls I was at school with, you were the only one with whom and with whose parents I had sought a close relationship. I remind you of this in order to answer a question which must surely occur to you: "How was it possible for you to enjoy the company of those Nazis?"

On the occasions when I talk to foreigners they constantly reproach me on this score: "But what about the systematic training of youth to hardness and hate? You had to become as hard as Krupp's steel, and you wanted to."

It was only recently, when I was in conversation with a fair minded Frenchman, that I realized how this 'training to hardness' can be seen from two sides. The complete quotation ran as follows: 'Tough as leather, swift as greyhounds, hard as Krupp's steel.' Hitler applied these words to German youth. I had always taken for granted that with these words he was expressing a certain attitude of sportsmanship as an educational ideal. Granted a onesided one, as I now realize — for the element of fairness is lacking — but I had always understood the 'hardness' which was required of us as a hardness in 'taking punishment'. I thought we should learn to be hard in bearing privations, frustrations or pain. But not hard in 'handing it out'! If my leaders had at that time required me to quarrel with my parents, who were indeed opponents of National Socialism, or to cultivate hostility towards my Jewish classmates, I should probably have soon found my way out of the Hitler Youth. A systematic training for hatred and hardness in administering punishment would have driven many of us away. The fact that we later learned, during the war, to be hard in handing it out as well, and the reason why we offered no resistance to the training for hate which was then being introduced I will discuss in another context. What first drew young people to National Socialism was not hatred — of 'enemy' tendencies or foreigners — but love of Germany. It was in the service of this love that they wished to make themselves 'tough, swift, and hard'.

So if I have said there were many fine people amongst my superiors and none who preached hate and brutality, you will understand me better. It was this that was the tragedy: that so many good people fell victims to the fascination of the Third Reich.

My superior at the Berlin head office, where I now worked, was in her early twenties. She came from East Prussia and after her Abitur school leaving examination she had gone in for professional youth work — against the wishes of her parents. Much in Petra's situation corresponded to my own. She too left her home as a 'wellborn daughter' and had a certain feeling of guilt about the comfort in which she had grown up. Now she lived in voluntary poverty and was happy to do so. Her initial monthly salary scarcely sufficed to cover her living expenses. She had taken a cheap groundfloor room in the neighbourhood of the Schönhauser Allee, but even if she had had more money she would still have wanted to live in this poor district.

Towards the end of the month she went hungry, but I never heard her complaining about it. She would then suddenly find it 'unaesthetic to eat so much'. One day a dog came to her. It was a neglected mongrel; a beast of little distinction. Her meals became still more frugal but she kept the animal until it died.

Petra was often homesick for the Courland Spit on the Baltic coast of Prussia, where she had spent a part of her childhood.

Nevertheless we joined forces in attempting to cultivate an artificial patriotism for Berlin in our propaganda work. At night I drew inspiration for this somewhat romantic feeling from the area between the Silesian Station and the Ackerstrasse. I often made my way through this quarter after late meetings. The midnight streets of this partly derelict district had an irresistible attraction for me. From the basement dwellings there rose a smell of poverty. Drunks staggered from lamp post to lamp post, and at certain corners stood the whores. On occasions they would shout at me mockingly: "What are you doing here, little one? Run home to mother!"

In those days I wore plaits and was so slight and childlike that I was taken for thirteen or fourteen, although I was sixteen and seventeen. These nocturnal walks were an escape from the protection of my parents. I was in the midst of 'Berlin, my home'. Probably the element of danger in the situation thrilled me, and perhaps I also enjoyed living out my loneliness unconcealed, among strangers and in the dark streets.

The poetic fruits of such 'night wanderings' have fortunately not been preserved.

As I attracted attention through a certain aptitude, I soon came into contact with the Press and Propaganda Division of the Reich Youth Leadership. The editor who was responsible within this office for the girls' section was one of the most striking people in the leadership of the Hitler Youth. Her intelligence and critical sharpness made her feared by all those who were addicted to hollow rhetoric and vagueness. But anyone who had the courage to make their own judgements and a taste for dry North German humour soon discovered that the prim and laconic exterior concealed a particularly sensitive and good natured personality. Colleagues of this kind did not find it easy to work in an office where there were ambitious schemers and toadies. During the war she became such a thorn in the flesh of important people that they got rid of her. In the course of a conversation I had with her a few years ago, she admitted that she had never read Hitler's *Mein Kampf.* She had also considered the 'virulent' anti-semitism to be simply a passing excess which the Party itself would one day disavow.

It may sound astounding that someone with this viewpoint should have been able to remain for many years in the ranks of the top leadership of the National Socialist Youth movement. I am convinced that this was not just one exceptional case. Many of us there were first and foremost in search of a platform for youth work. We were only secondarily interested in politics, and even then often only under duress.

I had friends who were music teachers, whose speciality was ancient music and the making and playing of old musical instruments. During their free time they took part in performances of Bach cantatas at church concerts, and during working hours they sang songs with Hitler Youth choirs which glorified Hitler and romanticized war. Often they only stayed in the Hitler Youth because it gave them the opportunity for systematic music teaching.

The fact that, through their collaboration in the National Socialist training of young people, they were bound to come into a position of inner conflict with the spirit of (say) Johann Sebastian Bach, whom they loved and revered, was not entirely clear to any of them at that time.

Now I have told you about some of my former comrades, with whom I worked for many years. Even today I have no need to be ashamed of their friendship. Naturally there were amongst us arrogant, self assertive, power hungry, scheming, calculating and very superficial people, but I must stress that in the youth leadership section they were not numerous. One could avoid them and stick to those to whom one felt drawn by sympathetic affinity. And one could hope that the unpleasant elements would be excluded more and more.

Something else must be clearly stated: I was not one of those who worked professionally in the Hitler Youth because they wanted a field of activity for their specialist abilities. I wanted to educate people politically and, indeed, on expressly National Socialist lines.

In an argument which I had with my father I quoted the example of a Hitler Youth leader. I had visited him in hospital after his third car accident and found myself faced with a mummy who was swathed in bandages almost from head to foot, but was nevertheless typing out reports with two fingers.

Referring to this tireless man, I said to my father: "Even if I work myself to death by the age of twenty-five I would not think of sparing myself. What matters now is for us to build a firm foundation for the Third Reich. We are needed now."

My father had often reproached me with frivolously neglecting my health. I had far too little sleep and worked constantly at high pressure. But there were many of us who did not learn until 1945 to do less than their utmost.

The senselessness of our pace of work was demonstrated by Petra. When I was in the Lower First Class I had to deputize for her for months because she had to go into a sanatorium to recuperate. At the same time I was going to school and making an exceptional effort to get through a syllabus which normally called for the diligent application of all one's energies. The situation was aggravated by the fact that my parents forbade me all activity in the Hitler Youth apart from the club evenings, as I was getting worse reports on my mathematical subjects. From now on I had to do my press work in secret and give myself scope for it by means of constant lying. You were often implicated in this. When I went to my office I would say: "L. wants to go over some maths with me."

A senior boy who lived in the same street as us was at that time my companion in work and trouble. He too had to keep his activities secret from his parents. His reason for becoming a National Socialist was unusual: his father was a psychologist in the Higher Education Service. As far as I remember he was a Freudian. He must have been so obsessed with his scientific concerns that he brought Freud into all the ordinary affairs of his family life. The son hated his father and rejoiced over the fact that the National Socialists had unmasked Freud as an 'alien thinker'. So what inspired the boy about our work was that 'here something practical was being done and there was no poking around in people's minds'.

One day I met him in the street in tears. We went some way together before he was able to speak calmly. His father had notified the school that he was leaving, although he had every likelihood of doing very well in his final Abitur examinations. In order to work in the Hitler Youth, his parents had explained, all he needed to know was the simple multiplication table.

On my eighteenth birthday I admitted to my mother that I had gone on working in secret and that I had lied to her on countless occasions. I had hoped that she would in future allow me to do my press work openly once more, in order to spare the strain on my nerves and my energy. My hope went unfulfilled. There came a grave crisis between my parents and myself which finally led to the decision that I should be sent to a boarding school in central Germany at Easter. The selection of the school was made by our senior B.D.M. leader. When I went to say goodbye to her, she said: "I expect you to do excellently in your Abitur examinations. The Hitler Youth needs people with a sound education."

During the past year I had felt myself to be already an independent adult engaged in a professional life. I found it bitterly hard suddenly to revert to the role of 'schoolgirl' again. There was only one thing that made me glad to leave Berlin. In this way I could allow my friendship with you and your family to fade away. I wanted to avoid the open breach, which — after years of evading the conflict — I nevertheless felt to be my duty, because one could only do one of two things: either have Jewish friends or be a National Socialist.

There is not much to be said about my year at boarding school. I was happy after the first difficulties of starting there. It was a princely foundation and had a consciously fostered Evangelical tradition. Christian educational concepts, embodied in the life of the school, conflicted with National Socialist regimentation.

The daily prayers, the grace at meals, the biblical pictures and the prominence given to religious instruction stood in contradiction to the brown B.D.M. dresses which were the school uniform and to the Hitler Youth spirit of the B.D.M. groups within the school. It did not quite come to open conflict between the two ideologies which met here; scarcely indeed to secret skirmishes. But it was just that which was ominous: the Christian teachers pretended to themselves and to us that one could be both at once without dishonour: a Christian and a National Socialist. They had not yet taken the measure of what was afoot in Germany, or they did not want to take its measure, because they would then have needed a great deal of courage in order to go on living as Christians. So people floated along in a confused jumble of Christian and National Socialist attitudes. If one later looked back on those teachers — even in this situation some of them earned one's respect and friendship — one could say to oneself: even X with his passion for Greek philosophy, or Y, who considered the Sermon on the Mount to be the supreme revelation granted to mankind, were ready to enter the Party. It was an alibi which they could use as a cover if doubts arose.

I have one more important memory of the summer of 1936. I spent the holidays in Berlin and saw many of the events of the Olympic Games. Because of my knowledge of English I was taken on to guide foreign youth groups. How well one got on with these boys and girls from all over the world! Political discussions were rare. If they came up, we swiftly reached agreement: let us live in our country according to the new laws we are seeking and you live in your country according to your laws.

For me the solemn moment when the teams of all the nations marched into the Olympic stadium remains unforgettable. As the French with their flags approached across the cinder track, an old man next to me wept: he was a veteran from the front in the First World War overcome by this display of reconciliation between the nations. The German nation cheered the sons of the nation which had been considered an hereditary foe. In all of us there was hope for a new future of peace and friendship.

The youth of the world had received a call.

Three years later the new World War broke out. How could one have imagined that the leaders of Germany would be driven by insane power lust to launch a war against those very nations whose youth they had so recently invited to the Olympic peace festival?

The summer after the Abitur was the most carefree period of my youth. I was called up for Labour Service in East Prussia from the beginning of April. While the train was still drawing out of the Silesian Station in Berlin I began happily to adjust my mind to the fact that this coming period of service to the National Community would give me a chance to leave behind the theory of my newspaper articles and get down to practice. My 'service' began a few minutes after the train had left the station, and I remember it with a grin. I had taken onto my lap a little girl of about two, who was one of a large family, in order to relieve her mother. She remained with me all through the night, for her mother did not show herself again. It was thanks to this child, who was dirty and neglected, that I arrived for my Labour Service with lice. With my sensitive nose suffering agonies — my nursling soon had her pants full — I found that the transfer from theory to practice put something of a strain on my 'social beliefs'.

Next morning I discovered I had been looking after the youngest offspring of a family of Polish seasonal workers. Though I felt that I had learnt my lesson for my overeagerness, I could not help seeing the funny side. What did not occur to me was that the Polish mother in her need was just as entitled to my help as any German would have been.

The camp was situated near the largest of the East Prussian lakes at D. on the Spirdingsee. It was installed in a worn-out house which was far too cramped. All the equipment was as shabby as the rooms, down to the patched straw mattresses, the threadbare clothing and the clumsy laceup boots. This poverty corresponded to the style of our life there. The day began at six o'clock with early morning physical training. At half past seven we went off to work on the farms, after half an hour of singing, during which most of us were in fact falling asleep again from exhaustion. At harvest time the farm work went on for up to fifteen hours a day; normally it was only meant to last seven or eight hours. In the late afternoon there was sport, political instruction, dancing or singing. The evenings were generally free.

D. consisted of the few farmsteads of a new settlement, packed closely together. Scattered over a wide area across the countryside were old peasant farms, several of which could only be reached in an hour's cycle ride. The new settlers and the peasants got on badly together. Amongst the settlers, for whom the state had paid out large sums of money, there were people who could scarcely speak German and who obviously lacked experience and industry. Their farms soon became neglected. Many of them considered it to be simply their due to have a girl to come regularly from the camp to help them, and took advantage of this cheap labour.

When one went out to the peasants who were long established there, one was at first treated as a guest and entertained, and one had to seek out the work — in the face of protests from the farmer's wife. For these highly conservative farmers the Labour Service was something newfangled and unwelcome. They did not credit city girls with the ability to work and they were afraid that we would be critical or poke our noses into their affairs. Their farms were large, weathered and very gloomy. In the cowsheds, which were only mucked out once or twice a year, one could hardly see one's hand in front of one's face, but in the farmhouses cleanliness reigned.

My first place of work was on a run-down settler's farm, the occupant of which was called Pissauwotzki. After a cool greeting I was sent to the fodder kitchen to do the washing. There I found a big tub filled with unbelievably dirty underwear. The grandfather was ill. I had already noticed how he spat against the kitchen wall. On his account we had to wash shirts and underclothes daily.

My first work in the fields was planting potatoes. It began on a cold, rainy morning. Just a few days before, the last snow had been lying in the furrows. The sodden earth clung to my boots in lumps, and the wire basket which I had to keep refilling from the sack of seed potatoes, felt like a ton weight on my arm. My hands went numb in the damp cold and as I had to put each potato into the ground individually, my back soon ached unmercifully. The farmer, who should really have been ploughing in front of me, was close on my heels. I could hear the horse snorting at my back and stumbled desperately on.

My exhaustion suddenly overwhelmed me so completely that I had to cry, but at the moment when the tears began to well up in my eyes, I started to whistle loudly. Not at any price would I let it be seen how I felt. After this ordeal on the first day, I went to work each day for weeks, worrying if I should be able to hold out that day as well.

On one of the old, gloomy farms I discovered the hold superstition still had over many of these people. On account of the First World War the farmer had scarcely been to school. We gradually embarked on a series of 'tutorials' which continued over several weeks. As we worked on almost all the jobs together, I tried to tell this man, whose thirst for knowledge was insatiable, what I knew from school about world history. One day his wife joined us while we were mucking out the deep litter shed. She was many months pregnant and could no longer do such heavy work herself. Suddenly she interrupted us to ask how it was that the child grew in her belly. While I tried to tell her something about the development of the embryo she listened to me attentively.

Next morning the farmer came to the camp and asked for another girl to be sent. He was sorry to break off the conversations with me, but his wife never wanted to see me again. I had said that the child in her belly breathed through gills. Now she was afraid of bringing a fish instead of a child into the world. Two weeks later she gave birth to twins.

Nor will I forget working at a farm whose occupants were dispossessed that summer. The father was no longer alive, the mother had become alcoholic, and the adolescent son was feeble minded. I helped to plant potatoes there as well. In the mornings the woman would set down at the edge of the field a litre bottle containing a liquid which reeked of methylated spirits. As soon as she had been up and down a couple of furrows she would revive her strength with a draught from the bottle. Later on the intervals became shorter and shorter. Finally she put the bottle in the wire basket with the potatoes so that she could have a drink at any time. She now sang the same verse of the hymn, *Jesus my hope* over and over again. This enlivened the simpleton in a most alarming way. He joined in with many loud yells, beating his horse in a manner that appalled me. Towards noon we laid the woman, who had collapsed into a furrow, on the cart. Her son drank the rest of the bottle. When I came back to the farm in the late afternoon, mother and son were lying in the barn, sleeping off their drinking bout.

Before the start of the corn harvest I had to work in the camp laundry and rubbed my hands raw on the harsh, dirty bed linen. It was thanks to these wounds that the farmer to whom I was then sent entrusted to me the pleasantest job I have ever done in my life. I did not have to help in binding the sheaves, but was allowed to drive the laden wagons from the field to the barn and then bring the empty ones back again.

One afternoon the farmer, meaning to pay me a compliment, said to me, "You're such a little shrimp, I can't think how you manage here. But you really drive those horses like an old trooper."

Like an old trooper! That was not very flattering to a girl in her teens. Next day I tried not to shout so much when I got to the big slope with the team of four. Instead of this I made judicious use of the whip. But the horses were used to being encouraged verbally — there was nothing for it but to go on shouting 'like an old trooper'.

In those weeks I experienced something wonderful. The physical exhaustion which reached its deepest point before the harvest and which had at times turned me into an almost apathetic lump of aching flesh, changed suddenly into a feeling of unquenchable joy in creation. I still had to drive myself but I was often so happy at my work that I sang aloud for joy. Since then I have had a profound respect for all those who perform physically hard work. Uncomplaining endurance of physical suffering, over the tireless routine of the decades seems to me to have the quality of a religious exercise.

The fact that I was able to carry on was not primarily due to my increasing physical aptitude for the unaccustomed work, but to aids of quite a different kind. I knew that the farmers needed us and I had come there intending not to spare myself. If the temptation to give in became very great, there was one final resort — to glance at the camp flag, or if it was not in sight, to call to mind one of the texts which expressed what we considered to be the purpose of our lives.

It costs me some effort now to describe experiences of this kind and I can foresee that you will only be able to read them with reluctance, but I do not think I have the right to leave out anything important. I often helped myself over the collapse by repeating the same verses ten or fifteen times over. They said:

"You must believe in Germany as firmly, clearly and truly as you believe in the sun, the moon and the starlight. You must believe in Germany, as if Germany were yourself; and as you believe your soul strives towards eternity. You must believe in Germany — or your life is but death. And you must fight for Germany until the new dawn comes."

Our camp community was a model in miniature of what I imagined the National Community to be. It was a completely successful model. Never before or since have I known such a good community, even where the composition was more homogeneous in every respect. Amongst us there were peasant girls, students, factory girls, hairdressers, schoolgirls, office workers and so on. The camp was run by the daughter of an East Prussian farmer, who had not overcome the narrowness of her background. But although she could hardly pronounce a single foreign word correctly, it would not have occurred to anyone to make fun of her. She brought us to the point at which we each recognized one another's particular value, after having come to know one another's weak and strong points, and everyone strove to be willing and reliable.

The knowledge that this model of a National Community had afforded me such intense happiness gave birth to an optimism to which I clung obstinately until 1945. Upheld by this experience, I believed, despite all the evidence to the contrary, that the pattern of our camp would one day be magnified on an infinite scale — if not in the next then in future generations.

At the end of my period of Labour Service, I spent three weeks alone cycling through East Prussia right up into the furthest German corner of the Courland Spit. No landscape has ever since fascinated me quite as much as the one between the Masurian forests and the Courland Lagoon.

4

I must break off my chronological account here to discuss a question which will become increasingly important in what follows. It had already preoccupied me in my early youth and I must trace its impact on me from then onwards until the time when it first confronted me with a challenge. I mean the phenomenon of anti-semitism. You will understand that I can hardly consider this apart from my memories of you.

During the first six or eight years following 1945 I dreamed of you frequently and all my dreams were similar. I was always meeting you and trying to speak to you, but you ignored me. Once I was riding past you on a bus and I was unable to get off. Another time I was running after you but you moved away from me faster and faster. In a third dream I came into a room and found you standing in the middle of it. I asked you to listen to me but you gave no sign that you could even see me. When I woke up I always felt that what stopped me communicating with you had its origin in some incapacity of my own. I was unable to express the guilt I felt towards you in a way which was audible to you.

It is hard to know now why I never managed to speak to you in those dreams. Perhaps this was an admission of a level of awareness far below normal consciousness. Consciously I still believed it possible to 'apologize' for the crimes against the Jewish people committed by us. That was why I sought you in my dreams. But when I stood before you, all possibility of bridging the gulf between us was denied to me. Every attempt at an 'apology', however it was formulated, was bound to miscarry. The wrong we had done to you and your kin was so terribly immeasurable that a truly sensitive heart could only have found one 'answer' to it — to stop beating. How frivolous and inappropriate was the wish to 'apologize'!

Please do not regard what follows as an attempt of this kind. I simply want to identify for you and for myself those conditions which, when they were fulfilled, made it possible for me to accept uncritically the immoral maxims of National Socialism.

The house in which my twin brother and I were born stood in a street off the Kurfürstendamm. As far as I can recall, the majority of the occupants were always Jews. My parents were only on friendly terms with our Gentile neighbours across the landing. This family consisted of a brother and sister and their elderly mother. The brother was a bank official, the sister a teacher. As children we liked all three of them very much. They were already National Socialists during the 'years of struggle' and the first expressions of anti-semitism with political overtones which reached our ears came from them. They clearly objected to having to live in a house in which Gentiles were in the minority. From odd remarks of theirs I gathered that Jews were 'foreigners': our neighbours pronounced the word with scorn.

On the floor below us lived the Lewys. They were the only Jews in the house with whom my parents had any kind of contact. We profited from them because we shared their telephone for many years. I remember Herr Lewy as a friendly old man with a fine, full beard. When we were at the nursery window blowing soap bubbles, he would smile at us. We knew that for religious reasons he would never let himself be seen without his black velvet skull cap and it was at his flat that we first marvelled to see a seven branched candlestick. The fact that the Lewys must not be disturbed on Saturdays because it was their holy day was something our mother never forgot to impress upon us. They were the only orthodox Jews in the house and I seem to remember that this made them more acceptable to our parents, probably because they came from a 'good old family' and did not belong to the *'nouveaux riches'*, let alone the 'foreign' families who had only come from eastern Europe since the war.

Contact with the other Jewish inhabitants of the house was limited to an exchange of greetings if one met them on the stairs.

Whether I had any Jewish classmates at my primary school I no longer remember: but at the secondary school Jewish girls at times made up one-third of my class. My parents often complained about this situation. Why it was lamentable I did not understand, but then our parents also complained about the unemployment, although we did not suffer from it ourselves.

I ask myself now how my Jewish school fellows struck me. First, almost without exception, by their physical and mental precociousness. They were 'ladies' already, while I felt I was still a child, and the ostentatious clothes many of them wore annoyed me. Not one of them came from a poor home. Most of them, indeed, were rich and there were some who sought to impress with their father's cars, in which the chauffeurs sometimes came to fetch them. The fact that these airs particularly upset me may have been connected with my mother's frequent complaints about *'nouveaux riches'*. If this expression refers to the time a family's prosperity dates from — and not to a style of life — then my mother came from a *'nouveau riche'* family herself anyway. Her father was a tradesman who had worked his way to the top.

As regards accomplishments, the Jewish girls were above average. True, the top girl in my class from the lowest form to the Upper First was always the daughter of a Catholic railway guard with a large family, but after her in almost all subjects came Jewish girls. They never formed cliques and one might well say that they were conspicuously well bred. Their good behaviour was for a long time a source of irritation to me, for until the Upper Third Class I regarded school as a playground, a place where one could get up to all kinds of silly escapades which would be prevented at home by parental discipline.

The first 'political conversations' I can remember having with other girls at school were provoked by a girl in my form whose father had been an officer in the First World War and belonged to the *'Stahlhelm'*[4]. These consisted of boasting about the 'exploits' of one's brothers or cousins, which were directed against the new German Republic and also, even before 1933, against the Jews. Gerda's brothers went out at night and tore down the 'black, red and mustard' flags from flagpoles with hooks fastened to long lines or daubed swastikas on walls. One day Gerda brought me a railway ticket which looked like an ordinary one. It was only on closer examination that I realized this was a 'political joke'. It carried the imprint 'To Jerusalem'. Underneath was written in smaller print: 'And no return'. We gave this ticket to Rahel K. for her father. We chose Rahel because she was a particularly goodnatured girl, somewhat simple in her friendliness. I do not know if you can still remember her.

I liked her very much. When our cruel joke threatened to have repercussions and before my parents were summoned to the school, I went to Rahel's mother and apologized. The kindliness with which she received me filled me with shame. From then on I refrained from tasteless jokes of that kind. I was then twelve years old.

I do not remember our having serious discussions about internal politics in class — not even at the time when I belonged to the Hitler Youth. One of our classmates, a girl whose company I found particularly agreeable, ran the school group of the Union for Germans Abroad *(Verein für das Deutschtum im Ausland)*. You will remember her, although matters like this did not interest you. Hilde Sch. was a pastor's daughter. I regarded her as my exact opposite, because the Union was joined by all those consciously bourgeois girls who had no desire to join the Hitler Youth. Despite this rivalry we got on well together as individuals. My membership of the Hitler Youth played no part in the life of the classroom. It did not even alter my attitude to the Jewish girls in the class.

A trivial episode from that period which has recently occurred to me throws some light on the situation. I was having an

---

[4] 'Steel Helmet': a right wing paramilitary organization.
Translator's note.

argument with Rosel Cohn, whom I had long disliked for her intellectual arrogance. She had a much sharper brain than I and I was losing the argument. I can no longer recall what the argument was about, but I remember that for a moment I was tempted to keep my end up by making a derisive reference to the fact that she was Jewish. I rejected the idea almost at once, not because I would have been ashamed to use such an unfair weapon, but because I thought: what an absurd idea! You would only make a laughing stock of yourself.

Rosel Cohn was a Jewish classmate of ours, but I did not really connect her with 'the Jews'. *Those* Jews were and remained something mysteriously menacing and anonymous. They were not the sum of all Jewish individuals, who included yourself or old Herr Lewy: they were an evil power, something with the attributes of a spook. One could not see it, but it was there, an active force for evil.

As children we had been told fairy stories which sought to make us believe in witches and wizards. Now we were too grown up to take this witchcraft seriously, but we still went on believing in the 'wicked Jews'. They had never appeared to us in bodily form, but it was our daily experience that adults believed in them. After all, we could not check to see if the earth was round rather than flat — or, to be more precise, it was not a proposition we thought it necessary to check. The grownups 'knew' it and one took over this knowledge without mistrust. They also 'knew' that the Jews were wicked. This wickedness was directed against the prosperity, unity and prestige of the German nation, which we had learned to love from an early age. The anti-semitism of my parents was a part of their outlook which was taken for granted. Our father came from the university educated middle class. In his day there were still not many Jews at the universities. They were widely regarded as intruders, particularly because their keen intelligence offered an uncomfortable challenge. My mother had grown up in the family of a tradesman 'by appointment to the Court', who had risen to prosperity through hard work. In such circles as these, fear of competition may well have led to the early development of a thorough going anti-semitism.

My parents certainly grumbled about the Jews, but this did not stop them having a genuine liking for the Lewys and having social relations with my father's Jewish colleagues.

For as long as we could remember, the adults had lived in this contradictory way with complete unconcern. One was friendly with individual Jews whom one liked, just as one was friendly as a Protestant with individual Catholics. But while it occurred to nobody to be ideologically hostile to *the* Catholics, one was, utterly, to *the* Jews. In all this no one seemed to worry about the fact that they had no clear idea of who *'the* Jews' were. They included the baptized and the orthodox, yiddish speaking second hand dealers and professors of German literature, Communist agents and First World War officers decorated with high orders, enthusiasts for Zionism and chauvinistic German nationalists...

When you came into my class at Easter 1933 from another Berlin school I made friends with you, although I knew you were Jewish and despite the fact that I had joined the Hitler Youth at almost the same time.

I had learned from my parents' example that one could have anti-semitic opinions without this interfering in one's personal relations with individual Jews. There may appear to be a vestige of tolerance in this attitude, but it is really just this confusion which I blame for the fact that I later contrived to dedicate body and soul to an inhuman political system, without this giving me doubts about my own individual decency. In preaching that all the misery of the nations was due to the Jews or that the Jewish spirit was seditious and Jewish blood was corrupting, I was not compelled to think of you or old Herr Lewy or Rosel Cohn: I thought only of the bogeyman, *'the* Jew'. And when I heard that the Jews were being driven from their professions and homes and imprisoned in ghettos, the points switched automatically in my mind to steer me round the thought that such a fate could also overtake you or old Lewy. It was only *the* Jew who was being persecuted and 'made harmless'.

Perhaps I should have been more ready to learn from the sum of my own observations if I had not had the example of this fatal schizophrenia before my eyes from an early age: there is much to suggest that I might. Your father — if you will allow me to cite him as an example — was a man who epitomized the complete opposite of what was then depicted to us as typically Jewish. He had been awarded both Iron Crosses during the war, and as a doctor he was much sought after by poor people because they knew that he would take the trouble to help them sympathetically even when they could not pay his fee. During my schooldays I never felt more at home with any of the families I knew than with yours. Here the two generations lived together in friendship, without this ever calling into question the authority of your parents. There was always an opportunity to join in conversations, whether about plays, books or current affairs, which had a real educational value for us children, not only because of their intellectual level but also because of the personal example expressed in your parents' attitude to every topic.

What bound me to you — apart from a spontaneous liking for you — was a shared interest in literature and philosophy. You thought more slowly and more deeply than I. With an intensity at which I marvelled, you would burrow into a question, remaining long silent and surprising me with solutions which went deeper, both intuitively and intellectually, than ones I could have found.

On the question of whether we ever discussed anti-semitism together my memory gives me no clear answer. Perhaps we avoided it. I was used to respecting your reluctance to talk about very personal matters, even though I did not share it.

But I certainly remember my telling you quite freely about my experiences in the Hitler Youth and your equally open descriptions of those of your brothers and sisters in their youth groups. They belonged to the illegal 'Federated Youth' to which the National Socialists were ruthlessly opposed. The leader of this group was known by the nickname 'Tusk'. It was said then — and as far as I can remember, this corresponded to everything you told me about him — that he had Communist leanings. Out of all the 'Federated Youth' he was the Hitler Youth's enemy number one. One day I learned from you that many of your brother's friends, when their group had been closed down, had joined the Hitler Youth. This confirmed something about which I had heard frequent complaints in the Hitler Youth — the infiltration of National Socialist youth by 'Federated' and indeed Communist elements. It was probably this circumstance which led me to review my own unclear position. I gradually felt its ambiguity to be unclean and oppressive. I reached the conclusion that it was not possible to be both a National Socialist youth leader and the friend of a Jewish family whose sons belonged to an illegal Federated-Communist group.

I also gradually lost touch with you physically, because I spent every possible free moment in the service of the Hitler Youth. And inwardly I had less and less patience with things that were not connected with this service.

I do not know if my behaviour hurt you. I fear it did. You never readily showed your feelings and I was doubtless blind to any modest indications that you were upset.

When I said goodbye to you at Halensee railway station, I felt that you had understood the situation perfectly. We made no mention of it. You offered your sympathy for the fact that I should have to surrender a great deal of my freedom at boarding school. I replied with empty phrases. Then we parted quickly, just as we did every day. At that parting I had wanted to 'make things clear', but now I found that the price of this 'clean break' in our outward existence had been an inner stain of guilt which was not to be obliterated. Nor can it today. In those days I thought burdening oneself with guilt must just be a part of life. You know the next part of the story from the letter I wrote to you shortly after my release from internment, but it belongs with the rest of this account so I shall mention it once again. It may be that my letter did not reach you in all the confusion of the postwar years. I have never received a reply from you, though I did not dare to hope for one.

When I was released from Labour Service in the autumn of 1937, the Gestapo tried to make me act as a kind of agent for them. On the day after my return from East Prussia someone who was working for them appeared at my parents' house and called every day for a week to put pressure on me. I learned from him that the illegal restarting of a youth group which would have 'Federated-Communist' tendencies was planned for November 1. The inauguration was to take place at your parents' house, because your brothers were amongst the leaders of the group. I was to observe the proceedings.

The Gestapo official explained to me that it had been established that I was the only reliable National Socialist who had had contact with your family and I was therefore expected to try and gain entry into the group in order to keep watch on it.

I bluntly refused this demand. It would be impossible for me to spy on former friends and, besides, I was not cunning or diplomatic enough for such a task.

For several weeks I was harassed daily and finally my National Socialist convictions were called into question. One day I was called before the senior leader of the B.D.M. in Berlin and she, whom I had known and admired for years, succeeded in convincing me that it was my duty to perform the task which was required of me. Nothing could be more understandable than my reluctance, but my former friends were conspiring to corrupt young people with the spirit of 'Federated-Communism'. Anyone who led young people astray from their National Socialist convictions was endangering the future of Germany.

I then tried to make contact with you again, under the pretence that I had abandoned National Socialism. I owe one of the best turns of my fate to the fact that I failed in the task which I had finally undertaken. It foundered on my incapacity in the role of secret agent. I have no doubt that it was written on my brow that I was lying, when I turned up at your house again and started abusing the Nazis. On the evening fixed for the inauguration of the group I obtained entry to your parents' house on some pretext or other. But I only managed to speak to the maid. Nobody else was to be seen and I lacked the impudence to stay in the face of the maid's refusal. The Gestapo official was waiting for me outside the house and dismissed me with a curse. I never heard anything from the Gestapo again. My unsuitability for collaboration with them was doubtless thoroughly proven.

It was only after 1945 that I learned from my chief superior in the Reich Youth Leadership that they had considered dismissing me from the Hitler Youth on account of this failure. I was finally kept on because my skill for the press work was needed.

The last news I received from you was brought to me by your father on the morning after that night when your house was searched and two of your brothers were arrested. While I had failed to warn you of the danger which I knew threatened you, you sought to protect me from trouble. You sent me word that they had seized your diaries in which you had reported our conversations. I was to make no attempt to deny your brothers' illegal membership of a 'Federated' youth group.

It is barely comprehensible now that being forced to spy on my friends did not open my eyes. I could see then, and should have recognized for what they were, the methods used against all youth groups who did not join the Hitler Youth. But it was only some fifteen years later that I came to understand the value of independent thought and freedom of action. In 1937 I wanted to devote all my energy to uniting German youth both inwardly and outwardly in the Hitler Youth. Every kind of 'separatism' seemed to me to threaten the future of the Reich.

The fact that there was a police force which kept a watch on the restarting of illegal Communist-Federated youth groups was no reason for me to lose my faith in the National Socialist system.

The ruthlessness with which I was required to spy on my former friends certainly disturbed me. Could the State, I wondered, demand that I act basely as an individual in its own service? It was just at this point that I should have been on the alert. I was not. We had learnt that for the sake of Germany no sacrifice could be too great. In this particular instance I did not feel justified in sparing my 'private feelings' or my own individual urge to moral purity.

I have never in my life suppressed anything so completely from my memory as I did that lamentable episode. I actually succeeded in forgetting this betrayal of you and our friendship until after the end of the war. It oppressed me doubly. Not only had I abandoned former friends of mine to a danger of which I should have warned them. From the other point of view I had also failed shamefully: I had lacked the strength to carry out effectively what I believed to be a necessary duty. I had slithered through a crisis without seriously facing up to it.

When I wrote to you again for the first time in 1948 I was far from having overcome my National Socialism, but I was bitterly ashamed of the betrayal of our friendship. I had only learned shortly before then that your brothers had suffered no grave harm after their arrest in November 1937. I was myself transferred to a post as chief press officer in Frankfurt-an-der-Oder just a few months later, and I was glad to get away from Berlin. The change of scene helped me to escape from my burdensome memories. During the years which followed I never allowed any of my experiences to prompt me to come to grips with the so-called 'Jewish Question' for myself. My anti-semitic attitude seemed to me a natural part of my National Socialist outlook. Basically the problem did not interest me. The programme of the National Socialist Party contained a whole series of points which were of equally little interest to me: for example the one about the abolition of usury. I never took the trouble to find out what it meant — very likely because I dislike anything at all reminiscent of mathematics. The fact that anti-semitism did not interest me can no doubt be traced back to my suppressed bad conscience. I did not want to be reminded of you or your family.

I did not read the Nuremberg Laws[5], which were enacted in 1935, until 1941 when I had to give a course on them at a Labour

---

[5] These deprived Jews of German citizenship and forbade them to marry non Jews. *Translator's note.*

Service camp. Previously I had been satisfied with a very imprecise knowledge of their contents. Doubtless this was because I did not want to know exactly what they contained. I did not want to be obliged to think about it. As I was employed in the Hitler Youth not as the leader of a group but only as a press officer I took part in hardly any 'ideological training'. The lectures which I did have to endure from time to time at leaders' conferences generally bored me so much that I only lent half an ear to them. Often, too, I laughed at them out loud or on the quiet. At the meetings of the Kurmark Hitler Youth which I went to from Frankfurt-an-der-Oder, a lecturer turned up dressed in hunting attire. He was supposed to be an expert on the secrets of the Talmud. In the small group of colleagues I was quite friendly with we called him 'Ritual-murder-very-funny'. This nickname was a quotation of his own words. His lecture consisted of a string of dark suggestions and mysterious allusions. He plainly avoided any reference to facts. Obviously he considered it more effective to leave his listeners to draw the conclusions he was hinting at for themselves. So, on the basis of his confused ravings, one was supposed to arrive at the conviction that the Jews had committed ritual murders in the middle ages and still did so today. Each time he had strung out the sequence of his 'evidence' before us, he asked us, with a movement of his hands which was supposed to mimic the gesticulation of an East European Jew, "No ritual murder?" and after a pause he then added himself, "Very funny."

We laughed at him and imitated him ourselves. Many of us must have realized that he was talking complete nonsense. But no one found room for the thought that the nonsense was a deadly poison which threatened the lives of countless Jews. Today I know that the fairy tales of ritual murder had to be invented and propagated amongst the people so that Müller the shoemaker should not get any rebellious ideas when his neighbour, Mayer the tailor, was taken from his bed one morning and never came back.

We should not have liked to be mentioned in the same breath as Müller the shoemaker, after all we were youth leaders, but the rebellious thoughts did not even occur to us — even though we did not believe a word the raving lunatic in the hunting suit told us. It was so easy to dismiss these things with a laugh. Thus one established one's own superiority.

We also believed ourselves to be above the methods of racial enlightenment employed by *Der Stürmer*[6]. This magazine filled me with nausea. I never held a copy of it in my hand, though I would sometimes glance at it on notice boards. At leaders' conferences it was openly said that it should not be given to young people. What we took exception to in it was not, of course, its basic political tendency but its scandalous lack of taste or educational insight.

The same goes for the bloodthirsty songs in which I joined after 1933 — the only line I can remember is: 'When Jewish blood spurts from the knife...' After the Hitler Youth had ceased to be an instrument in the struggle for power and its educational role came to the fore, such songs were hardly sung any more. We became concerned to maintain a certain 'level of culture'.

---

[6] An anti-semitic weekly published by Julius Streicher, which made much use of cartoons. *Translator's note.*

5

After my return from Labour Service the question of my choice of profession had to be resolved. If it had been financially possible I should have studied German and philosophy at the university, but meanwhile my father had become unemployed. The English firm he had worked for had been forced to close its Berlin branch. The reason given was that many of the men who ran it were Jews. From now on we had to manage on the rents which my mother received from her inherited property. I cannot remember having heard of the system of part time studies then, or I should have tried to follow it. My efforts to obtain a scholarship were unsuccessful. It was explained to me everywhere that the educational requirements of the 'old guard' Party members had to be met first. But if I was prepared to work full time for the Hitler Youth for two years, my application would also be given sympathetic consideration. All this seemed quite reasonable to me. I thought it right that the 'foreign' enterprise, which my father had worked for, should be forced to close its Berlin branch and I took my place in the queue behind the more deserving 'old guard' without a murmur.

My full time work for the Hitler Youth began with a job which lasted only a few months in the press and propaganda department of the Berlin district of the B.D.M. I found a superior there with whom I soon began to quarrel. As a journalist she worked to a certain routine but her character was not what I expected of a youth leader. The things that annoyed me most about her were her unscrupulousness and her unreliability. On the door of her room there was a bright notice bearing a saying in Frisian which meant: 'Pure heart, clear head'. She was an enthusiast for everything Frisian, because she took a pride in her own nordic appearance.

I suppose before you emigrated you must have had more than your fill of the cult of the nordic race which was being built up at that time. I had swallowed the racial teaching with scientific trimmings, which was offered to us in our last years at school, with the same indifference as that with which I mastered chemical formulae or the laws of mathematics. I was not one of those unfortunate people who suddenly found themselves in mortal danger on account of their own lack of 'nordic characteristics' and so I found it easy to ignore this problem in my daily life.

I was, indeed, able to make fun of the 'nordic racket', which I regarded as one of the National Socialist movement's teething troubles. It was only occasionally, when I found myself mildly surprised to realize that most of the people I respected were, outwardly at least, anything but 'nordic', that I took the matter more seriously for a moment.

My Berlin superior who raved in Frisian about a pure heart and a clear head belonged in the same category as a certain sports instructor who had to put up with a lot of ragging because he was earnestly searching for a 'nordic girl' whom he could make the mother of his children. In the group of B.D.M. leaders I became friendly with a little later we called these people 'n[2]' (nordic ninnies) or 'b[3]' (blue eyed, blond blithering idiots).

While I was still at school I went to a wedding ceremony in the woods near Potsdam. I belonged to a choir which was to take part in it. In a clearing there stood an altar on which a fire was burning. Two women in long white robes held bowls filled with bread and fruit. While one of these 'priestesses' had long blond hair which fell about her shoulders, the second had an ordinary 'perm' and wore earrings, as many of the local girls did.

Unfortunately I cannot remember the words of the dialogue spoken by the young couple. The man wore the uniform of an S.S.-Führer[7]. The girl was dressed in white and wore a crown of flowers. Both stood before the altar with heads held high and addressed one another in quotations from the *Edda:* 'Thou, fairest of women...', etc.

The fairest of women was small and fat and had dark, nervous eyes. The quavering of her voice marked her as no Brunhilda. Afterwards my friends and I often laughed heartily about this wedding.

In the years which followed I often went to weddings of youth leaders which showed a feeling for style, and at which the attempt was made to rise to the seriousness of the occasion in the content and form of the ceremony. Certainly the idea that the marriage was concluded as a duty to the nation was emphatically central to them. But there were also young couples who disliked all formulas of that kind and chose the texts for their wedding ceremonies accordingly.

The religious content of these ceremonies was very general, indeed one must call it muddled. If we had been called irreligious we should all have protested with conviction. We looked down on the churches in whose dogmas God — as we thought — was humanized. But we should have found it hard to express the content of our own religious notions. I can perhaps say that we believed in a Creator God who was revealed to us in the order and beauty of nature and whose mysterious being also touched us when we were confronted with great works of art. We also included this god — though without any precise idea of the manner of his working — in the lives of the nations and of our own nation.

When I considered the First World War as a child, I had always reflected on the plight God must have been put in by the prayers of people on both sides. To whom should God listen, since each nation prayed for its own victory? He had not listened to the

---

[7] An officer of the S.S. (Schutzstaffel); Hitler's personal élite guard, which ran the concentration and extermination camps. *Translator's note.*

Germans, because Germany had been defeated. Was I to conclude from this that the German soldiers had fought on the wrong side? Or did God reward the wrong side with victory? Or did He not care at all about the fate of nations?

The question was unanswerable.

At the 'ceremonial hours' in the Hitler Youth or on Labour Service, which I attended and for which I often selected the form and content myself, verses were spoken which had the force of prayers. With their poetic language they were only another way of expressing what we sought to say in our music: our thanks for the community in which we lived, for the 'new start' in the life of our nation, for the harvest, for the birth of a child or for the beauty of the summer. This thanksgiving included at the same time the promise that we would strive to serve well the community into which we were called.

In all this we were very naïve. The question of whether God might possibly be on the side of those who were opposed to National Socialism did not occur to me once — although a variant of this very question (prayers in wartime) had taxed my brain as a child.

We were so filled with the joy of being allowed to contribute our efforts and so proud of the responsibility which we were allowed to bear, despite our youth and inexperience, that the idea that God could perhaps be against us would have seemed to us absurd. In every new success — the 'return home of Austria', for example — we saw a sign of His benevolence. It was encouraging and uplifting to see oneself as enjoying God's protection. One's own antlike efforts thereby almost acquired a halo. But how was one to react when one came into contact somewhere with the régime's acts of violence? How did I react later, for example, when I passed the ghetto at Kutno? On the other side of the fence the Jews lived in the ruins of an old factory. I could see their misery very clearly.

If my 'divinity' had had for me the quality of a primitive tribal god I could still have felt myself to be under his protection even in this situation. But it was not so. The danger of recognizing the injustice in such acts of violence committed by us (and thereby being cured of National Socialism) would have become a burning one had I not at the sight of these unhappy Jews, fiercely suppressed any kind of metaphysical consideration.

Early in 1938 I was transferred from the post in Frankfurt-an-der-Oder to one running the press and propaganda section of the B.D.M. in the district of Kurmark. The section had long been neglected and I had to build it up from scratch. I will not bore you with a detailed account of my work. The following is just to give you a general idea. The district I was responsible for included the country between the Elbe and the Polish frontier, excluding Berlin. I first found myself a team of colleagues in the area sub-offices within my district, where cooperation with the local press was to be established. Apart from this, editorial collaboration on youth publications and their distribution had to be organized. Film showings for young people had to be brought to every village and there were always fresh events — sports meetings, for example — for which posters and other publicity material had to be prepared.

I must digress for a moment to say that while my letter is unintentionally expanding to become a kind of presentation of accounts, I find the old language, or rather nonlanguage, returning with my memories and trying to corner me. The 'Thousand Year Reich' had its own terminology, and not only to designate its ranks, forms of organization and special subjects (like 'racial science'). There were also the typical rhetorical formulas of the Führer's speeches and Goebbels' proclamations and the jargon of the civil servants. Read an issue of the *Völktscher Beobachter* and you could make a dictionary of it. As I write, these expressions come to mind almost automatically, although I try hard not to speak of *Einsatzbereitschaft* ('enterprise-readiness'), *in der Arbeit stehen* ('standing to work'), *deutsche Mädeln* ('German maidens') and so on. But I cannot avoid this terminology altogether — a *Kreisleiter* (area leader) remains a *Kreisleiter* — and indeed I do not want to (though perhaps I am making a virtue of necessity), for the spirit of the time, its evil spirit, can be recognized much more directly in its own language than in a 'translation'.

At my new post I met with what might now be called an ideal working team. It was run by a woman who had started by studying theology and had then qualified as a sports instructor. Of all the National Socialist youth leaders I came to know, she was the closest to my ideal. With such a good example before one's eyes it was easy to forget that there were also ambitious humbugs, braggarts and narrowminded fanatics amongst us. Of course we all belonged basically in the latter category, to a lesser degree, for even a woman as highly moral and intelligent as the head of our office never overstepped the limits of thought and feeling laid down by our 'world view'.

I now worked in Frankfurt-an-der-Oder for almost two years and, because our team was made up of pleasant and able people, it was a happy time. As I write this, I am oppressed by the thought of what your experiences must have been during the same period. With what bitter feelings must you have left the country, which you regarded as home just as much as I did? How it must have galled you for you and your family to be suddenly marked off as a kind of sub-person! Almost everything I am writing here seems to me trivial. I am tempted to cross out every second sentence because I think: how trivial, if one looks at the whole picture! But our great and terrible mistake, the consequences of which, amongst others, were that Germany was torn in half and that today there are hardly any German Jews, was made up of countless small mistakes. A person who does not study them will never be able to understand how the whole picture fits together. It is my deep wish that you should understand, though it is my constant fear that this wish may be an importunity.

Writing articles or organizing meetings gave me little pleasure. I have already written somewhere that I considered propaganda to be basically superfluous and only did this work because I believed that those who gave it to me were better able to judge of its necessity than I could.

What I and my friends enjoyed was being allowed in our work to help young people to build the future National Community. With this aim in view, it did not matter whether or not the individual jobs were enjoyable. The idea that through the training of children we could educate our nation to become a community in which a spirit of brotherhood prevailed also helped us to swallow much that was unpalatable.

Today idealism has become suspect amongst us — which is partly our fault. Idealists too often lack a sense of the ethically negative aspects of their ideal. We found it wonderful that we did not have to work 'for our bread and butter' like most people in professional life. One day I said to a pastor, "We enjoy the same advantage as you. We feel our work to be a vocation."

I remember clearly that I always found it unpleasant to have to receive payment for this work. But I needed the money because I had to live off it. The fact that the salaries were low — my starting salary was eighty Reichmarks and in Frankfurt I earned 220 to 250 Reichmarks — seemed right and proper to me. Only a very few of us had had a professional training which qualified them for their work and, thanks to our youth, we were completely lacking in experience of life. The administrative apparatus was later built up more and more, and then many specialists came into the Hitler Youth as professionals. For example, where perhaps before a photographer might have been in charge of the physical training of a group, this job would later be taken over by a young gymnastics instructor.

Nevertheless the untrained personnel probably remained in the majority by far. But this did not seem an important defect to us. One was not a youth leader because one had studied a trade, such as, for instance, printing, but because one was a National Socialist and a 'natural leader'. Specialist training in education was replaced by youthful enthusiasm, tireless 'enterprise-readiness' and imagination. Willingness was worth more than a state diploma.

It was only in later years, when I was running a Labour Service camp in the Wartheland, that I found my lack of fundamental training to be a hindrance in my work. There were situations then which I could not handle, because I was not well enough trained for them as a teacher or a psychologist.

The knowledge that our work was voluntary was an important additional reason for being happy in it. When we were obliged to give a written undertaking to stay in the service for at least two years more because the turnover of staff was becoming too great — I think it was in 1940 — I protested. I had no doubt that I should stay in my job for more than two years but in doing so I wanted to feel free. Ultimately I asserted my voluntary status: I extricated myself from my contract of service and continued the same work as before, unpaid. What I needed for my living expenses I earned on the side by selling articles.

It was only after 1945 that I began to wonder why I would not have granted the principle of voluntary status, which I was so eager to preserve for myself, to all my fellow countrymen as well. Perhaps I considered, without ever making a conscious calculation, that it was the privilege of the leadership caste. The National Community could not, in fact, consist of brothers and sisters with equal rights.

Although my actual press and propaganda work gave me little pleasure, there were many experiences in the Frankfurt days which were far from unpleasant. I think of the tented camps in summer beside one of the lakes of the Kurmark or a long trip through Austria after its 'return to the Reich'. I went to all parts of the country then, because I had the task of collaborating in the adaptation of the 'illegal' Hitler Youth activities (from the period of its being proscribed) to the methods which had been developed in the Reich. I was overwhelmed as much by the beauty of the Austrian landscape as by the joyful triumph of my comrades, many of whom had been to prison for their political views.

If I think of the national rally of B.D.M. leaders at Bamberg in the summer of 1938, then once again I can only recall this feeling of happiness — to be allowed to belong to a community which embraced the whole youth of the nation, even that part of it which was forced to grow up outside the national frontiers. Many leaders who were *Volksdeutsche* from abroad had left their homes in secret. What made us so happy at this was not the numerical size of our community, but the feeling that no one was excluded from it any more — neither our Austrian comrades, nor even those who were German leaders in Transylvania or Banat. The feeling of being young, of belonging together, of understanding and loving one another in all the variety of our characters, which resulted from our different origins — and above all the feeling that we had a common task — how should it not fill us with overwhelming joy?

In this joy there was still no harsh note of hate or arrogance. The war had not yet begun. We were still not 'orientated' towards the conquest of our neighbours and amidst our own jubilation we did not hear the muffled cries of fear and distress from those people who lived in our country and were persecuted as enemies of the régime.

Now, when I sometimes talk about those days to people who were on the other side of the barricades before 1945, I can always feel their resentment as soon as I mention, for example, the tremendous amount achieved in the intensive and discriminating musical education of young people in those days. I can understand this resistance very well. It would be much simpler if it could now be said that in the Hitler Youth they only bellowed bloodthirsty horror songs and played military marches. But this was not the case and the position is similar in other fields.

The fact that so many of us find it hard to square our accounts with the past is also directly related to the fact that in those days every one of us invested a great deal of positive achievement and drew benefit from the positive achievement of his fellows. These memories obstruct our view. One must tear aside the flowers, if I may use a somewhat bold image, in order to be able to recognize that the roots were poisonous. Millions of men died from this poison, among them the German soldiers and the victims of the bombing raids. But my example was that of our musical education and activities. The general comments followed in anticipation of your reaction. You may remember that I always got low marks in music. It was part of my family tradition to be unmusical. When I left school I could hardly sing a scale. In the summer of 1938 I heard a performance of Bach's *Art of the Fugue* in St. Thomas' church, Leipzig, to which I am indebted for the fact that music is today my chief consolation in life. For then a door really opened before me. The concert took place during the Reich music festival of the Hitler Youth. I was sent there — despite my protests — to report on it for our papers. For days I went from one concert to another. The programme ranged from the Gregorian chant to choral and instrumental music which had been composed within the Hitler Youth itself.

After my ears had been opened at that unforgettable concert at St. Thomas' church I made the surprising discovery that not only could I listen, but I also had a critical appreciation of music. I knew almost no technical terms, but what I said in my layman's language coincided with the judgement of discriminating musicians.

You may well comment that if I had heard the *Art of the Fugue* outside this Hitler Youth performance my ears would still have been opened.

This is certainly true. Provided I had felt the same inward receptiveness at a 'neutral' concert. I did not go to concerts voluntarily, because I thought I was too unmusical. But my point in giving this detailed description is that if one sought it, one could also find within the Hitler Youth satisfaction for one's deepest cultural needs. And sometimes, as in this case, one found it even where one was not looking for it. The fact that this was so bound us with our whole being to the Hitler Youth. Even at the time when the war was destroying almost all the beauty of our lives.

As I give you my account of the year 1938 I think I know what you are waiting for. I have kept it back until the end because...

but I have not the courage to say something which you might interpret as an excuse...

On the evening of November 9 1938 I took part in a demonstration in front of the old gothic town hall in Frankfurt. I cannot remember now the details of this event. It was one of the routine occasions which I generally allowed to pass over my head in boredom and indeed regarded as a waste of time for people like myself, who had no further need of 'orientation'. I only remember that the Frankfurt S.S.-Führer asked my friends and me after the demonstration if we felt like coming with him as something else was planned for that night.

Perhaps he took some of us into his confidence. I myself did not hear what was proposed. I only know that everyone said, "We're not coming. We're too tired."

Next morning — I had slept well and heard no disturbance — I went into Berlin very early to go to the Reich Youth Leadership office. I noticed nothing unusual on the way. I alighted at the Alexanderplatz. In order to get to the Lothringerstrasse I had to go down a rather gloomy alley containing many small shops and inns. To my surprise almost all the shop windows here were smashed in. The pavement was covered with pieces of glass and fragments of broken furniture.

I asked a patrolling policeman what on earth had been going on there. He replied: "In this street they're almost all Jews."

"Well?"

"You don't read the papers. Last night the National Soul boiled over."

I can only remember the sense but not the actual wording of this remark, which had an undertone of hidden anger. I went on my way shaking my head. For the space of a second I was clearly aware that something terrible had happened there. Something frighteningly brutal. But almost at once I switched over to accepting what had happened as over and done with and avoiding critical reflection. I said to myself: The Jews are the enemies of the new Germany. Last night they had a taste of what this means.

Let us hope that World Jewry, which has resolved to hinder Germany's 'new steps towards greatness', will take the events of last night as a warning. If the Jews sow hatred against us all over the world, they must learn that we have hostages for them in our hands.

With these or similar thoughts I constructed for myself a justification of the pogrom. But in any case I forced the memory of it out of my consciousness as quickly as possible. As the years went by I grew better and better at switching off quickly in this manner on similar occasions. It was the only way, whatever the circumstances, to prevent the onset of doubts about the rightness of what had happened. I probably knew, beneath the level of daily consciousness, that serious doubts would have torn away the basis of my existence from under me. Not in the economic but in the existential sense. I had totally identified myself with National Socialism. The moment of horror became more and more dangerous to me as the years went by. For this reason it had to become shorter and shorter. But now I am anticipating. On the 'Night of the Broken Glass' our feelings were not yet hardened to the sight of human suffering as they were later during the war. Perhaps if I had met one of the persecuted and oppressed, an old man with the fear of death in his face, perhaps...

6

At the outbreak of war I was taking a course at the Reich school for B.D.M. leaders in Potsdam. The school lay in a parklike garden by the lake and was an ideal place for young people with a taste for natural beauty — and for the exciting vitality of a community — and who also needed to be able to work in peace.

Those last weeks of peace have left a memory which I can still only grasp in terms of a mood, as though we had resolutely turned our backs on the pressures of the political situation and devoted ourselves exclusively to beautiful things.

I can remember frequent evenings when we rowed out onto the broad lake. In the late summer of that year there was an overwhelming brilliance in the pure blue skies and the riotous colours of the gardens. We stayed on the lake until the shore became invisible and the stars emerged out of the depths of the green glowing sky. Our conversations were in no way different from those which young people in all ages have always had at such moments of emotion at the mysterious beauty of nature.

The news of partial mobilization came as a stunning blow to us in our retreat. Since 1933 we were used to political sensations, but this time we felt that more was at stake than at, say, the 'return home of Austria'.

We belonged to the generation that had grown up after the First World War. The war memories of adults and the harsh consequences of defeat had hung over our childhood like evil shadows. Although we did not know from our own experience what war meant, the inkling we had of the suffering that lay ahead made our hearts heavy.

I remember the silence that suddenly spread through our gay company. One scanned the faces of the others: what could they be thinking? Everywhere the same fear was delineated.

Naturally everyone in that company knew that each of the others was ready to endure the privations imposed by a war for as long as his strength endured. None of us doubted that Hitler would avoid war if he could possibly contrive to do so. "He went through the First World War as a soldier," we consoled one another, "so he knows what misery he is trying to prevent. So long as he sees the slightest spark of hope for a tolerable peace, there will be no war." If it should come to war, then Germany would not bear the guilt for it but her enemies, who would not allow all the Germans to live together in peace and prosperity in one Reich.

We believed this and so there was not one of us who did not identify himself with every one of Hitler's commands. We parted without saying much after the head of the school had given expression to what we all felt in a few brief, quietly spoken sentences.

Do not be impatient if I attempt now to depict the state of mind in which I entered the war. It very likely corresponded to that of many gullible compatriots of mine. You may justly call them complaisant. Our later attitude cannot be understood without taking into account the assumptions with which we started.

During the Sudeten Crisis conjured up by Hitler in the autumn of 1938, thousands of Germans had left their homes in fear of acts of violence by the Czechs. The fact that this panic mood was systematically stirred up by German propaganda in order to keep the Sudeten German pot on the boil was, of course, only known to a very few Germans at the time. I often visited the refugee camps, several of which were in the area where I worked. The Hitler Youth had sent boys and girls to the camps to give all kinds of help. The misery of the old and sick refugees in particular moved me deeply. All this strengthened my naïve belief that the German nation could not be responsible for the world political crisis. It seemed unthinkable to me that German

74

policies should have deliberately created a situation from which such suffering by refugees like this was bound to result. Besides, we considered that Hitler had demonstrated his intelligence by his successes of the past years, so it could not be the ineptness of his policies which had led to such an aggravation of the situation — it could only be the power lust and envy of our enemies.

In those days I and my friends would make such unreal calculations time and again. The combination of true and imaginary facts on which they were based determined our attitude to the war.

Almost all of us knew a family who had been driven out of their home in the east after the First World War. Anyone who had crossed the Polish corridor in order to get to East Prussia must have been struck by the senselessness of tearing the country apart in this way. Every summer groups of young people travelled to the eastern provinces from all parts of Germany and saw how the frontier ran through the middle of farms and divided old villages into a German and a Polish half.

I have often stood there myself and felt what an injustice is done to the people who are the victims of such boundary making. Already before the war I had a sense of the particular misfortune of such frontier areas in which the political frontier does not correspond with that of nationality. In the age of national wars their fate was bound up with an inevitable tragedy, from which there was no way out. The victor is compelled to drive out the defeated. And the defeated will agitate for revenge until it is they who drive their former enemies from the farms. In the terrible circle of retribution an end only seemed foreseeable if one of the two groups could definitely prove itself to be the stronger. To hope for a voluntary surrender of territory either from a victorious or from a defeated nation seemed in our eyes to be Utopian. In 1939 it was the Germans who had most recently been wronged and who hoped for a revision. After the Polish campaign it was the Poles who were wronged. I became fully aware that we were committing wrongs against them in the later years of the war, when the memory of the wrong suffered by the

Germans was slowly fading. But I bowed to the tragic and, as I thought, inevitable law governing this country that ran: He who will not suffer wrong must commit wrong. Only he who possesses the power and exercises it can be master of this country.

At the outbreak of the war I was utterly convinced of our superior moral position. The news of the 'Bloody Sunday' at Bromberg, on which (according to the German Press) 60,000 German nationals were supposed to have been murdered in an appallingly savage manner, thoroughly justified a war against Poland in my eyes. Should not a stop be put to such bestiality?

With regard to the number of German nationals who were killed then, I have since found the following passage in the book by Martin Broszat *National Socialist Policy in Poland 1939 to 1945* (published on behalf of the Institut für Zeitgeschichte's series of quarterly magazines on contemporary history, Number 2): 'In the days immediately following the outbreak of war the rage and hatred of the Poles, justifiably embittered by Hitler's attack, was often vented blindly on *Volksdeutsch* German nationals living there. In several places inhabited by Germans — particularly in Bromberg on September 3 — Germans were shot in large numbers by the Polish Militia and Army. After the German occupation of the country it was established that altogether some 6,000 Germans, mainly from West Prussia, the Province of Posen [Posnania] or Upper Silesia, were dead or missing... But justifiable grief over this event soon merely served a raging campaign of hate propaganda, and finally became the alibi for a policy towards Poland whose simple aim was the systematic extinction of the Polish people's own existence. In public the officially established number of killed and missing Germans was immediately multiplied by ten on Hitler's personal instructions. All relevant German offices were told that in future the figure of 58,000 was the one to be quoted...'

It can hardly be possible now to establish how many Germans were murdered then, and the figure is not relevant here. But there is another significant point: my clear recollection was that we had only made the attack on Poland *after* the news of the 'Bloody Sunday' in Bromberg had reached Berlin. In point of fact the events happened in the reverse order. But my version, which I held to until a few months ago, was much better for easing our bad political conscience.

I mention this so as to give you a specific example of how difficult it is even for someone who genuinely wants to, to cut through the undergrowth of their own minor and major political mistakes.

In the first days of the war I went to Schneidemühl, near the Polish border. I cannot recall now what I had to do there, but I still remember the journey itself very well. My horror over the outbreak of war had abated and had given way to grim resignation. Out in the fields the last of the harvest was being brought in. The harvest carts and the lorries full of young soldiers became jammed together at the level crossings. There were sunflowers in bloom in the peasants' gardens and corncobs drying on the south facing walls under thatched roofs. The people on the train were one single large family, preoccupied with the same worry and full of hope for a swift end to the war. Everyone was more than usually ready to give up their places to exhausted travellers and to share their provisions. The eyes of the women and girls, filled with secret fear, dwelled on the faces of the soldiers, particularly the young ones: Will you come home safely? Will the one I am waiting for come home safely?

Then I had an unforgettable conversation with myself. As I looked out of the moving train at the late summer landscape a voice inside me suddenly said: "It is war: now you have nothing more to fear." "What do you mean?" I asked, "I don't understand." For some time there was silence within me and then the voice replied: "When you are dead you have nothing more to fear — have you?" "No," I said, "I haven't." "Well, for yourself you are now dead." Everything that was *I* had been absorbed into the *Whole*!

This release from the ego and simultaneous identification of myself with something greater than myself, the nation or the

National Community, created an inner attunement which protected me throughout the war like a Palladium: not from physical dangers, from the bombs, the Polish partisans or later from the Russian snipers, but from the greatest mental danger — fear.

I often had the impression that I was less susceptible to the terrors of war than many of my 'comrades', the people who went through dangers with me. I was not often afraid, although I am by nature anything but brave. As a child I was afraid of every dark room for years and never went to sleep without making sure there was no burglar or bogyman under the bed. And for a long time after the war the mood which dominated my life was one of agonizing fear.

But during the war I felt myself in a mysterious way to be invulnerable. I had no fear about myself. What happened to me did not matter. The whole which I served was not endangered by the dangers which threatened me. And I only began to have fears for this whole in the very last months of the war.

As I write this, I wonder how I should judge that selfless existence in retrospect, and I do not mean from a political, but from a personal point of view. Many people, especially young National Socialists, must have lived through that time as I did, with this almost monastic asceticism in regard to themselves and in devotion to the Reich. Although they spared themselves less than most others, they were better protected. He who has a reason for living can bear almost any way of life. But the question must now be examined from another angle: did not such a selfless existence also imply a dangerous loss of contact with ordinary people? Does it not always imply this, whatever the motive for it may be, and in particular when an idol is being worshipped which the misguided devotee takes for a god?

Certainly I threw away many valuable opportunities to broaden my personality because all my energies were driven in a single direction. The fact that it was a misguided, ultimately an evil direction was the misfortune of people who were not the worst of our generation.

It was late in the afternoon one day in November 1939 when I arrived at Posen (Poznan) for the first time. The Hitler Youth leader of the Mark of Brandenburg had been put in charge of the Wartheland Hitler Youth and had asked me to take on the press work in the new district.

At that time I had just decided to go onto the editorial staff of a newspaper as a volunteer in order to complete my training as an editor. In accordance with the most recently established regulations, this training was an essential qualification if one wanted to be responsible for the publication of a newspaper or magazine. It was therefore in the interests of the Hitler Youth that I should qualify as an editor so that I could later become active as an editor for their publications.

The invitation to work in the 'Wartheland'[8] tempted me because something new had to be built up there. When I was promised that I could do editorial work for the Hitler Youth at the same time I agreed to go to Posen.

I remember my arrival there clearly. It was cold, dark and rainy. A young woman whom I had asked the way to a certain street gave me a hostile look and turned her back in silence. After this setback I had no more desire to ask my way. I climbed into one of the horse-drawn cabs which were waiting by the station in a long line. These oldfashioned vehicles reminded me of the bonnets of Salvation Army girls. As it turned out, I had chosen a particularly antiquated specimen: stinking shavings poured out of the torn upholstery and rain streamed into my lap through the leaky roof. The clatter of hooves upon the cobblestones reminded me of films about the days of coaching but that was the only idyllic element in my situation. As the cold rain poured into my face, I had my first intimation of the hostility of the land in which I now wanted to work.

---

[8] The Wartheland or Warthegau was the district of German occupied Poland round the river Warta. *Translator's note.*

After inquiring at the office of the Hitler Youth I was taken by a taciturn man to the house where a room had been requisitioned for me on the third floor. When I rang the bell the front door opened at once. I was expected. An elderly woman took me to my room. A bed had been made up for me there on a sofa. Although the room gave an impression of cleanliness, it gave off a strong musty smell. The people had clearly given me their best room, which was rarely used or aired. It was no different from the lower middle class living rooms which I knew in Germany. There were plush armchairs and lace mats and *art nouveau* twirls on the furniture.

That night I slept little. I was freezing cold in the unheated room. I had opened all the windows because the musty smell made it hard to breathe. In the rooms next door I could hear men and women talking softly together, and often children cried. I had the feeling that a great many people were sheltering in the house. At one point a short burst of shooting roused me from half sleep. I groped my way shivering to the window. They were still talking next door. As I looked down onto the street, the feeling crept over me that I was shut away in a tower with my escape barred by enemies. A little later I got up again and pushed a chair against the door. It had no lock.

I lived in the same room for about three weeks. I gradually gained the impression that the other rooms in the house were occupied by Polish refugees who probably lived in painfully cramped conditions. When I rang it was always the same woman who opened the door to me. She often asked me anxiously in broken German if I was satisfied with my quarters. I found these conversations distasteful. I did not know how to treat the woman. When I moved out she begged me with tears in her eyes to stay. She was clearly afraid of the next compulsory lodger. The thought then occurred to me that the refugees whom I had never seen, but whom I had heard all the more clearly, must be hiding in the house.

Although in the lower middle classes the Polish and German populations differed very little from one another, I developed a keen eye for telling who was a Pole and who a German. One sought in vain amongst the people one came across for Poles of the intelligentsia or prosperous middle class. It was only in the last years of the war that I was informed that this class had taken flight to central Poland and today I know that even this was hardly the case: most of the members of the Polish intelligentsia were deported or killed by the Germans. The few who may have remained must have stayed in hiding, disguised as poor tradespeople. The fact that one nowhere encountered Poles of the upper classes led me to the false conclusion that the Polish nation consisted of workers, peasant farmers and lower middle class tradespeople. No wonder, I said to myself, that they had repeatedly had to suffer long periods of foreign domination. They were clearly not capable of forming a ruling class which could carry responsibility for any length of time.

This line of reasoning made life easier for me as a member of the enemy occupying power. In the Posen area I felt quite at home and regarded the Poles as grudgingly tolerated intruders, who would remain only so long as we needed them. In the eastern regions of the country the situation was different.

Here the position of the occupying power was unmistakable, although this almost wholly Polish region was also designated as German territory. Even if one did not want to admit it, one had a clear feeling that a German future for the eastern Wartheland could at best be considered as a very distant prospect.

What distinguished the Poles one came across in Posen and the nearby districts from the *Volksdeutsch* Germans was — apart from a preference for certain somewhat garish colour combinations in the women's clothes — the way they expressed their state of mind. One could tell by looking at the Germans that they felt themselves to be the conquerors. The Poles had misery written on their faces. In their eyes one encountered all gradations of antipathy from cool reserve to hatred. Even the few who behaved subserviently had an oppressive air of dejection.

The feeling of suffocation, which was hard to escape, also came from the decay of the town itself. During the first late autumn when I roamed through it with my senses undimmed it seemed to have a particular smell of saturated clothes, stale bread, unwashed children and cheap scent. One was constantly going down the same dark, narrow streets past tenement houses with flaking plaster, crossing broken pavements in the hollows of which puddle after puddle collected. Children emerged from stinking yards with rags wrapped round their feet, visibly starving. They pursued me in my dreams. During the first winter of the war Posen was still swarming with begging children, but old people and cripples also held out their hands to us. To begin with I walked past these hands, without putting anything into them. When an old man fell down in front of me with his face in the snow just as I was about to give him a coin, and remained lying there like a log of wood, I was overcome with horror. I was afraid to take hold of him and turn him on his back. The sores and skin rashes of many of these beggars led me to believe they suffered from terrible contagious diseases.

I lived near the fortress, a fortification built in the previous century. Often great mountains of coke and coal, intended for the use of the soldiers, lay there in the street. These stores were guarded by patrolling sentries. On many evenings I watched Polish children creeping up to the coal in the darkness and filling small buckets or sacks. If they were spotted, the soldiers ran after them firing warning shots, or chased them with a barrage of coke. Any who were caught were beaten. At first my sympathies were entirely on the side of the children. I gave them to understand by signs that they need not be afraid of me, but they mistrusted my uniform. They scuttled back silently into the darkness on their ragbound feet. One afternoon I wrested a girl of perhaps eight from the hands of a sentry. In her fear of being beaten she had to let fall her bucket and held both arms folded over her head. When she felt herself released she gave a little cry and ran away. I had bent down for the bucket. Before the soldier could stop me, I threw it into the bushes where the children generally waited hidden. The soldier glared furiously at my silver-trimmed uniform coat. He could not make head or tail of my intervention.

In a very short time I was describing as politically naïve the 'uncontrolled' way I had reacted to this encounter with human misery.

A comrade who was a *Volksdeutsch* German had criticized my 'thoughtless sympathy'. In so doing she expressed what I had already dimly felt: the Poles — even if they had been militarily defeated — remained dangerous enemies; their strength lay in their biological superiority; it was a kind of suicide for us to try to save their children from starvation.

One day, I cannot remember when, an order came from the district headquarters forbidding all Germans to give alms to Polish beggars. I still continued to disobey this command sometimes, in order to mitigate a little the pain which the sight of starving people caused me.

During the first weeks at Posen an image surfaced in my memory and from then on stuck in my mind. I must have been still at primary school the day I pulled a map out of our letter box which pleased me because of its gaiety. The countries of Europe stood out from one another in bright colours and on each country sat, crawled or stood a naked baby. I showed the map to my father because I wanted to know the significance of the babies. He explained to me that each of these children was a symbol of the birthrate of the country. The German families had on the average far less children than, say, Polish families. That was why only a frightened little girl sat on the patch of blue that meant Germany. On the yellow patch, just next door to the right, a sturdy little boy was crawling on all fours aggressively in the direction of the German frontier.

"Look at the boy," said my father. "He is bursting with health and strength. One day he will overrun the little girl."

The picture map stuck in my memory. It kept alive in me the feeling that the Poles were a menace to the German nation.

Later in 'racial science' classes in the upper school the emotional lesson was 'scientifically' reinforced. You will remember how we compared the birth rates of the Slavonic nations with those of the German nation and were instructed about the 'average qualities of the east European races'. Amongst them, so we heard, the intellectual and particularly the creative element came to the fore much more rarely. The noble, refined and intellectual qualities were everywhere in danger of being suppressed by the brutality of the primitive. That was why the Nordic nations were threatened with annihilation by the biological superiority of the Slavs. Primed with these views I came to the region which had been for generations a battlefield in the nationalist struggle between Poles and Germans. What I saw and heard seemed to confirm the National Socialist theories: the foreign nation seemed to consist only of manual workers, poor peasants and lower middle class townspeople, and the few Polish families I had a chance to study had substantially more children than corresponding German families.

It must have been in that first winter of the war that I went to a meeting of the organization which had for years been the mainstay of the *Volksdeutsche* in West Poland. The members of the association met in Bromberg for the last time in order to resolve on and solemnly to celebrate the dissolution of their league. It had fulfilled its purpose, of giving the Germans of the Diaspora a means of supporting one another. The meeting took place in an atmosphere of joy over the German victory, which had fulfilled all these people's hopes. Their homeland had become a part of Germany again. But many of them had had to pay dearly for the victory. A horrifyingly high percentage of the women around me were in mourning. They had lost their husbands, sons or brothers on 'Bloody Sunday' at Bromberg. The Poles must have directed their bloodbath just below the leadership stratum of the German nationals. Wherever one sat down at a table to listen to people's conversations, there was talk of the terror of the first days of the war or of the 'March to Lowitsch'. At the outbreak of war the Poles had sent many of the Germans who were a particular thorn in their flesh to central Poland. The procession of misery had been set free by the German army near Lowitsch.

I had made the journey to Bromberg by car with former Youth leaders of the *Volksdeutsch* Germans who were now working with us in the Hitler Youth. We came through villages where my companions told me that every male inhabitant over the age of fourteen had been killed by the Poles. At one village inn the landlady told me in tears that she and her old mother were the only surviving members of the family.

I could not verify these stories then, nor can I now. I have written elsewhere that even today Polish and German accounts of those events are contradictory. Apart from this, I must not omit to mention that many of the Polish atrocities were provoked by the Germans. Hitler waited for the Poles to give him an opportunity to stage a military intervention in defence of the German minority.

Particularly in conversation with Jewish friends, we are shy of lamenting the sufferings undergone by our fellow countrymen during the war at the hands of their enemies. I can only agree that such complaints against Poland should not be given too much prominence, not even with regard to the East Germans who were driven from their homes at the end of the war and later. We forget so easily that one Pole out of every five died in the war.

My reason for nonetheless reporting these events to you in detail is that, for me, they were a painful political education. What I read in the newspapers about the 'Polish Terror' had left little impression. The fear and sorrow in the eyes of the survivors were more eloquent. Then I acquired the fateful ability to suppress the spontaneous sympathy I felt for the sufferings of members of a foreign nation. Early in 1940 I had an experience which opened my eyes to the state of tension in which many of the *Volksdeutsche* lived at that time. I was driving through the country with a comrade who had been a German Youth leader for years in the Gnesen area and now belonged to the Hitler Youth. Near his home village a farm cart had stopped plumb in the middle of the road. Probably the farmer had fallen asleep on his cart. I suddenly saw my companion reach for the riding whip which lay beside his seat, fling open the door and leap out into the road. Before I could stop him he was beating the deaf farmer as if he had taken leave of his senses. When he came back his face was white and twisted. I realized that it would be pointless to call him to account straight away for his brutality. But even when I tried to do so an hour later he stepped on the brake and said furiously: "You can get out if there's anything you don't like."

I was his superior and I had hitherto found him to be reserved, certainly; but never an unfriendly young man. Soon after this occurrence I lost sight of him, for he was called up into the army. One of his former colleagues told me later that the Poles had tortured to death his mother and his brother or sister (I cannot now remember which). After that I had a better understanding of the impulsive acts of many of the *Volksdeutsche* which disgusted me. But it was also amongst their number that one often met very moderate and reasonable people who knew, from long years of living side by side with them, that the Poles were 'people as well', like all of us, and who tried to treat them accordingly. I say 'tried', because these reasonable people must often have been afraid of being found guilty of fraternization, which was severely punished. Many of those who like myself had been posted to the east from the 'Old Reich' may also have made the discovery that it was hard to maintain the victor's attitude of detachment from the foreign nationals and often difficult to suppress one's natural feelings of sympathy. It was this circumstance which made it necessary for the Party leadership to stiffen our backbones.

I very rarely found time to read the instructional material from the District Headquarters, because I considered myself to be sufficiently well instructed already, but I do remember one item in the material. It aroused my interest because it was passed on in confidence amongst the particularly reliable leaders. This sheet contained a copy of a letter from a Polish priest to a Polish woman. The official religious life of the Poles had completely succumbed to our drastic measures, but one was constantly hearing of Catholic priests remaining hidden amongst the people and not only looking after their souls but also acting as secret political resistance leaders.

One of these priests had written to a Polish woman, whose husband had been taken away by the Germans to do forced labour, roughly as follows: "The Germans have determined to destroy the Polish nation. Our leaders have been killed or forced to live in hiding in the most demeaning circumstances. Countless men, both workers and tradespeople, have been parted from their families and sent abroad. At this time of national peril it is the willingness of Polish women to make sacrifices which will decide our future. What we need above all is children. We must not now at any price lose the lead we have over the Germans, thanks to our high birthrate. For this reason Polish women who may perhaps live for many years to come in separation from their husbands, must not hesitate to bear children whose fathers are decent Poles. Such a liaison would not be interpreted as unfaithfulness towards the husband." The letter closed with a declaration that in behaving thus the Polish women would not be guilty of adultery in the eyes of the Church. I cannot recall the way this last part was argued and expressed.

The authenticity of this priest's letter seems questionable to me now. I think it is possible that it was invented by the Party Leadership in order to lend support to a particular political theory. At that time the Germans were far more sensitive and susceptible to arguments from the field of population politics than the Poles. The secret leaders of the Polish Resistance very likely knew that the biological strength of their nation need give them little cause for concern and, apart from this, almost every Polish child born then grew up in a world of hunger and oppression.

The letter was so accurately aimed at a weak spot in the German's self esteem — the bogy of belonging to a 'dying race' was an ever present obsession then, thanks to the appropriate 'teaching' — that one could well believe it had been concocted as an irritant to arouse hatred.

Nothing else I learned about the Polish Resistance in the course of the year made such an impression as that priest's letter. It increased my fear that all our efforts for the final Germanization of this borderland would be a fruitless labour of love if we could not match up to the vital strength of the Polish nation. Henceforward whenever I was 'in danger' of allowing my behaviour towards the Poles to be tinged with pity I would remind myself of that letter. I told myself that if the Poles were using every means in the fight not to lose that disputed eastern province which the German nation required as *'Lebensraum'*, then they remained our enemies, and I regarded it as my duty to suppress my private feelings if they conflicted with political necessity. The notion that our so-called *'Lebensraum'* could be secured at the expense of the neighbouring nations caused me no moral discomfort. It is true that we had fears for the biological survival of our nation, but we were confident of its unique qualities of leadership. A group which believes itself to be called and chosen to lead, as we did, has no inhibitions when it comes to taking territory from 'inferior elements'.

I have examined myself at length and I think I can say that I did not hate the Poles. Most of the people who had recently come to the country and who had formerly never been victims of racial hatred must have fared as I did. However, I can also remember sometimes coming across 'Reich Germans' (that was the name for people posted there from Germany) who so completely embodied the whole ideal of the Master Race, proclaimed by the National Socialists, that for them every Pole was a kind of slave. These people disconcerted me at first by their completely self confident manner: did they never have any doubts about their attitude? I wondered. At bottom I found them uncanny. I had heard almost nothing about psychology at that time but I felt that those 'Reich Germans' were working off personal neuroses in their political behaviour and I found that repulsive.

It is true that I quite quickly lost my own initial openness towards the Poles. For the reasons I have already mentioned, enmity between the nations seemed to me a bitter necessity. And one could not uphold it if one did not consistently shut oneself off from the men and women of the enemy nation.

This situation caused a strain on one's nerves. One felt oneself obliged — except when one was amongst no one but Germans — to keep constant check on oneself. It was probably an illusion, but one never lost the feeling of being watched by the Poles, as if they were only waiting for one to compromise oneself, by showing fear, for example.

One night when I was going home through lonely streets and witnessed a shooting affray between German policemen and drunken Poles, I did not dare to take shelter in the front hall of a house. Perhaps, I thought, a Pole was standing at a window behind the curtains who would have derived satisfaction from seeing me fling myself down in the dirt from fear. Nor did I ever quicken my step when young Poles, excited by my uniform — these days they would be called hooligans — ran after me in the dark alleys of the old town and shouted things at me which sounded unfriendly.

You will say that I obviously also felt it was my duty to behave like a member of the 'Master Race'. That is to some extent true. I did not like the phrase. It sounded too pompous to me. But my pride at representing Germany in this territory would not permit me to betray any human weakness *vis-à-vis* the Poles.

The constraint of this way of life became particularly noticeable when one travelled back into the 'Old Reich'. When on the westward journey I crossed the former national frontier at Neu-Bentschen, my inner tension every time disappeared so noticeably that it was as if a rigid mask had been taken away from my face. I suddenly had the feeling that I could be myself. I could even smile at the foreigners I met without thereby betraying my political naivety, and I could share their worries, their fears and their joys quite openly.

Then when I had to make the journey back to the East I was filled with conflicting feelings. I was afraid of the cold armour behind which I must so often hide and yet I rejoiced in the strong fascination which the work in that country held for me.

At times when I was not particularly exhausted, the joy was always greater than the fear. I was glad to be allowed to work in the Wartheland and I would not have wanted to change places with anyone in Germany. My colleagues and I felt it was an honour to be allowed to help in 'conquering' this area for our own nation and for German culture. We had all the arrogant enthusiasm of the 'cultural missionary'. Many of the southeast Prussian villages which I had come to know during my period of labour service had been just as poverty stricken and agriculturally backward as the villages we were now visiting. But in those days we had carefully suppressed our cultural missionary's arrogance. Our glorification of the peasant in the ideology of 'blood and soil' prevented us giving rein to our feelings of superiority. In the Wartheland, which was said to be so backward only because of the years of Polish domination, one could enjoy to the full the awareness of having a cultural mission.

As you see I am striving to get on the track of the element of a 'double moral standard' in our reactions, but as things were it is only too understandable that we should have enjoyed a great part of our work.

Bureaucracy was not yet in command there: almost everyone was a little king in his own field of action. There was room for boldness, imagination and enterprise, and although all our sense of responsibility was focused on the question, 'What serves the need of your nation best?', there was still room for personal initiative. Even the atmosphere of hostility in one's encounters with the Poles was not always a cause of depression. One often felt it as a stimulant.

How could young people, in particular, fail to enjoy such a life? It is true that if one visited the eastern parts of the Wartheland it was impossible to imagine oneself to be standing on lost German soil which had simply to be reclaimed for the Reich. This country was Polish through and through. Hitler had not reclaimed it, but conquered it in battle. We knew that might had triumphed over right there. In those days we should probably have agreed that 'the right of the strongest' had triumphed in the struggle for *Lebensraum*.

Those of my friends today, who then already foresaw to what excesses Hitler's power lust would rise, find it barely comprehensible that I should have served this power policy so willingly in the Wartheland. But remember our history lessons, even those we had before 1933. Who were the great men of world history whose deeds were still extolled to us after many centuries, although they had waged war after war? Napoleon, Caesar, Alexander...

We had learnt how England had conquered a world empire for herself, how the French acquired colony after colony. And we believed that now at last Germany's historic hour had come too, and that the dream of her greatness would become a reality in our own lifetime in the Reich of the 'Führer'.

I know from experience that only a very few of the people who held aloof at that time can understand the irresistible fascination words like 'Reich' and 'Führer' had for us. I also know that many people who suffered under this 'Führer' can scarcely endure statements like the ones I am making here. But should I omit them because of this?

Our existence at that time was for us like a great adventure. We were all the happier because we had not sought out this adventure ourselves in order to satisfy our own desire for excitement. We felt that we had been summoned to take part in a difficult and noble service, by which we believed ourselves to be fulfilling our duty towards the 'Reich'. For the individual it meant more than an increase of personal self esteem. All through our childhood the lament over Germany's defeat in the First World War and her misery in the postwar years had never ceased. I believe that growing up in a country where people's minds are dominated by such a mood has a fateful effect. Young people do not want to have to be ashamed of their fatherland. They depend more than older people on being able to honour, admire and to love it.

The fact that we were allowed to perform a kind of 'colonization work' in 'advanced posts' there healed the wounds which our sense of honour had suffered in our childhood and early youth. Germany required us not merely to do a job of work but to give our entire selves. This feeling rose on many occasions to a sensation of intoxication. I do not have to remind you that young people as a rule find little joy in sparing themselves. They want to be required to give themselves entirely.

It goes without saying that in this situation we were inclined to romanticize our existence in the 'front line', and developed much of the colonial's presumptuous arrogance towards the 'stay at homes'.

But the daily tasks required of us, which often forced us to go to the limits of our strength, had a sobering and balancing effect.

I was the first Reich German B.D.M. leader to be sent to the Wartheland, and for a long time I was the only one. It is true that I had no leadership task — I had simply come to Posen to run the press department for the Regional leadership of the Hitler Youth — but I quickly made close contact with the local *Volksdeutsch* B.D.M. leaders and was drawn into their work.

They were all in for a disappointment, for which I slowly tried to prepare them: one fine day a staff of tried and tested Reich German B.D.M. leaders would come to Posen and push the old-established Youth leaders back into the second or third rank. The *Volksdeutsche* were allowed the honour of having been early fighters for the German cause in the Diaspora and having gone to prison for it, but they were not wanted on the pinnacles of the leadership.

I have scarcely any memory of my work in those first weeks at Posen. It must have consisted of establishing an office — partly for the B.D.M. leadership, partly for the press department. I only know that we had a house, which was standing empty and which was said to have belonged to a Polish officer, requisitioned as a hostel for the B.D.M. leaders. My memory gives me more precise information about the setting up of a school for leaders.

Someone had drawn our attention to an abandoned country house which was supposed to have passed back and forth between German and Polish owners several times during the past generations. It lay in a western district, near the former German frontier. Its previous occupants must have abandoned it suddenly, or perhaps they were surprised there by the advancing German troops. The furnishings of the house testified to an old and solid culture. I came back to the house again one day when they had begun to move the furniture. In the great dark panelled library all the books had been torn out of the shelves and lay in a forlorn heap on the floor. Somebody told me they were going to be pulped. I began to rummage round in the mountain and I came upon the most beautiful book I have ever possessed, even if I was not its rightful owner; a collected edition of the works of Shakespeare in English, published in the first half of the nineteenth century. It was printed on India paper and had a soft red leather binding and gilt edges. What particularly fascinated me were the book's scurrilous illustrations. I took it secretly, uncertain whether I was guilty of an act of plunder. But should one let something so precious be destroyed? I would have been only too glad to go on rummaging in the heaps of books for hours, but one could not give up one's time to such things. The book remained in my possession until the Germans left Posen. It must have fallen into the hands of Polish or Russian soldiers along with all my other books. Perhaps it found another admirer amongst them, who saved it from the flames. It was the only piece of someone else's property I ever appropriated.

My work as press officer for the Hitler Youth was confined to writing reports about the local German youth and the beginnings of Hitler Youth work in the Wartheland for the Reich German newspapers or youth magazines.

All of us who were later to build up specialist departments within the youth leadership cooperated at first in taking stock of what we could adapt from the prewar youth work, and in the first stages of building up Hitler Youth units and establishing hostels, offices and schools. This probably sounds more splendid than it was. In general it consisted of driving across country in a rickety car, abandoned by the District Headquarters because it was too unstable, to meet half a dozen boys and girls in a village somewhere. I have never in my life been so cold as on those drives in my first winter in the Wartheland. The roads were little used and the snow was not properly cleared. One was repeatedly stuck in snowdrifts and forced to dig the car out. If that did not work one could, under some circumstances, tramp through the snow for hours until one had found a farmer who helped to get the car going again with his horses.

When one arrived at one's destination one found a pathetic handful of boys and girls clustered close round the stove in a village school room. One of these groups, when I came into the room, was even listening piously to the life story of a Polish national hero. By the light of a paraffin lamp the oldest girl was reading aloud from a Polish newspaper that was two years old. These children had no German reading matter. In any case they could not have made use of it, for up to the outbreak of war they had been forced to go to Polish schools. However, one should not generalize about the situation in different localities, because there were in Poland before the war a great number of public and private primary schools where both Polish and German were taught.

For most of these boys and girls I was the first person from Germany they had ever set eyes on. The things one told them about the life of children of their age in the 'Reich' must have sounded to them like a fairy story or a confidence man's yarn.

One could only say to them: "Don't be impatient. In two or three years' time you will no longer be the only German boys and girls in your village. Soon the Germans will be coming from the Baltic from Volhynia and Galicia and many of them will be settled here. Until then you must make every effort to learn to read and write German. You don't want to find you are behind the others who come here from other countries, do you? Many of them have been luckier than you. They were able to go to

German schools. But your advantage is that you are at home here. You know the country. You must become the best farmers."

When one drove away two hours later one by no means always had the feeling that one had at least found a tiny nucleus for a future youth group.

Lodz in the first winter of the war has stayed in my memory as the ugliest city I have seen in my life. Like many of the older industrial cities — it has a large textile industry — it gave an impression of squalor. Even in the city centre neglected tenement buildings alternated with one-storey wooden houses. Perhaps my memory deceives me, but I think the snow was hardly ever cleared away there at that time. It blocked the roads in yellow-grey heaps and lay on the roofs under a layer of soot. By far the greatest section of the population, the Poles, lived in poverty. There are few people who are indomitable enough to avoid looking outwardly squalid if they have to endure grinding poverty. That is doubtless the reason for the dreary picture which has stuck in my memory: ragged people trudging wearily through the filthy snow, children holding crusts of bread. The black market flourished in this city. Even amongst the Poles there were people who became rich through it, but the bulk of them lived in misery.

When I first visited the office of the Hitler Youth I also met the Kreisleiter there as well. At the end of our conversation he said to me: "My secretary will give you a list of the shops where you can buy everything you want without coupons." I answered ingenuously that there was nothing I needed. It was only later that I realized this indication of the sources of provisions had been a kind of test to see if I had come to 'Litzmannstadt'[9] to work or to 'shop'. When I discovered that Party high ups and officers had come to Lodz specially to hoard without restraint, I swore to myself that I would never buy so much as a skein of darning wool there.

---

[9] Litzmannstadt was the German name for Lodz from 1939 to 1945. *Author's note.*

I was of the opinion that the shrinking stocks of textiles should be left for the non National Socialists. For the people who could not see why the war was necessary — and I was thinking for example of my parents — the many shortages meant a heavy sacrifice. For 'us' it was not important to have new clothes or to be able to smoke or drink coffee. These deprivations did not hurt us.

Of all the *Volksdeutsch* Germans I came to know in the Wartheland, the headmistress of the German High School in Lodz made the strongest impression on me. So far as I knew, this woman had been in charge of German education in central Poland before the war. I can still see her open, intelligent face, with the imprint of intellectual work and an expression of deep sorrow. Since the days of her prewar work she had been the particular friend and adviser of the youth leaders, but she must have been more out of touch with their work than any of us — and also more than we could imagine.

Only once at her home did I spend an evening with her in undisturbed conversation, and that evening she admitted her worries surprisingly openly.

Never before, and also never since, had a person who saw things with critical detachment had the courage to speak to me openly. I must admit that there are some people older than me whom I silently reproach for this 'sin of omission'. But I must agree with you if you object here that it might have been a mortally dangerous undertaking to try to open my eyes or those of someone like me. Even someone who had known me better and had trusted me to act with decency as a human being, would have had every ground for caution. There was no means of knowing in advance whether I should not have felt in duty bound, if someone had revealed themselves to me as an 'opponent of National Socialism', to denounce them as such, despite my personal sympathy.

It would probably have taken an extremely careful and patient approach to convince me that I was on the wrong road. This headmistress in Lodz either had no opportunity for this, or else she did not seek one. She was, like me, a busy woman.

On the evening I am talking about she gave me to understand that she considered our behaviour towards the Poles to be wrong. They were people like us and should be respected as such. The way the Jews were dealt with was equally dangerous and shameful. One could not lock them up in ghettoes as if the Middle Ages were to be conjured up once more.

I can see before me the woman who had the courage to appeal to my independent moral judgement and intellect.

Beneath her white hair she had a young, narrow, rather fresh face in which there was a certain expression of boldness. She came on to say later that it was a mistake to suppress religious education in schools and in the Hitler Youth. I think it is possible that it was her own Christian convictions which made her try to warn me but I could not say for sure.

She herself was probably caught in a difficult inner conflict, for one could clearly feel that she had been glad at first to be able to work in her homeland as a German teacher unopposed. But for the seizure of power by the National Socialists within Germany and without their military expansion, the situation in central Poland would never have altered. Now that she had come to know National Socialism at close quarters, she might be horrified and deeply disillusioned, but nevertheless she felt definitely obliged not to break off contact with those of her old friends who had become blind followers of Hitler. If I understand her rightly, she strove to have a moderating influence.

I did not take her warning to heart until it was too late — after the war. In 1941 I parted from her regretfully. How hard it must be, I thought, for an older person to grow fully to accept National Socialism. Unless one identifies oneself with it entirely, one cannot understand the necessity for all these severities, and probably they cause one distress, even if they do not affect one directly. The thought that most of all made me sad concerned my friends and myself, and there was an element of self pity in it: if so exceptional a person as this woman did not understand us, who, out of the previous generation, could understand us at all? The many officials who made a business of their Party membership were abhorrent to us. One could not wish to be understood by them. But where could we find advisers whose personal and intellectual eminence would help us to become more mature? Must we create everything out of ourselves?

I learned recently that the woman to whose warning words I was deaf at that time was horribly wounded in the flight from the Russians and was finally left lying in the forest, where she froze to death.

7

This 'letter' has remained in a drawer of my desk for two months. I had lost the courage to go on with it. I wonder if you can understand why.

At the house of some friends of mine I met an American doctor of German origin, an elderly, pleasant, ebullient man, of whom I only subsequently learned that he had left Germany in 1935 because of racial persecution. We became involved in a stimulating conversation about the problems of modern art. It was stimulating for me because this doctor was defending a surprisingly conservative viewpoint with arguments that testified to a superior education and training in logic, to which I had almost no reply. I could only defend modern artists by saying that I liked them. You will not be surprised that I therefore had to admit defeat.

You left Germany in 1938 or '39. I very much hope you still found a way after that to continue your formal education. Many people of our age and generation did not. I am one of them. Just when we had reached the stage at which we could have learned to think and acquire intellectual equipment, the period began when thinking was regarded as a 'biologically negative' activity of degenerate brains. We had no education. All we ever had was experience — much too much of it: at all events more than a person could digest in the space of a dozen years. For this reason many of our experiences failed to bear fruit. They have left us with no more than a sense of grievance.

But that was not what I wanted to say; forgive the digression. I was talking about the American doctor whose intelligence and education caused me one of those defeats which people of my background often have to stomach. In the course of the evening the doctor got into conversation with another man who turned out to be a former career officer in the German army. This officer was talking about his wartime experiences on the Eastern Front. Perhaps he knew the man he was talking to was a Jew. He had a tormented way of speaking that was unpleasant to listen to. Suddenly he came to one of those notorious acts of reprisal against the partisans. On this occasion a village in the southern Ukraine was razed to the ground by German soldiers.

I could feel the resistance of the American doctor. He was very annoyed at having to listen to this story. But at the same time I sympathized with the officer: he did not seek to excuse himself but to explain how it had happened that he had become involved in these appalling events.

Later, the doctor, who knew nothing about my own political past, said to me: "Why should I have to listen to that man cleansing his soul in public? People like that ought to leave me in peace!"

Perhaps you can understand why this remark for a while took away the courage I needed to return to this letter.

Nor have I, meanwhile, been able to think of any answer I could have given the doctor on behalf of the officer, or of myself. So I continue to write, despite my fear that you would also like me to leave you in peace. Such an attitude would be only too easy to understand with regard to what I must tell you now. But I should not have dared to begin this letter if my fear were not counterbalanced by hope.

In 1940 I went with a senior Hitler Youth leader on an official journey into the eastern districts of the Wartheland. In the course of it something happened to us which has made me remember this journey, unlike countless others I made.

At the village of K. we crossed a bridge which was swept away a few minutes later by the flood waters of the Warta. It was a wooden army bridge. The posts were cut through by the floating ice and now it hardly stood above the water level. Where it normally reached dry land there was an expanse of water. We only perceived our situation when we had already reached the middle of the bridge, and there was nothing left to do but to accelerate and risk trying to cross the flooded terrain. The car stopped in the middle of the water. The wheels seemed to be spinning in a void. The water had reached the top of them and one could see it rising. As we were preparing to climb out of the windows and onto the roof of the car, a sentry standing on the bank gave the alarm. With excited shouts some men came running out of the nearby houses. They were gaunt people, dressed in black, mostly bearded, and their fluttering assiduity reminded me of a flock of crows. They fetched a team of horses, launched a boat and finally brought us safely ashore.

We had landed on an island in the Warta on which the local Jews had been herded together in ghetto fashion. They ran round our car excitedly and as they hastened to clean off the slime they talked loudly together with many gestures. Just as we were about to get in again a young man pulled me back by the sleeve of my coat because he had found some more dirt in the car which he wanted to clean out first.

After that we drove away without a single word of thanks. I think I can remember exactly how I felt then. The whole time I had avoided looking any of these people in the face. It was as if I were ashamed for them. Did they not know how much we despised them and that the Germans meant them no good? Under these circumstances how could they fall over themselves completely in their eagerness to help?

But I was also ashamed of our own arrogant ingratitude. It was unworthy to treat these men, whose swift intervention had enabled us to reach land almost dry shod, like machines which only existed to tow us ashore.

You do not know the East European mentality. Perhaps you too find the behaviour of these men, as I have described it to you, incomprehensible. In the penultimate year of the war an old Polish woman kissed the hem of my coat long and fervently — although I kept trying to shake her off. She had been afraid that I wanted to turn her and her family out of their house, and when she understood that I only wanted to spend the night on the floor of her kitchen (the beds would have been too dirty for me) her joy at being spared once more inspired her to make this 'obeisance'. On that occasion I had got lost and I was myself much relieved to have found a lonely farm as a refuge for the night.

The behaviour of the Jews on the ghetto island was basically motivated in much the same way as the absolutely groundless gratitude of the old Polish woman. These poor people, who lived in fear and misery, were acting like the child in the story: they stroked the savage beast which threatened to destroy them, hoping thus to overcome its savagery.

One day in the first year of the war I found myself standing unexpectedly before the Kutno ghetto. If my memory does not deceive me, it was located in the grounds of a sugar factory shot to pieces in the fighting, not far from the station. My path led me along beside a high wire fence, in front of which an armed sentry patrolled. Behind the fence lay the ruined factory building. In many places one could see through holes in the walls right into the inmost rooms. Everywhere a roof offered shelter from the rain the families were huddled together. I looked into a burst boiler, inside which the prisoners lay close together in the straw. On the wall of the boiler a great cross had been painted in red paint which had run in bloody tears. A gruesome piece of irony: was this boiler the Jews' hospital? Many men, women and children lay on the bare earth. Some had managed to bring straw with them; a few, feather beds. All were enveloped in an oppressive lethargy. Perhaps most of these stricken people already felt too hopeless to talk to one another and walk about.

The only exception was offered by a few ragged children who stood close by the fence with hands outstretched through the wire netting, begging. There was one adult amongst them, a man whose silly grin led one to suppose that he was feeble minded. A shapeless peaked cap hung over his prominent ears.

As I passed I observed that someone had thrown a paper bag over the fence. The children pounced on their booty. Then I saw one of them holding a matchbox.

I had looked round anxiously at the sentry. Would he intervene? It was one of the young *Volksdeutsch* auxiliary policemen in plain clothes, who were mobilized everywhere for semi military duties. He looked at me just as anxiously as I did at him. My uniform indicated that I belonged to the leadership caste of the Party. He was probably afraid I might tell him off for his laxity.

I hurried by, and from now on cast no more glances through the fence into the Jews' camp. As it was, I had only dared to glance fleetingly into it. The wretchedness of the children brought a lump to my throat. But I clenched my teeth. Gradually I learned to switch off my 'private feelings' quickly and utterly in such situations. This is terrible, I said to myself, but the driving out of the Jews is one of the unfortunate things we must bargain for if the 'Warthegau' is to become a German country.

On my way back, which took me past the ghetto again, I heard loud shouting from a long way off. A ragged old Pole was standing by the fence, shaking his raised fists at the Jews and screaming curses at them. The children had drawn back in fear. Only the feeble minded Jew hung about grinning by the wire netting. This scene seemed to amuse the sentry. He came slowly up to the shouting Pole from behind and lifted off the old man's hat with the muzzle of his rifle. Then he jammed it onto the head of a little girl who was standing by, gaping. Finally he gave the shouting man an almost amiable kick and told him to move on.

As I continued slowly I heard two German railwaymen talking together. One of them said: "I have to show this to all my friends who pass through. They all want to see it. Just a few hundred Jews on a dump, a nasty bunch — filthy and no respect. Dozens of them often stand up here begging by the fence."

103

I glimpsed a greedy look of curiosity and uncanny satisfaction on the face of a red-cheeked bumpkin. A strong feeling of nausea drove me from the spot.

Everything I saw and heard there sickened me. The sight of the Jews did so for two reasons: both because I had learned that they were the most dangerous enemies of Germany, and because their wretchedness offered the spectacle of a human fate which might, for all one knew, be one's own as well some day.

The shouting of the Pole jeering at defenceless people was sickening too. But the most sickening thing of all was the shameless conduct of the railway officials. They went up to the fence like people going to look at caged animals at the zoo — to satisfy their curiosity and to be pleasantly amused. But that is a bad analogy, for one looks at the animals without delighting in their suffering and without arrogance.

You may perhaps feel inclined to interrupt me here to remind me of what I said with reference to the 'Night of the Broken Glass' — the fact that, unfortunately for myself, I was spared the experience of being moved by the sufferings of the persecuted. But here, you will say, they should have been fully before my eyes.

True, but by then it was too late for me to permit myself to recognize that I supported an ideology whose very core was a primitive and, in its effects, criminal racial madness. The war had started. Since I had seen the sufferings of the German community, some of whom had been killed by the Poles, I believed I had learned that one must harden oneself against the sight of human suffering.

English friends with whom I have occasionally discussed this period have asked me why it was not too late for the *Art of the Fugue* to uncover my latent sensitivity, if it was for the misery of the Jews. But we open our hearts willingly to that which is beautiful and brings us happiness, even though it is only a chance beam of light. Yet it is also just as natural for us to reject that which is dark and painful to us. And if the suffering we encounter is understood rightly or wrongly to be the inevitable consequence of the situation — in this case the war — about which we cannot permit ourselves to become confused, then we are more than ever inclined to seal off our hearts hermetically.

On my way through Kutno I also came through streets where the Jews had lived before they were herded together at the sugar factory. One could still read the names over the doors of the houses and shops, and in almost every case I could establish what trades the expelled occupants had followed. I can only remember one specific example: I read that a man named Jakob Biggeleisen had been a shoemaker. Others had been butchers, tailors, blacksmiths, tinkers, stove fitters and so on. These discoveries surprised me: clearly the Jews there did not think themselves too good for hard manual work. But had I not learned that they were too lazy and snobbish to perform exhausting physical work with their own hands?

Significantly I avoided going on to ask what in heaven's name these humble tinkers and shoemakers could have to do with the dollar millionaires of New York. If Jewish capital was harrying Germany all over the world, as our newspapers made us believe, why did it follow that Jakob Biggeleisen with his wife and children must be hounded out of this miserable shack in which he had his workshop?

A person who has never lived under the tutelage of an 'ideology' will find it hard to understand how it is possible for such pressing questions not to be asked. But you will remember what I told you about the headmistress of the Lodz High School. Her objections to National Socialism were certainly convincing. I closed my mind to them, just as I closed it to the urgent questions which pressed themselves upon me here in Kutno.

Here, as there, a different attitude could perhaps have led to suicidal consequences. If I had inquired further, I should have become inextricably entangled in conflicts which would have caused the total collapse of my 'world'. Clearly our subconscious energies — and I can speak here for many of my companions — were fully concentrated on protecting us from such crises. In

1940 I also had repeated opportunities to cast a fleeting glance into the Lodz ghetto. It consisted of a quarter which was cut off from the rest of the city by a fence. One of the main roads out of the city led straight through the ghetto. One was not allowed to go down it on foot, but trams and cars used it constantly. At the time when the ghetto had just been set up, the fence which sealed it off from the street consisted only of fine wire netting. On the other side of this fence there were crowds of pedestrians trying to catch a glimpse of freedom from there. The side streets into which one could see were empty of people.

I still remember my first impressions of a drive along the ghetto street. I said to my companion at the time: "Look at these people. They are walking about as if they were on the Kufürstendamm in peace time."

To my surprise there were quite a few well dressed men and women amongst the prisoners. I saw costly fur coats and carefully made up faces. But what not merely amazed but annoyed me was that the detainees were obviously not required to do work of any kind.

The Germans in Lodz told one another that the Jews had great hoards of gold, jewels, furs and cloth hidden away and that one could only force them to hand over their treasures by threatening to cut off their supplies of provisions.

When I had to pass along the ghetto street again some time later, it was shut off on both sides by a continuous high wooden fence. Doors were let into it at long intervals, and they often opened for a moment: a ghetto policeman, swinging his truncheon, would hustle a couple of pale, hollow cheeked Jews across the roadway to be swallowed up by another door on the opposite side.

One of the girls I worked with had an opportunity to go into the ghetto during the first year of the war. She accompanied the Kreisleiter of Lodz on a tour of inspection of the Jews, for no other reason than simple curiosity. For the same reason I envied her this opportunity. She wanted to see something of the customs of the Jews and their way of life. At that time the inhabitants of the ghetto did not have to endure any torture, apart from the fact that they were penned up together.

I remember her account quite distinctly. She first saw a ritual bath for women and then the slaughter of some poultry. Then her companion had taken her to see a rabbi who lived in a garret surrounded by old sacred books and objects.

He was still only a young man, but he must have had a fascinating aura of true religiousness and spirituality. If my memory does not deceive me, the Kreisleiter ordered him to perform a complicated prayer on the spot, like an oriental prince commanding an acrobat whose skill he wishes to show off before a guest, "Turn three somersaults!"

This situation made my friend so ashamed that she felt like sinking through the floor. The rabbi obeyed, but in every one of his movements he must have expressed a profound contempt for the man who had ordered him to pray.

In the course of the prayer the young man seemed to forget his surroundings, even his scorn for his enemies. My friend said later: "As I looked at the rabbi, I gained an idea of what it can be like to pray. Confronted by this young Jew, I had a feeling of utter defeat."

As you were reading that page you may perhaps have wondered if I would not have received the stimulus for an inner *volte face* if I had myself witnessed that prayer.

It will disillusion you, but the answer must be: No, I do not think anything like that would have happened. My friend was sensitive rather than thick skinned and she remained... just as blind as myself. It is from such experiences that one can recognize the terrible power which so called ideologies can exercise over young people. Once they have surrendered to them, they see without seeing and hear without hearing.

8

When I was posted to Posen I had made it a condition that I should be given the opportunity there to complete my training as an editor. Months passed before the *Ostdeutscher Beobachter* announced that it was prepared to take me on as a volunteer. This newspaper was published and edited at the building of the former *Gazetta Polska*. The *'O.B.'* was the official Party organ for the district and together with its subsidiaries in Lodz and Hohensalza it constituted a press monopoly in the Wartheland.

Every one of my colleagues there, without exception, considered that women were out of place on an editorial staff, except as secretaries. Even if you are only familiar with the broad outline of events in Germany at that time, you will doubtless know of the general tendency which existed in the Party towards a state dominated by men. Most of the male leadership held the view that women's activities should be strictly confined to the family and social spheres and that their education should be correspondingly limited.

With regard to this opinion, which I considered retrograde, I entertained the suspicion from the first that in many cases they upheld it because they were afraid of competition from women. I was in agreement with many of my female comrades that we should under no circumstances yield to this tendency. During the war the 'market value' of women who could be employed outside the home rose constantly in any case. We could see that we should now be used in many posts as 'substitutes' for men who had been called up and who would oust us again after the war as troublesome competitors.

In those days it was considered fashionable to denigrate and mock the movement for the advancement of women, and the female champions of women's rights in particular. I had never taken the time to study these questions properly and I definitely reacted against women who set themselves up as agitators and made inflammatory political speeches. But I was firmly resolved to struggle for equal rights for women as soon as the concern for the very existence of our nation had ceased to call for all our energies.

My new colleagues, then, to return to my story, were more or less 'militant champions for men's rights', and the reception they gave me was correspondingly friendly. Months later one of them admitted to me that at the last 'woman free' editorial conference they had agreed to drive me out again as quickly as possible. I believe they had even jokingly promised a prize to the one who managed to get rid of me in a semi respectable manner. Excessively rough methods could not be considered, because I had been taken onto the editorial staff at the request of Party headquarters.

My colleagues' peculiar enthusiasm for me also had personal causes. Most of them had left their families behind in the 'Old Reich' and enjoyed a carefree bachelor existence there. As I had neither the time nor the inclination to become involved in their private lives, they regarded me as a discomforting — because critical — outsider.

Nevertheless we settled down together surprisingly quickly, for two reasons. My colleagues soon discovered that I was a fully capable member of the staff, not a beginner like the other volunteers, and furthermore they were pacified by the fact that I did not take it upon myself to lecture them on morality.

I noted that most of them got drunk readily and many of them had affairs with their secretaries — which never prevented them writing tender and anxious letters to their families in Germany — but I was not shocked. In those days I held to a kind of theoretical double moral standard. Any effort to reform these men, I told myself, would be completely wasted. One would

have to be very unworldly to believe that most men of this kind
live ascetically and unadulterously. My colleagues could do what
they liked; I was only interested in our work together. But I
expected a completely different moral standard from my
comrades in the Hitler Youth. In my view, a youth leader had a
duty to set an example in his personal life. And this included not
succumbing to the misuse of alcohol — above all not in wartime.
I expected this exemplary conduct of basically everyone in the
Party who held any position of responsibility. I had been
disillusioned to realize that it was a Utopian demand. For me the
fat bellied, drunken *Ortsgruppenleiter* (local S.S. group leader)
or Labour Front official had gradually become a type I hated
more than any enemy of the Party. One day, I believed, these
third rate Party bosses would die out and then a generation would
take charge who had learned to practise voluntary self discipline
as youth leaders.

My new colleagues did not belong to this 'Party boss' category.
They were journalists, not government officials, although they
produced the Party newspaper. There was more abuse and
mockery of the Party amongst them than I had experienced in
any other circle. Presumably the attitude most of them had to
their leading articles which followed the Party line was 'He who
pays the piper calls the tune'. I had no sympathy with this
attitude, but it soon turned out that one could work with them
very well. We helped one another and in general a pleasant
atmosphere prevailed in the editorial office.

The prime difficulty of my position lay in the fact that I had
three tasks, each of which was a full time job for one person. I
was a volunteer on the paper — and at times I had to look after
the features department single handed — but apart from this I ran
the press and propaganda sections of the B.D.M. headquarters
and the Hitler Youth headquarters.

I never had a free Sunday — or even a free hour — to myself,
and as a rule I had to make do with five or six hours' sleep.
When I came home from the newspaper office at about three in
the morning I was so tensed up that I could not get to sleep for

hours. I gradually got into the way of drinking a measure of strong alcohol before going to bed. I hated the taste of it but I needed it as a sleeping draught. I got up at eight and did Hitler Youth work for several hours before going in to the newspaper office about eleven. After lunch I had some more time for my youth work. Then at four o'clock the real day's work on the newspaper began.

I gradually managed to write my Hitler Youth articles there as well, without my colleagues noticing. Whenever I was sent out to get a story or visit a function, I could generally manage to take off some extra time for my 'sideline'. Basically, of course, I regarded the newspaper work as a sideline, but nobody in the office must notice this.

Being obliged to switch my thoughts continually backwards and forwards between the various duties I had taken on was more of a burden than the renunciation of all free time. I was used to this from the age of sixteen. But I had not sufficient time for any of my jobs. I therefore had to improvise constantly and to reckon all the time with the nerveracking risk of things going wrong.

Many of my friends were in a similar position. We cultivated a technique of management which differed from the one that has now come to the fore in modern business life, amongst other things, in that it could call upon 'idealistic' impulses. Fanatical hard work had become a passion for many of us. We probably used it to create a self assertiveness which we lacked.

As I was thinking over what I have just written, one question occurred to me which I thought you might ask at this stage: Why did we hurl ourselves into this fanaticism for work? Might the fact that we did not want to have time to think have had something to do with it? Or was the reverse true — that we had no time to think, just because we worked at high pressure the whole time?

I am afraid I cannot give you the answer. But something else comes to mind which belongs in this context. At a reception on the occasion of his fiftieth birthday Hitler is said to have expressed himself as follows: "My colleagues sometimes complain that I maintain too swift a tempo and thereby overturn developments which should be completed slowly. I know that this is so but I must ask you to keep pace with me. The Third Reich must be built up and secured while I am still at the height of my powers. What we cannot achieve now will never be achieved."

I can no longer remember who reported these words to me. They were quoted amongst us occasionally and never failed to impress me. Hitler is right, I thought, we must not spare our strength for a single minute. In their enthusiasm for the Führer most Germans are still ready to make every sacrifice that he demands of them. It is only at this historic hour that Greater Germany can be built. Then when Hitler dies we shall only have to hold on. Then the inspiration he has given us and the general willingness to make sacrifices will be extinguished. This conviction lay behind all that I did and drove me along from minute to minute.

At the beginning of May 1941 I took my editorial examination. I regarded it as a pure formality and I had not prepared myself for it at all. As far as I remember, I could only answer a fraction of the questions which were put to me. The first question, and the only one I can recall, ran: 'Which orders and decorations does Hermann Göring possess?'

At first I thought this question could not be intended seriously and I tried to give a humorous reply. But then one of the examiners who had come from Berlin informed me that every German journalist should know the answer to this important question.

In the field of economic policy, which was clearly the favourite department of one of the examiners, I failed completely and my knowledge of foreign policy was very indifferent. I knew something of the 'blood and soil' literature on the subject, but I provoked disapproval by permitting myself to make a sarcastic remark about this. When it came to the history of the Nazi Party and the provisions for the training of youth I was able to 'shine', and I acquitted myself well on technical questions and in a short practical test in the composing room.

During my time as a volunteer I had several times visited the women's Labour Service camps in the eastern sector in order to report on them. I had been pleased by what I saw there. The fact that the Labour Service took girls into its camps for half a year meant that it had much more intensive educational possibilities than the Hitler Youth. Apart from this, its work in the villages which had been re-populated with German settlers from Eastern Europe seemed to me to be a particularly necessary and sensible type of war work for women.

I have already told you that my press and propaganda activities always seemed to me, on the other hand, to be somewhat superfluous. I lacked the quality of the born propagandist, who believes he can change the world with the battery of equipment at his disposal. Apart from this I was never quite sure if my work was not simply a contribution to the greedy competition for publicity between the various organs of the Party. I would have regarded that as not merely superfluous but ludicrous and worthless.

As my work in the Hitler Youth for the past year had been unpaid, I could not be made to stay. At the end of my period as a volunteer I 'deserted' to the Labour Service, or rather, I obtained two years' leave in order to take over a job as a leader there. At that time it was possible to enter the Labour Service with the immediate rank of leader on a probationary basis. I made use of this and was taken on as a probationary *Maidenführerin* (leader of maidens) with the prospect of being able to run a camp myself in the near future.

Before that I made a short visit to Lake Constance, where my parents were on holiday.

As I left Lindau station on the morning of June 22 1941 after an all night journey and walked towards the lakeside, I could hear snatches of a loudspeaker broadcast. In a beer garden by the lake a group of holidaymakers were gathered round a wireless set.

I went into the garden and suddenly recognized the voice of Adolf Hitler. He was announcing the invasion of Russia by German troops. I remember very clearly that I was afraid. Had we not made a treaty with the Russians? And, above all, had not Germany once before been ruined by a war on two fronts? Would we be able to hold out this time, with the double burden to eastward and westward? What fate had awaited Napoleon in Russia? In my readers at primary school there had been terrible pictures of the retreat of the French soldiers through the Russian winter... Would Hitler be able to conquer what had been denied to Napoleon?

The people round me had troubled faces. We avoided one another's eyes and looked out across the lake. Its farther shore was shrouded in mist under a grey sky. There was something cheerless in the mood of that cloudy summer's morning. Before the broadcast was over it had started to rain. I had a sleepless night behind me and I was cold. I walked along the shore in a fit of depression. The water lapped, grey and indifferent, against the quayside.

There was one thing the invasion of Russia would certainly mean. The war would be prolonged for many years, and there would perhaps be immeasurably greater sacrifices.

That morning hour on June 22 1941 was the only moment up to 1945 when I seriously asked myself whether Hitler had acted wisely and responsibly. His breach of the agreement with Russia staggered me for a moment, but then I told myself that he must have reasons which would justify his conduct.

At the beginning of August 1941 I went to the camp where I was to do another three months' service 'in the ranks'. I had been able to arrange to go to a camp where the leader was an old friend. It was one of the so called 'Eastern Venture' camps which were set up where the German peasants were still in a tiny minority. For this reason these camps were only staffed by twelve to fourteen girls. It would not have been possible to find work on farms within easy reach of the camps for any more than that.

Apart from the camp leader, who was twenty-three, there was also a nineteen-year-old housekeeping assistant. All the others were 'work maidens' who already had three months' service in a camp farther west behind them and had volunteered for the tougher 'Eastern Venture'.

The war had ravaged our village. There were farms of which it had left nothing but smoke blackened ruins. Most of the farms under cultivation looked neglected. Many people lived in mud shacks from which the plaster had come away in ugly patches. Here and there the thatched roofs were deeply sunken in, doors and windows gaped like black holes. The Polish inhabitants must have guessed that they were going to be driven back to the eastern part of their homeland. What was the use of exhausting themselves working for the foreigners who would move in after them?

The farms of the few German peasants were better cared for, but even they showed traces of the war and of the poverty which had reigned for generations.

Our camp was based in a house which differed from the others only in that it had been kept in better condition. Before the war it had housed a police station.

It was a house like one in a child's painting, and we loved it at once. There were luxuriant cushions of moss on the steeply pitched thatched roof, and to the left of the door stood two old trees. Inside were the dining and living room, the dormitory, the wash room, the camp leader's room, a kitchen and a small room for the housekeeper. All the rooms were too small for their intended purposes and we had to squeeze in very much on top of one another, but it was cosy nonetheless. We used paraffin lamps for light, but the paraffin ration was so small that it only lasted for half the month. When we could not get hold of any candles, we had to manage in the evenings — and during the autumn in the mornings as well — in the dark.

The camp leader came from a prosperous middle class background. Her father was a merchant and had had Jewish friends. When the war came she interrupted her studies, not out of enthusiasm for the National Socialist slogans but because Germany was in need and she wanted to help. She shared this attitude with many men who found it quite natural to become soldiers, although they had no particular sympathy with National Socialism.

I was a friend of hers and I wrote her descriptions of my experiences with our peasants which she still has in her possession. These are the only writings of mine dating from before 1945 to which I still have access. In contrast to what I have so far written to you, they have the virtue of being authentic documents. For this reason I should like to quote from some of them now. They are rather long winded, but if I were to try to abbreviate and alter them, the feel of them would be falsified, and you know how important it is to me that you should gain a picture of the content of my life at that time. If you take the trouble to read them, you may also understand why the positive effects of the work we were doing then kept our attention diverted away from all the negative side of it.

Perhaps you will be shocked by the frankly expressed self confidence, not untouched by arrogance, of the youthful 'colonizers'. You may also find it difficult to understand the attitude which was typical of us at that time: unquestioning willingness to perform an extremely arduous service in order to help our 'compatriots', coupled with blindness to the sufferings of the 'foreigners'. Please remember in all that you read in the following pages, that I do not seek to justify what happened at that time, but only to make it as clear to you as I can.

On the subject of my work for the Sch. family, who were of Volhynian-German origin, I noted the following:

'... The house is a new building. It has only one room and a kitchen. The third room is not finished yet. In the winter Herr Sch. is going to lay floorboards there. He hopes his wife will be home again by then. She has been in a pulmonary hospital for months.

'"You must not be alarmed, Fräulein. There has been no woman here for four months and seven children make the place untidy."

'The little man stands there with his hands clasped in front of his chest and looks at me anxiously with his bright eyes. I later observed that he always adopted this posture whenever he spoke of Hitler. Then he was often overcome with such emotion that tears came to his eyes. It was remarkable in what oldfashioned, almost biblical sounding German he would express his praises. He was firmly convinced that the Führer would think of him quite personally and see to his children's welfare as soon as the war was over.

'Apart from the little iron fireplace there are only two old beds and a rickety table in the kitchen. The beds are also used for sitting on. There is a third bed in the living room, so nine people have to sleep in three beds. The farmer's feeble minded brother sleeps in the barn. I was afraid of him at first. He only makes inarticulate noises and he has the build of an orang outang. When he eats he grunts like an animal and plunges both hands into the dish. Once when I cooked a chicken he swallowed the bones.

'There is just one girl amongst the seven children. Hilde's trust can only be won slowly. She is thirteen but she has the body of an eight-year-old and the face of an old woman. Since her mother has been ill she has been running the household alone. For months there has been nothing to eat but boiled potatoes for lunch and watery gruel morning and evening. Bread is expensive and it can only be bought for Sundays.

'But today we are making vegetable stew. I bought the ingredients, at my own expense. Little Wilhelm-August appears at the kitchen door every five minutes, pushes his round, close shaven head round the corner and asks with a delightfully mischievous smile if the meal is ready yet. I reply every time: "Soon, Willimann!" and pretend to chase him. Then he runs off as fast as he can on his stocky little bow legs, crowing with pleasure.

'At lunch they look into their tin bowls in astonishment: no boiled potatoes today! But they don't need any further invitation. Only Helmut sits in front of his bowl with his head bowed. When I try to coax him he gets up slowly and goes into the corner. He sits there on a bed with his face to the wall. Hilde takes his food to him but he won't touch it. The first morning I arrived he ran far over the fields, like a hare, until I lost sight of him. His older brother says of him: "Helmutchen is the saddest of us."

'After washing up, I want to mend his trousers. They are full of holes and it is beginning to turn cold. While I am busy with this, he has wrapped himself in one of his mother's aprons and sits very still beside me. It is only when I start to tell a story that some expression gradually comes into his pale face.

'His twin, Herbert, is a wag. When I was hoeing potatoes with the feeble minded brother he kept creeping round us. As soon as I looked up, he flung himself flat on the ground and covered his face with his hands. Later on I was running after him with a piece of bread and butter. (I always bring a few slices from the camp for the children.) Finally he fled into the tool shed and crept under a cart. When I followed him under there as well, he closed his eyes tightly and opened his mouth wide for me to push the bread between his teeth. I lay there with him until he had finished eating it. Suddenly he threw his arms round my neck, bit my nose and roared with laughter.

'Eduard, the eldest boy, is sixteen already. He is a handsome, intelligent lad. Ever since I have known him he has been going round in an old top hat. Heaven knows where he found it. He even wears it at meals, with comic pride.

'... The children become more trusting from day to day. I can hardly do any job without lots of little hands wanting to help me...

'Every day it is a new pleasure to work for them and to set the house and garden thoroughly in order for them. Soon everything had reached the stage where I could look beyond the day to day work and think about the future. The children only have very worn out, almost ragged clothes. I calculate this way and that with Herr Sch. to see how we can best divide up the little money there is and the clothing coupons on their ration cards, so as to cover essentials. At first he was ashamed of his poverty, but when he realized how seriously I intended to care for his family's future, he discussed everything with me...'

While the Sch. family had been moved from Volhynia to the Wartheland, the E. family, who feature in the next account, had lived for generations on the same farm. They were long established people of German stock.

'... Today on outside service I visited the farm of Farmer E. for the first time. Four children have already died in the family. The fifth is only three months old and also in danger. It is terribly thin and pale. Its little legs are so thin one is afraid they will break when it kicks.

'I have been sent here to do all in my power to prevent the fifth child dying as well. The wife uses two Polish maids in the kitchen and does not seem to do much work herself. She was unwilling to give me any work either. Finally I scrubbed out the living room and kitchen, although I was rather cramped by the two Polish maids, who were busy sewing and peeling potatoes. I only wanted to show the woman that I have come to work...

'Today I have peeled potatoes, cleaned vegetables and stoned cherries. In the afternoon we were in the fields. The wife talks Polish to her husband much of the time and to the maids all the time. After every sentence I ask what she has said. Perhaps she will get used to talking German, if only for convenience.

'The baby is fed on watered milk. The moment it cries it is rocked and given a drink. Frau E. considers regular feeding unnecessary. When the crying gets on her nerves I believe she gives the child a "sucking bag" filled with sugar into which she puts a few drops of schnapps. As soon as I come on the scene the sucking bag disappears. But I have seen it lying on the cupboard. It smelt of alcohol.

'The child is wrapped up so thickly in clothes that one can scarcely see its face and little hands. I make every effort to convince the woman that if she feeds and treats her baby in this way it will probably share the fate of its brothers and sisters. But she only smiles at my advice. I have the impression she does not take it seriously. When one of my friends made similar reproaches to a Volhynian-German peasant woman she received the disconcerting reply: "But the dear Lord needs little angels too."

'During the last few days I have helped in the kitchen and twice cooked the midday meal myself, worked in the fields hoeing turnips and, above all, looked after the child.

'Now it is given carrot juice every day. But if I don't watch out, the woman pours away the juice which I have prepared ready for it to drink and then lies to me that the child has already drunk it.

'For a week I tried using friendliness and patience with her. Then on Friday I told her emphatically that she was responsible for the life of her child and therefore must not simply ignore wellmeant advice. Her reply was just as emphatic: "I shall treat the child the way my mother treated me."

'The farmer's wife is very familiar with the Polish maids. She fools about with them all day and allows them to keep kissing the child. The farmer — he is the local *Ortsvorsteher* (headman of the village) — observed, when I remonstrated firmly that he should surely speak German in his own home, "German or Polish, it's all the same to me."

'I was tempted to explain to him that a man with such views was unfit to be the headman of a village. But I did not do so. The other *Volksdeutsch* farmers certainly think much the same. It would be equally senseless to use compulsion or threats here. The people must first learn to be proud of their German nationality.

'The apparently pro-German attitude of the Polish servants is also remarkable. One of the maids — who has more say in the running of the house than the farmer's wife — sings German songs all day. In a dreadful thick accent, of course. For example: *Es zittern die morschen Knochen*[10]. This would be her favourite, of all things! I have forbidden her to sing songs of this kind. I find this pro-German attitude of the Poles quite odd. It cannot be honourable.

'If only I can keep the child alive. I have grown so fond of it already. It is so pitiful I feel very sorry for it. Every day we carefully do a few exercises together, so that the little arms and legs can grow stronger.

'On Saturday I fled behind the barn with the little thing, because the wife follows me everywhere and will hardly allow me to take the child out into the air for half an hour every day. For the first time I dared to undress the child completely and to let it kick naked in the sun for three minutes (by the clock!). I coated it lightly with cream and during the sunbath (the sun was not very hot) I took care to keep its little head in the shade all the time. Just as I was about to wrap it up again, Frau E. appeared

---

[10] National Socialist song: 'The rotten bones of the world tremble before the great war' etc. *Translator's note.*

and made a great scene. Now she will not let me near her child any more...'

I gave up outside service there after that because the woman really would not let me near her child and I was not needed for the other work. The little girl died the same autumn.

As I was five years older than most of my fellow workers I was given the most difficult tasks. I have a vivid recollection of a young Volhynian-German couple who were expecting their first child. These people had been less than six months on the farm, which had formerly belonged to Poles, and the move seemed to have stunned them like a body blow. Perhaps, also, they were not used to working. Here is my account:

'... When I arrived at the farm in the morning they were still in bed and both the cows stood hungry in the shed. One had the impression that the woman was about to give birth at any moment. She herself did not know when to expect the child. At all events she had made no preparations for the birth. She had neither clean sheets, nor nappies, nor a bandage.

'The bed in which she slept with her husband consisted of a straw mattress, a filthy old quilt and a pair of ragged grey sheets.

'As I had been sent to the house with an express commission to make the necessary preparations for the birth, I applied myself to this work at once. In the farthest corner of the attic I found an old cradle underneath a lot of junk. I replaced the damaged boards, dug out a piece of cloth for the mattress and bought, at my own expense (the people said they hadn't a penny to spare for this), a dozen nappies and two bandages. Then I mended the tattered bed linen and boiled it several times so that it should be ready for the birth. Every time I left them I told the husband not to forget to drive into town and fetch the midwife as soon as the labour pains began. There was a law there which made it a punishable offence not to call in a midwife or a doctor at the birth of a child.

'After we had been waiting for the child for two or three weeks I saw one morning that the cradle had been hacked into pieces, which now lay beside the firewood. The mattress had been torn to shreds and thrown on the dungheap. Where the nappies were I could not discover but the woman was lying in bed between the clean sheets. My first thought was that the child had come into the world stillborn and, in his grief at this, the father had destroyed all the preparations for the birth. But I was quickly able to ascertain that the woman's condition was still the same.

'I met the man in the cowshed. "What in heaven's name have you done to the cradle?" I asked him. "Have you bought a new one? And where are the nappies?"

'"My wife has given them away," he answered sullenly. "When a child is expected you mustn't make any preparations for the birth, otherwise it dies."

'I was speechless. When I had got over my surprise I went to the wife. She looked at me with hostility. I asked her as amiably as I could how she was feeling but before I had finished speaking she shouted at me: "It's only because you bought nappies and fixed up the cradle that the child won't come. Perhaps it's dead already."

'I soothed her carefully. I felt sorry for her. "Look," I said, "do you really believe God will take less care of your child simply because I have bought the nappies?"

'But it was impossible to talk about such things calmly with her. When I came back from the fields at midday a few days later, she was in labour. I bade her husband fetch the midwife or see to it that a neighbour fetched her. But he refused to do so. "We need no midwife. The child will come into the world the way we came into the world."

'I knew from other families that the Volhynian-German women had formerly brought their children into the world in their husbands' arms. Lack of hygiene during the birth was considered to be one of the chief causes of the high death rate for babies in just this community. Although the man would gladly have stopped me, I harnessed the horse and hurried off to the town. I had to look for the midwife and when we returned to the farm two or three hours later the child was born. It lay beside its mother wrapped in an old shirt of its father's. The bed linen had meanwhile got as dirty as if it had been in use for a year.

'That evening I went with the other girls to the mother's window and we sang a few cradle songs. Then I took the woman flowers and pastry. The man was busy making a box out of some boards which would serve as a substitute for the cradle...'

While I was copying out this old account for you, I became aware, in certain places, of a definitely uncomfortable feeling. Perhaps you will react in the same way. It is remarkable how unquestionably superior to the farmer's wife I felt. She must have been about the same age as myself, if not older. At all events, I treated her with the mild indulgence one normally reserves for a sick and innocently obstinate child. We must have adopted such behaviour basically because excessive demands were being made on us almost all the time. We had to force ourselves to adopt an air of outward superiority, irrespective of whether we were inwardly mature enough to deal with a situation or not.

In this way, bit by bit, one probably (without noticing it oneself) lost any sense of proportion between what one was really capable of, on the basis of one's experience and capabilities, and the tasks one 'took on'. And so one found that the things one attempted generally 'came off'. By expending a considerable amount of will power and enthusiasm, one made them work. In this way, without being basically arrogant, one manoeuvred oneself into assuming a certain 'infallibility'. The psychological consequences of this, both for the individual and the cause (that of the Third Reich), could only be highly dubious. Here was a nucleus for the most varied types of National Socialist hubris. The fact that after the war many supporters of the movement found it such an endlessly difficult process to free themselves of the old wrecked ideas has some of its roots here. It costs a bitter spiritual effort to gain detachment from a high period in one's own life when, without being initially particularly self-assertive, one has grown into a kind of 'infallibility' in the service of something one believes to be great.

Just one more account:

'One morning a peasant woman sent back the girl who was working for her with a request to the camp leader to come quickly, as her husband wanted to kill himself. My friend mounted her bicycle and sped into the neighbouring village. On the way she called over a fence to me where I was weeding: "Come quickly, Herr K. wants to kill himself."

'When we got near his farm we saw him run out through the back door and across the fields. What could we do but run after him? His wife stood at the kitchen window and made a great lament. We followed the fugitive and found him at long last in a loft, tying a rope to one of the beams. After some time we had talked him round sufficiently to induce him to come with us. He gradually admitted to us what had made him so weary of life. The family had only been settled there a few months before. The good man, who now sat before us like a heap of misery, had indeed a deep sorrow. He had fallen in love with a Polish girl, and he knew that liaisons of this kind were severely punished. The girl was the daughter of a Pole who had previously occupied one of the farms. She had returned to the village secretly after the expulsion and worked in K.'s house as a maid.

'The farmer was a man in his prime, tall and broad-shouldered, with a powerful red face. In his wretched state he uttered lamentations in words which recalled texts from the psalms. He said: "I am like a flower of the field and the Lord has resolved to cut me down."

'His despair both touched and amused us and we finally persuaded him to go back with us to his farm. There his wife made him a good meal and in an atmosphere of calm we advised him what should be done to prevent the affair becoming a public scandal...'

Finally I should like to quote part of a letter I wrote at that time, which describes my feelings for the countryside where we lived.

'... It is remarkable how my feeling for this country fluctuates. When I am in Berlin I am homesick for it. Then I speak of it as "our country". It is the land on which we work and prove ourselves and we are often happy in this work. That is why we love it. But on days like today I am afraid of it and I would almost say I hated it.

'Nothing but stubble fields, rank pastures, waste land and unmade roads that threaten to swallow one up. They eat into the farmland on both sides, because every vehicle hugs the edges where it is firmer. The whole countryside is as formless and blurred as these roads. In the dull autumn light not even the horizon presents a clear line; it, too, merges into an undefined sky. Scattered far and wide, little farmsteads cower under poplar trees, which only have leaves at the very tops of their tall stems.

'It is hard to feel at home in this landscape. There is an emptiness about its spaciousness. It lies before us without creative movement. But perhaps that is the wrong word. This country is certainly not "empty" although it is only thinly populated. I mean something else when I say that the sensation keeps forcing itself upon me that we are surrounded by an "emptiness" which drains the strength out of us, body and soul. What this country lacks is that heritage of history which speaks to the people of the present time through the monuments and traditions of former periods. Where are the cathedrals, where the castles, the abbeys and town halls? Where the buildings of old merchant companies and the patrician houses? Has this country produced no people in the course of the centuries who gave expression to their piety, their civic pride or their sense of beauty and proportion in buildings?

'Last Wednesday I went for a cycle ride across country in my free time. On the way I found the remains of a castle from the time of the knights of the orders. It stands on a hill on the banks of the Warta, from which you can look far along the river in both directions.

'I ran about amongst these remnants of old gateways and towers. Seven hundred years ago history was made here, and we must seize hold of it. But can our people still summon up the strength of blood and spirit to bridge such a time span?...'

A few months later I was reminded of that afternoon. I had been summoned to a course of lectures at a school for leaders of the women's Labour Service. Amongst the lecturers who spoke to us was a top man from the *Reichsnährstand* (the 'Reich peasantry', the National Socialist agricultural organization). He indulged in bold and, as I thought, irresponsible prophecies about the extension of German *Lebensraum* to the east. As he raved about how the German peasant would secure the country for our people as far as the Urals, I lost my self control. I sprang to my feet and interrupted him.

"What utopian nonsense! You can only make plans like that sitting at a desk. Who knows if we can ever make the Warthegau into a German country? In three generations the east will drain our strength with its space and emptiness..."

The violence with which I had interrupted left the lecturer speechless. Our school leader tried to intervene.

"Please defend your point of view more objectively. What do you mean?"

"I find it hard to talk objectively about this question, which is a daily source of anxiety to me. I have been living in the Wartheland for over two years and I have travelled round a lot. I am often oppressed by the feeling that the true German nation is thinly stretched over this huge area like a net. If the net has to be stretched much farther, as far as the Urals, it will become so fragile that it will break in countless places."

The man from the *Reichsnährstand* smiled indulgently at my passion and my 'lack of faith in the German peasant'. He was not prepared to engage in a discussion with me. The notion that Germany's eastern frontier must be pushed back to the Urals fascinated him. I got up and left the room, remarking, "I refuse to listen to such nonsense!"

In the corridor my anger and despair at this extravagance overcame me and I burst into tears. I do not know if you can imagine yourself in my position: after that episode the image of the net of German life stretched over foreign territory, breaking at every end and corner, became a kind of obsessive fantasy. I suppressed it, telling myself that an unrealistic conception like 'Germany as far as the Urals' would soon come into collision with Hitler's good sense.

At one time, probably not until the summer of 1942, I felt so drained by what I called the 'emptiness' of that country and I had such a longing for a beautiful old town, that I spent two days and nights on the train, just to be able to wander through Würzburg for eight hours.

I left Lodz on a Friday morning and arrived in Würzburg on the Saturday morning. I had loved the town since I first saw it as a child. I walked for hours over old bridges, through cloisters and churches, admired the splendour of the Bishop's palace, strolled through the alleys of the old town and finally climbed up to the little chapel on the other side of the Main. In the evening, as the valley glowed in its richest colours, I rode back to the station in a horsedrawn carriage. When I think of the journey back by train, I believe I must have sat there for a night and a day without opening my eyes. I did not want to lose a single one of the images I had in my mind. They must become fixed there before other images drove them out. Who could tell how many years I should have to live off that store of beauty, which I had absorbed in a few hours?

In describing my visit to Würzburg to you, I began to wonder again where my thoughts should seek you now. The people who had to leave Germany in similar circumstances to yourself are scattered over the whole world. I know of German emigrants in Iceland, Haiti and the Brazilian jungle. Or do you live in an Australian city or on a farm in Paraguay?

At the end of October 1941 we had to leave our camp base with the two old trees by the door. There was already snow on the ground, and apart from the kitchen stove we had no means of heating the house.

When we said goodbye to our peasants there was much weeping and embracing. We had to promise repeatedly that a fresh team would move into our house the following spring.

From the notes I have already quoted, I learn that we struck our camp flag with the following quotation from Fichte: 'Shall we not rejoice at the broad field that opens before us? Shall we not rejoice that we feel strength within us and that our tasks are endless?'

The field which now opened before me offered few attractive possibilities for development. I was sent to a big camp just on the old frontier. There I no longer went out to work with the farmers but had to acquaint myself with the various departments of camp organization. I had to spend most of the time with the catering staff (for some eighty people) because I was less qualified for this work than any other.

Then in January 1942 I went to that course of lectures for Labour Service leaders, at which I learnt, to my horror, that Germany's eastern frontier was destined to run along the Urals. I was thoroughly bored on that course. I can only remember trivial details — the fact that the course leader, who was lively and had a sense of humour, was very good at getting us to sing with her. She could have got us out of bed in the middle of the night without protest to sing the old three-and four-part songs which we enjoyed so much.

Only the newspapers reminded us that we were living through the third year of the war. Thousands of German soldiers were falling victim to the Russian winter, for which they were not properly equipped. Meanwhile we worried about learning recipes, the texts of youth education laws and historical dates.

After 1945 many people affirmed that the women's Labour Service was basically an institution with social-educational aims rather than political ones. This view bears out my own feelings about it at the time: in my eyes the lack of political direction in it was lamentable.

The women representatives of the Reich Labour Service administration who visited us at the camp seemed to me to be people who only wore the National Socialist uniform by chance. Most of them had been trained as teachers. They were clearly only interested in social and educational questions and not at all in political training. Their basic specialist knowledge distinguished them favourably from many high ranking B.D.M. leaders, but they had a 'bourgeois' aura about them which disturbed me.

In the so called 'heart to heart' at the end of the course when the school leader talked to each of the girls who had taken it, I said quite openly that while we had been served up with the usual helping of ideological training, I had received the impression that the corps of women's Labour Service leaders was a patriotic association for 'wellborn daughters' with a penchant for education. I had felt the lack of a strong element of National Socialism on the course, both in the classes and in the communal life. I should also have preferred there to be some encouragement of a fresh and more critical — and therefore more independent — attitude of mind, whereas my experience had been that we were being trained to acquire a kind of civil servant mentality.

10

Early in 1942 I took over the running of a camp myself for the first time. I was glad to be given a small 'Eastern Venture' camp because there were only a dozen girls there. All of them had volunteered to go to the Eastern sector and were prepared for the particular demands it would make on them. Our camp village was about twenty-five miles from the chief town of the 'Kreis' (area) and the nearest railway station. It was five miles to the village where the nearest Amtskomissar (a German administrative official) was to be found. This village contained some two thousand inhabitants.

The Amtskomissar, his deputy, two policemen and the postmaster and their families were the only Germans among them.

When I presented myself to the Amtskomissar he said to me: "A gang of Polish fire-raisers has been hiding for months in the forest which starts beyond your camp. Apart from that, one of the Polish women in your village must be the ringleader of a resistance group. Keep your eyes open and report to me at once if you notice anything suspicious. In any case the village will be vacated soon. We need it for the German settlers."

What the gang of fire-raisers could do I was soon to discover in a drastic manner. One day when I had business at the post office in the Amtskomissar's village, the whole village turned into a witches' cauldron. While the fire alarms were still sounding, black columns of smoke arose above the thatched roofs in a number of places. The houses, which a moment before had stood there as if deserted, spewed forth an apparently endless crowd of people. They all rushed about shouting in panic. Those who had not lost their heads completely led their cattle out of their stalls or dragged their furniture out into the open. Women carried bedclothes out into the market square and fought one another for places of safety where they could lay their children or invalids. Dogs, pigs and cattle plunged in fear through the human turmoil.

While I was standing pressed against the wall of a house in order not to be hurled to the ground, a woman suddenly clung to me. She was almost naked. Her face was hidden from me by dishevelled red hair but I could hear her whimpering.

As a child I had once witnessed a mentally sick person having a fit on a Berlin tram. Since then I have always been overcome by an indescribable horror at the sight of a mentally deranged person.

I did not see the face of the woman who was clinging to me, but sudden terror gripped me. A madwoman! I thought, and at the same moment I hurled her from me with all my strength and fled into the middle of the market place.

For a minute, perhaps, I was in danger of being carried away by the general panic. Then a cold calm swiftly came over me.

I do not enjoy thinking about that burning village. Perhaps I should try to make it plain to you why not. That day I encountered the evil in myself, without knowing it. It is only years later that I have recognized it, in retrospect, for what it was. Viewed externally, what I did then was even good. I roused the people from their fatalistic despair and made them try to save their houses from the flames. But of course I was not thinking about the misery they would suffer if their homes were destroyed — I was thinking that they would be a burden on German supply arrangements.

There was nothing strictly evil in this consideration. What was evil was the lack of feeling with which I moved amongst these unhappy people. I saw their fear and distress as if in a film: in no way did it touch me myself. I remember well that I had a particular clarity of vision. I wanted to observe precisely how the desperate person behaved in a situation like this. That shyness which normally protects our fellow men in distress from prying eyes had turned into its opposite, into a ruthless desire to probe.

And as I drove the people on, pushing and dragging them and threatening them with a stick (what a sight that must have been!), I was filled with a cold, almost intoxicating feeling of superiority. I fought against their fatalism and their despairing panic and against the fire. And in this fight, in which I myself had nothing to lose, I felt as if I were measuring my strength against some unholy power.

In the heavy air raids I experienced during the later years of the war I often strove with all my strength to be ruled by cool judgement amidst the general panic, because I wanted to help. But then there was no part of evil in me. I remember that in the town of D. I tried to push an old and exhausted man out of the danger zone. And then he was burned to death all the same. He was too weak and I could not carry him. I dragged and shoved him because I was suffering with him. And I suffered with him because I felt that he belonged to the great family of my National Community.

The Poles whose houses were burning were my enemies. I did not suffer with them, even if I acted outwardly in their interest.

Anyone who sees his fellow men in such distress and can only recognize the enemy and not the neighbour becomes himself defenceless against the powers of evil. It is only many years later, looking back on those events, that I understood this.

The fire was fought with a stirrup pump and chains of buckets. These would never have been formed if the Amtskomissar's two constables had not intervened with rubber truncheons and pistols. Gradually the Poles overcame their paralysis and let themselves be driven onto the roofs of their houses to combat the showers of sparks from there. The men formed groups which dragged up every vessel they could lay their hands on, filled with water, in the effort to isolate the seats of the fire. But everywhere there were still women kneeling in front of the burning houses tearing their hair and shrieking in despair. Many of them were praying. On all sides one heard the same cry: "U Jesus! U Jesus!"

One of the policemen had asked me to stay beside the pump to prevent the Poles abandoning it. In the first place it was to be used to protect the Amtskomissar's house from the flames. Before running off the policeman pulled a pistol the size of the palm of his hand out of his trouser pocket. "Would you like this, to be on the safe side?" "No thank you," I replied, "I wouldn't know how to use it."

He clearly seemed to think the situation was dangerous. I did not know what I was supposed to be afraid of. Besides, I had broken off a stick for myself out of a fence after I had half lamed my hand striking a copper boiler. I wanted to take it away from a man so that it could be used for a chain of buckets. When he held onto the pan I aimed a blow at his hands and hit the handle.

The village would probably have vanished from the face of the earth if a heavy fall of rain had not helped the fire fighting. That evening the Amtskomissar, who had been at the chief town of the Kreis all day, reported that fires had broken out there and in other places at the same time. In this way bands of Polish saboteurs, who thought nothing of setting fire to the roofs over their own fellow countrymen's heads, were trying to upset the general supply position. Many Poles were more afraid of them than of the Germans. For these reasons they often did not dare to put out a fire where it was started. These partisans had already taken fierce revenge on those who tried to cross their plans. They had quite recently 'liquidated' a German government official who had become known for his unusual sympathy towards the Poles.

The talk that evening with the Amtskomissar took place in the yard amongst his piled up furniture. The things had been brought out into the open in case the worst happened, and had not yet been put back into place. The little round man stood before an oil painting in a golden frame: a sunset over a heath. His wife was complaining loudly that a pair of valuable boots of hers had been stolen. I saw at least three or four pairs of high boots made of soft leather lying about on the plush covered furniture. "It's the last straw. I'm going back to Germany tomorrow. Who on earth could stick it here?"

It was plain that her husband would have been only too glad to go with her. He gazed gloomily at the purple glow of the sunset over the heath.

The village in which I was to set up my camp was like most of the villages in that part of the country. There were scarcely two dozen straw thatched wattle and daub houses with unkempt, irregular front gardens running down to the main street. This street was like a broad strip of wasteland emerging from the plain, where it had no clear edges, flowing along a narrower bed between the houses and losing itself again on the other side of the village in its sprawling breadth.

The village of B. did have something unusual to offer; a church dating from the first decade of this century. Its size and tasteless decoration dominated the poor peasant shacks in a way that seemed to us grotesquely incongruous. The house which had been allotted to us for our camp base had formerly, so it was said, been the priest's house. It stood opposite the church and the garden bordered an old overgrown cemetery. On many days Polish funeral processions came through the village. One could hear their singing from a long way off, shrill and mournful and always with the same monotonous melodic line. I was amazed every time at the number of people following the hearse — a farm cart with the coffin laid on it. One never had any idea where they had all come from or where they disappeared to afterwards. It was as if the forest swallowed them up. They wore threadbare mourning clothes, and they were lean and wretched. Their faces had the voracious, cunning expression which starving people almost always acquire even when they have not surrendered to selfishness. In the cemetery they lowered their dead into the earth amidst the scrub and weeds. If one looked for it an hour later one could scarcely find the place. I never observed a priest in the funeral processions, although the German villagers always claimed that one had spoken prayers at the graveside.

The church was closed. I cannot remember now who gave me the key. The window panes were smashed in and somebody must have removed the altar. Later on I found a chest containing some huge brown altar candles in the vestry. I took them back to the house. Although they gave very little light and smoked a great deal they were some help to us when the paraffin ran out. I never saw people kneeling in prayer before the door of this church as I did before the porches of many churches in Posen. Even in the winter months, figures wrapped in rags often knelt there for hours at a time. The sight disturbed me. I could almost say that those kneeling people were the only Poles I hated. I hated them because they took God so seriously. It meant nothing to them to provoke the anger of the Germans, and their prayers seemed to be so fervent that they could no longer feel the bitter cold in which they knelt. Must God not love them for this?

But I am afraid I have digressed again. Back to my report.

The former priest's house in which we were to live was in poor condition. Hardly a single window would shut, and none of the doors. Our furniture had been unloaded in the biggest room before I arrived in the village. Now I was waiting for the 'work maidens' to come so that I could get the house arranged with their help. But instead of them came a telegram from which I learned that the camp where they were undergoing training for the 'Eastern Venture' had been put in quarantine for scarlet fever.

I can no longer remember how many weeks I had to remain alone. It was an uncomfortable time, amongst foreigners who watched me, I felt, with hostility. At night I often listened uneasily to the noises in the empty house where none of the doors would shut. And the proximity of the graveyard where cats ran wild was not exactly comforting.

I got local Polish women to help me set the house in order. To my surprise they were eager to do so, although they were not paid for it. They were probably curious to come inside their former priest's house.

I often got a few men to help me as well. They had to put the doors and windows in working order or mend the fence. On these occasions I would go into one of the neighbouring houses, and when I found a man I would tell him in sign language to follow me. I never knew one of them to hesitate even for a moment. Our relationship was simple: I gave the orders and these people carried them out. Nor was it ever necessary to shout or to use any kind of emphasis. Time and again, though, when I gave an inept order, I found the Poles, who understood practical matters better than I did, making counter-proposals. "Nix gutt, Panni, nix gutt!" they would say, and then they showed me how we could do it more efficiently.

I found this complete lack of friction in my dealings with them uncanny. To this day I cannot really explain the reasons for it. I often wonder what gave me the authority which I seemed to possess in the eyes of these peasant farmers and artisans. I felt none of the confidence which their willingness to work for me seemed to suggest.

When I could not make the Poles understand me, I had to seek the help of a so called German, a wily old fellow who cringed before me in an odious manner. He was supposed to have lived in Chicago for forty years and returned shortly before the war. I could never verify his German origin, and in any case he spoke as little German as the Poles. But I could talk to him in English and he could then make himself understood by the artisans. He was the only *Volksdeutsch* German in the village. The few other Germans who had already been moved in came from Bessarabia and spoke only 'Swabian' and Russian. One day I had a hitch with my interpreter. I had asked him to arrange for several cartloads of stones to be brought to our garden — there were enough of them lying at the edges of the fields. The area round the well was to be temporarily paved with them, so that we could walk from the house to the well and back without getting our feet wet.

When I came back from visiting a farmer, there were two Poles busy shovelling stones into the well shaft. The well was our only source of water. If it had been made unusable we should not have been able to open the camp.

In my rage I threatened to report the two Poles to the Amtskomissar for sabotage if the well was not put right within twelve hours. They understood at once and fetched reinforcements. I doubt if they had intended to play a trick on me. Probably the interpreter had misunderstood me. When the camp team finally arrived, almost all the farms in the village had shortly before been taken over by German settlers from Bessarabia and Galicia. Our fellow villagers had previously lived on farms of some size, some of them very prosperous. They would keep trying to prove to me how prosperous they had been by showing me the photographs they had brought with them. By now most of them had idled away a year or more in camps and had acquired a longing for work like a burning thirst. They made no bones about the fact that the poverty of their new farms appalled them — but nevertheless one did not hear them complaining.

"In a few years we'll have it as lovely here as in our old home," they said. Their fanatical industry infected us all. When we heard them ploughing or mending the roofs of barns on moonlit nights we wanted to get up too. The girls were continually asking me to let them stay out on 'outside service' for longer than my instructions allowed.

Our village headman was an old man and hard of hearing, who gradually, without a word, handed all his duties over to me. I became 'parish clerk', 'justice of the peace', 'doctor', 'teacher' and finally even 'priest'. Unfortunately I also had to be 'village constable'. That was the only task I disliked performing.

When the Polish farm servants were too lazy or too cheeky or when they stole things, the farmers' wives, whose husbands had been called up, brought me in to help. I would put on a stern face and make all kinds of threats. The worst threat I could make was to report them to the Amtskomissar. The people knew then that in certain circumstances that could mean being sent to the 'Old Reich'.

Once I brought myself to box the ears of a young lad. People said in the village that he came from Warsaw and was a student, but he seemed to me too young for that. The farmer's wife he worked for had fitted him out with her absent husband's clothes and had given him not the servant's room in the stable but a room in her own house.

He had repaid her trouble by stealing corn every night from the granary. He was probably collecting provisions for a resistance group. (At that time many cattle disappeared from the fields at night.)

I had decided to report the boy to the Amtskomissar, but when he stood before me — a lad with a handsome, intelligent childish face covered in freckles — I could not bring myself to do so, although this neglect gave me a bad conscience. He understood my words very well and suddenly sprang to the hearth, snatched the fire hook out of the firewood chest and held it out to me. Let me beat him with it myself, but not report him. Then I slapped his face with my hand and threatened him: "If you steal once more you will be reported without fail!"

Fortunately I never had to report him.

The settlers did not put their trust in me straight away, but I soon had the chance to win it. Certainly I had a good deal of good luck on my side. Daniel was the first to help me.

One day I found him lying sobbing in the ditch. He was eleven or twelve years old. His left foot was wrapped in a mound of filthy rags. I put him on the saddle of my bicycle and brought him back to the house. There I undid the rags. His foot was a shapeless blue object. Someone had put a compress of elder leaves smeared with chicken dung on a wound. I went to his parents and told them to take the child to the town at once. But they did not think it necessary to go and find a doctor. I therefore set off with Daniel myself. I hardly dared to hope that his foot could be saved. It was saved. Daniel spent many days in my room, and although in handling his foot I had to cause him terrible pain he was as devoted as a dog.

Later on I bicycled round the surrounding villages several times a week with my medicine bag visiting my 'patients'. But first I had to eliminate the competition of a faith healer. The opportunity to do this came with an epidemic of diarrhoea, which threatened the lives of almost all the babies in the village.

The quack was an old woman who came from Galicia: she must have done strange things. I only know that when the children were brought to her she took certain measurements with a hair and then burned the hair and made the child eat the ashes.

When I had persuaded the headman — whose twin sons were getting worse and worse — to abandon this hocuspocus and try 'those little black pills' (charcoal tablets) instead, the first breach had been made. The two children quickly got well.

That gave the man the opportunity to go with me to visit the quack. He stood by with a look of troubled officialdom, while I explained to the woman that her work was forbidden in Germany on pain of severe punishment. We had other and better ways of fighting disease.

One Sunday morning soon after that, I tried to talk over with the peasants the reason why we had had to deal so severely with this old woman, who quite possibly believed in her cures herself. On these mornings most of the men from the village gathered in the school and a few women always came with them. We discussed the most important questions together and then I told them the latest news of the front and of political events. We also went in for a certain amount of adult education. For example, we would study a map of the world and I would tell them about foreign countries.

I shall never forget how old grandma Müller, a ponderous woman for whom the school benches were too narrow, tried to measure the distance between her home in Galicia and her new home with a straw. Then with the same straw she wanted to measure how much farther the distance was between Posen and 'the land of America'. Her son lived in 'the land of America'. He had emigrated shortly after the First World War. When she had measured as far as the middle of the Atlantic her courage deserted her. Not even in her worst nightmares had she imagined 'the land of America' to be as unattainably distant as that.

On many Sundays we invited the villagers to our morning ceremony. These occasions were just as popular as the Sunday afternoon parties when we danced, sang, told stories and played games with our guests.

The older people in particular, who sorely missed their church, were glad to come to our morning ceremonies. I personally had gradually absorbed all the mistrust of the Church which the Party cultivated. I had never really taken the trouble to come to grips with Christian teaching, but more and more I felt an undefined hostility towards the Church.

This hostility only differed in its political emphasis from the attitude of rejection which had formed in me when I was going to confirmation classes. The churches were opposed to National Socialism. I had not verified this assertion. I took it over. It was in the air.

Despite this position, however, I believed that the existence of the churches was essential for the religious needs of many humble people and that it would be a political blunder to allow the settlers, who were already exposed by their move to a considerable mental and emotional strain, to go hungry in this respect.

To begin with our morning ceremonies were simply conceived as periods of assembly for myself and the girls. We too needed a kind of faith, and we tried to find a form which expressed the values of the life we led. There were plenty of themes for us to choose. We celebrated the holiness of bread, of the home, of work, of maternity, and so forth. On another occasion we would centre our thoughts round political themes — for example the vocation of the 'Führer' of a nation.

We soon found that we must also share these periods with our farmers, with whom we were constantly striving to form a closer community. Now we tried to find simpler words and songs. We quickly discovered that our guests could make little of the verses and poetic prose passages in which we had indulged extensively so far. They wanted to be spoken to personally about their own fate and their daily sorrows and joys. What else could I do but introduce a kind of sermon into the middle of our meditations? It cost me some effort to do this, but after the first few attempts I enjoyed this as well. At that time there was hardly a task which I should not have enjoyed. The country people sat in front of me with their hands clapsed and their eyes fixed on my lips. The women's eyes often filled with tears.

Faced with such a receptive audience it was not difficult to find simple words which came from my heart and spoke to the hearts of these men and women. I was fortunate never to have to say anything that I did not fully believe in my innermost self, and I found it a particular advantage of my position that in the often difficult work we performed during the week, my girls and I could vouch for the things I tried to say on Sunday. It was only because we did not spare ourselves physically any more than they did, that I felt justified in giving this spiritual leadership.

Afterwards the girls would often tell me with a laugh what the villagers had said about it the next day. For example: "The Frau Führerin talked as lovely as the Reverend Father used to."

The Frau Führerin was then twenty-four years old and in no way a particularly mature person. On the contrary, I often found that I was hardly older in myself than my seventeen- and eighteen-year-old girls. I had no illusions about the fact that the ability I had to play the diverse roles I was called upon to fulfil in this village community was not derived from my own innate superiority. When there was a dispute amongst the villagers, which was occasionally the case between the members of different national groups, Bessarabians versus Galicians and so on, and I had to settle it, I did not feel my situation was at all a comfortable one. But I was called in by the people as the representative of the National Socialist government, and as I felt myself to be this, I saw no possibility of refusing the summons. Besides, nothing mattered to me more than that the people with whom we lived and for whom we worked should be happy there. They must never think: 'If only we had stayed in our old home.' They must learn to love the land into which Adolf Hitler had summoned them.

When I was dealing with old farmers and their wives who had so much more experience of life than I had, I was very much aware that my position was in one sense 'fraudulent', and it worried me. But I had a job which I had to and wanted to do. And the question of whether the way people saw me outwardly corresponded to what I was in myself must have nothing to do with it.

At that time the word 'humility' acquired a particular meaning for me. For many years I had disliked it. I felt it belonged to the special vocabulary of Christianity and indeed to that category of concepts which were the hardest to reconcile with the idea of a 'heroic life'. The word 'heroic' I also found unpleasant. I never used it. It sounded to me too rhetorical, in the same way as 'Master Race', but I was in sympathy with its meaning.

Perhaps I can explain to you what I now began to understand by 'humility' and why it was important to me. I thought of it as the necessary inner attitude for my situation and my task. I had to have the courage to serve, even where the feeling of my own inadequacy might have persuaded me to refuse to serve. And in performing it, I must not hide my inadequacy from myself; I must keep it clearly in mind. My task was greater than myself. It was not entrusted to me but rather I must entrust myself to it, in full consciousness of my own weakness, and I must hope that from it I should derive the strength I needed. When this idea became clear to me one day I felt liberated and fortified. I stopped thinking about my own position and simply devoted all my energy to my work.

However, I encountered new conflicts when we had the first death in the village. The women's Labour Service camps often helped in arranging name givings and marriages — I cannot remember if we had had occasion to do so — but how were the newly settled peasants to solemnize the burial of their first dead?

They had no cemetery, no church and no priest. Nor was there a layman amongst them who felt called to step into the breach. When the death of an old man was imminent there was general unrest and indecision in the village. I had grown accustomed to assuring the villagers that one day the question of a church would also be settled for them. Of course, I did not believe that the way it was settled would be in accordance with their wishes, but I did not tell them that. I simply wanted to spare them all inner worry for the time being, so that they could devote themselves to building up their farms undisturbed.

As you can imagine, my assurances were now very little use. "Have we to bury the dead man somewhere like a cow's carcase?" grumbled the peasants, and I had to agree with them. I offered to arrange the funeral myself with the girls. There was nobody else there who could have helped them.

We rehearsed a passage from *Kein Hälmlein wächst auf Erden,* and I prepared a short speech. I no longer remember what I said but I remember hesitating for a long time about whether to bring in a passage from the Bible. I came across it when I was leafing through the Bible at the bedside of the dying man: 'Then the Lord thy God will turn thy captivity, and have compassion upon thee, and will return and gather thee from all the nations, whither the Lord thy God hath scattered thee...'

It would have been tempting to relate this text to the fate of the Germans of Eastern Europe, but I left it out. I do not know why, now. Probably I had scruples about involving the Jews of the Old Testament, even without mentioning them by name, in my reflections.

When I had finished speaking, an uneasy silence reigned all round me. I saw the same uncertainty beginning to appear in all their faces. Many of the women clasped their hands and raised them to their faces. I knew that now I should have to lead them in prayer. I had made no provision for a prayer in my programme. I had probably avoided thinking about it because I was afraid of deciding. Now, I had no option. I must say the Lord's Prayer.

While I was speaking I had felt the sun rise directly above my head, pricking me as if the sky were full of thunderclouds. I was overcome with weakness and sweat ran from every pore.

I had hardly ever said the Lord's Prayer, even when I was younger, and I was convinced that I should get so far and then not know how to finish it. It was not until I heard the people round me softly joining in that I lost my nervousness. This embarrassment about speaking a prayer had nothing to do with the fact that I believed all kinds of Christian activity to be forbidden. (It was only after the war that I learned from my former chief that joining in Christian ceremonies in this way had not, in fact, been forbidden to Labour Service leaders.) My conscience was never troubled by disregarding orders if I was convinced that their observance did not correspond to the needs of the moment.

Officially the women's Labour Service was an institution which was designed to fulfil an educational and — in the field of farm work — a social purpose. In contradiction to this 'official line' I considered it necessary that in the Eastern provinces it should especially be a political instrument. Where there were conflicts between a requirement which was in the broadest sense political and the dictates of the Labour Service, I would decide without hesitation in favour of the political objective. I naturally avoided publicizing this practice. I regarded the discussions with the responsible authorities which would have arisen from this as an unnecessary waste of time and energy.

Even the arranging of the funeral was a 'political objective'. Should I have avoided getting involved and thereby been guilty of allowing a nucleus of discontent with the authorities to become established amongst the villagers?

But our decision to cooperate was not simply based on political expediency. We had a strong feeling of community with our villagers and we felt they had a right to solemnize this moment with us in a dignified manner.

There were personal reasons for my wanting to avoid the prayer. My inner attitude towards religion was very confused at that time. Sometimes I indulged in a romantic type of pantheism, sometimes — for example at a morning assembly — I would simply appeal to a personal God. In all this I had the feeling that I was not devoting enough attention to this most central question of human existence. I had neither time nor energy enough to do so.

At times a request formulated itself within me which ran something like this: "You eternal mystery above us all, give me time until after the war. Now I have to work all the time. You can see I have to. But later on, when we are at peace, there will be nothing more to stop me thinking about You."

In this personal situation I had the feeling that I was doing something dishonourable when I spoke a prayer over the old peasant's grave.

11

That summer we also came into close contact with the process of resettlement — that is to say, the expulsion of Polish farmers and the settlement of families of German racial origin on the vacated farms. I cannot pretend to enjoy telling you about it, but this is a chapter I have no right to omit.

At the first light of dawn a horse and cart would take us to the village where the Poles had been given orders to leave during the night. An S.S.-Führer explained to us what our function was to be. We were to clean out the empty houses, to make them ready for the incoming German farmers who were generally expected the same day. For months the Poles had known that one night they would be driven out of their homes within the space of a few hours. Understandably, in these circumstances, they had allowed their property to become neglected and many of them may have deliberately helped the process along. There were floors on which the dirt was trodden down into a layer so hard and thick that we had to take a pickaxe to it.

Our girls would probably have refused to work in a German house which had sunk so low, and I could scarcely have expected them to do so. But here, it seemed, the dirt could not daunt them and we set to work with ardour. The fact that most of the houses were filthy confirmed us in our arrogance: here were the results of the notorious 'Polish management' and we considered it high time that 'orderly German farmers took over the country and the farms'. (Later when there were also some amongst the settlers who — although they were not threatened with expulsion — neglected their houses, we did not find it hard to turn a blind eye. We excused them, saying: These people must be given the chance to get over the emotional shock of the move before severe demands can be made of them.)

When we pictured how distressed the newcomers would be at the dirty houses, the work gave us pleasure. As soon as the rooms were tolerably clean we made a stew in readiness to receive the German peasants. Then we went on to the lighter cleaning jobs and continued with them until the new occupants arrived.

To begin with we saw very little of the Poles when we arrived at the villages early in the morning. Sometimes one of the carts packed high with them passed us in the half light, and then one could look the other way.

But one morning, when we were once again woken up and brought to a village which was being cleared, the S.S. officer who was in charge of the operation explained to me that he no longer had enough men at his disposal, and he hoped that we would step into the breach. During the past few days his section had again been combed for men who were fit for active service, and he did not know how he would manage to carry through the resettlement without our help. He could only afford three *Volksdeutsch* auxiliary policemen, and he would spread them out over the village. We must do the rest of the work. The Poles were still busy packing their things. They had until six o'clock to assemble their farm carts on the road out of the village. Every family could only take what there was room for on a cart. A specified minimum of furniture must be left in the houses for the future occupants. I must divide the girls up round the farms at once and they must ensure that the Poles kept to the regulations.

My first reaction was fury that we should be expected to do this 'man's work'. I knew very well that my superiors would give me every support if I was not prepared to perform the task that was required of me. And if I *were* prepared to do it, it was fairly certain that I should have to take a sharp reproof. (I got it by the way, posthumously as it were, ten years after the war when I was telling my former chief about this.)

What was I to do? I could have explained that we were not auxiliary police: we would wait until the Poles had left the village and then we would do our work.

But what would that have meant for the German settlers? Most of them would have arrived to find almost empty houses. Again and again I had heard complaints from the men who had previously helped to expel the Poles from a village, about how cunningly they managed, even when one stood over them, to take things with them which were on the minimum inventory of what must stay in the house. Could I be responsible for the settlers coming to empty houses, simply because we refused to do such a tough job?

Finally I asked the girls themselves whether they were prepared to go round to the farms in these circumstances. Not one of them hesitated for a moment.

I think I know what may have been in your mind while you were reading the last passage. You will be thinking that some of the girls must certainly have felt afraid or disgusted at the job they were being given, but they were ashamed to admit to these feelings, as their comrades would probably have looked down on them.

But if you consider that all the girls in my camp had volunteered for the 'Eastern Venture', then perhaps you will believe that most of them were plucky and some of them even a little eager for adventure. I myself never felt any fear in this job and my confidence must have been transmitted to the girls. They would sometimes say to me: "When we see how calm you are, we feel quite safe."

I hesitate now, because you can probably have no way of imagining yourself in our position, but I want to try to tell you something which lies beyond what can be communicated in rational terms. There is no doubt that we all felt we stood there in the name of 'Germany's mission' and that this mission afforded us safety to act and a mysterious protection.

My English friends, whom I have mentioned before, interrupted me angrily when I tried to describe this situation to them. "Say what you like," they exclaimed, "it takes more than Germany's mission to turn decent people into bandits."

But without becoming involved in a detached psychological discussion here, one must say that this is precisely the terrible truth — that it did *not* take more than this. In point of fact we let ourselves become the accomplices of a policy of hatred and banditry — but does that prove that we ourselves were contemptibly cruel?

You will perhaps remember that at school no one ever gave us a wholly unambiguous interpretation of the attitude: 'My country — right or wrong.' Of course, our teachers would tell us, it did not testify to a particularly humane concept of justice, but nations that wanted to conquer world empires could not afford to be very squeamish about morality.

During the war we dreamed of founding a German empire. Without noticing it ourselves, we gradually slipped into the attitude that the end justified the means.

There was not one of us who did not find the situation that morning highly unpleasant. But were soldiers asked if they wanted to mount an attack? We felt we were soldiers on the home front. During the war countless men had had to learn to kill the members of enemy nations in cold blood, although by inclination they might be sensitive, considerate and kindly people. And they learned to do so because they believed that in this way they were performing a service for Germany, and because it is easier to achieve an attitude which goes so much against the grain of one's own personality if one acts in a group rather than as an individual.

I know now that taking part in this 'special action' against the villagers who were being expelled was harmful to the girls. They were certainly a particularly lively group, but they were not heartless. In the task they were given they had to force themselves to play military roles more suited to men. It required

150

a different temperament from ours to watch unmoved as whole families were driven from their ancestral farms. And now, in addition, to have to intervene if these people, whose future was bleak, secretly tried to take their cherished possessions with them under the eyes of the people driving them out... Before the girls went round to the farms I said to them: "What we are asked to do will be hard. But remember that after the last war the German peasants had to leave *their* farms." (The fact that they could also opt to remain was not known to me at that time.)

While the girls stuck to their posts at the various farms, I cycled round from farm to farm so as to put in a presence at each one as often as possible. Sometimes I had no choice but to make the Poles unload one of the carts and then to specify exactly which things could be loaded up again and which must be left behind. As the Poles often did not understand my orders, or did not want to understand them, I had to resort to the less ambiguous language of gestures. At the same time I would arm myself with a stout coat-hanger, and I recommended this Amazonian weapon to my girls as well.

As I stood beside the carts which were being unloaded again on my orders, I saw all round me looks of impotent hate and clenched fists. I heard the furious and despairing protests in a language which I did not understand and often I thought: Now one of them will reach for his knife behind your back.

I had given the girls strict instructions: "Make sure you never turn your backs on any of the men, especially the young ones, and keep a careful watch on what is happening in front of you." As there were two of them to a farm, that could more or less be managed.

I myself turned my back deliberately and with exaggerated calm on just those Poles who were particularly furious and threatening. That would indeed have been 'brave' if I had been at all afraid, but at that time I was not at all afraid.

Whenever we asked an S.S.-Führer where the Poles whose expulsion we had witnessed went to, we were told that they went

151

to farms vacated by German settlers or that they were resettled in the 'General Government'[11]. These answers satisfied us. I have already told you how good we were at giving awkward questions a wide berth. Our subconscious generally took very good care to see that we never became involved in dangerous discussion at a conscious level in the first place. Even if we had pressed on to the realization that there could not possibly be enough farms standing empty in the General Government for all those who had been expelled and that many of them would be abandoned to homelessness and the direst poverty, this discovery would still not have worried us. The Poles were our enemies. We must exploit the moment when we were stronger than them, to weaken their 'national substance'. Such arguments were called 'political realism'. I never admitted to the fact that we were basically planning to commit 'genocide'.

Thinking back during the last few days over my collaboration in the resettlement operation, I remembered an experience from the summer of 1941 that is more relevant in this context than it might seem to be. I will tell it to you and you will soon see why it has surfaced in my memory just now.

Before I joined the Labour Service in the summer of 1941 my editorial office in Posen sent me to southern Styria and Croatia to get a story. The Yugoslav campaign had only just finished and I was to write about the 'return home' of the southern Styrian region, which had formerly belonged to Yugoslavia. In doing this I was to compare the particular 'national' problems of this country with those of the Wartheland.

On my journey through the frontier district between southern Styria and the new state of Croatia I had a dramatic experience. The Slovenes who were settled in that area were, I learnt, to be moved out because a 'frontier wall of pure German blood' was to be built in the extreme south of the Reich.

---

[11] The central area of Poland left between the German occupied and Russian occupied zones in 1939. *Translator's note.*

One could easily recognize the Slovenian farms by their gaily decorated farmhouses. The whitewashed walls were painted with broad bands of bright colour round the windows and doors.

In my wanderings I had travelled a good way into the thinly settled area. Suddenly I met a ragged tramp who was clearly not in his right mind. He addressed me in an incomprehensible language with wild gestures, and was obviously becoming more and more enraged. Finally he threatened me with the stick he had been using as a walking stick. There was nothing left for me to do but run away as quickly as I could. The tramp came after me, and there was no doubt that in the long run he would catch up with me. As he had cut me off from the direction of the village I was forced to run farther into lonely countryside. At length I saw a Slovenian farm ahead of me beyond a small wood. I was greatly relieved and ran into the garden. The man abandoned his pursuit and slowly trotted off.

After this fright I needed to reassure myself that sane people were near at hand. I went into the house and knocked on the kitchen door.

It was opened by a woman whom I asked in sign language for a glass of water. I remember this old Slovenian countrywoman as one of the most beautiful people I have ever met. Details escape me now, but I can still see the silhouette of a tall figure with a bearing that was at once proud and graceful. The face beneath the white hair must have had a kindly, sorrowful expression, for it left me perplexed. While I drank the water and ate the bread, which the woman had set before me without being asked, I saw her walking round the kitchen and taking up many things in her hand before either setting them down again or putting them in a big hamper. I understood at once that this was in preparation for her expulsion, and I began to feel very ill at ease.

When I got up, she indicated with a vague gesture the Party badge which I wore on the lapel of my cloak. Then she beckoned me to follow her. We walked in silence through every room in the farmhouse, through the barns and the stables. Once again I no longer recall the details — I can only remember that I thought:

These peasants live and work just the way they did a hundred or two hundred years ago. At the same time I was amazed at the orderliness which prevailed everywhere and the sense of beauty to which the design of the old tools and implements bore witness.

I have never discovered what may have caused the woman to take me on a tour of her property. She walked slowly in front of me in her severe, dark dress, probably that of a widow in mourning, and when we entered another room she would invite me with a gesture of her hand to examine it all at my leisure. Perhaps I was mistaken, but I felt sure she meant to say to me: 'Look about you. All this has been the home of my family for generations. But you and your friends will expel us and drive us into misery.'

I followed her with increasing embarrassment — there was no bitterness or even reproach in what she was saying to me wordlessly, but only a sadness which made me feel heavy hearted. Finally she took me past a little hedge of yellow roses to the garden gate. When she held out her hand to me, I could see her face only dimly, through a mist of tears. I ran off miserably in the opposite direction to the one I had taken when I was pursued by the tramp.

It is difficult and perhaps, indeed, impossible to tell you how I felt at that time. There was no room amongst my ideas for the notion that neighbouring peoples could live side by side other than as rivals for power. During our childhood there was no end to the lament about the plight of the Germans in the lost border territories — Alsace-Lorraine, the Poznan region and West Prussia, the Memel territory, the Hultschiner Ländchen, North Schleswig, Eupen and Malmédy, the Saar district, Upper Silesia. We were taught early, if you remember, that when she lost the war, Germany had been robbed of valuable lands by her French, Polish, Lithuanian, Czechoslovakian, Danish and Belgian neighbours. The catchphrase 'the bleeding frontier' had been painfully impressed upon us. The effect of our whole upbringing — even the one we received before Hitler's seizure of power — was to teach us to regard patriotism, the love of the Fatherland, as one of the highest ideals of human civilization. And the more deeply we identified ourselves with the Fatherland, the more anguish we felt over the 'bleeding frontier'. In those days I held it to be a law of nature that in the rivalry between neighbouring nations there could only be the oppressor and the oppressed. How could one desire anything else for one's own nation, I felt, other than that it should not be amongst the oppressed? If that moment of history had given us the power, should we not use it in order to consolidate it?

Nobody, it was true, could keep an individual from feeling affection for a member of a neighbouring nation. The 'Slovenian problem' did not affect me personally. I had nothing to do with these people; I was not involved in their expulsion. This allowed me to regard it with rather more detachment. I could note objectively, for example, that their farms were clean and I had an open mind in my encounter with a particular individual. To this extent I could see things here, to which I would be blind in my dealings with the Poles. I was bound to consider the Poles 'inferior', otherwise I should have lacked the callousness I needed to help in driving them out.

But I should have thought it equally senseless, with regard to the Slovenians, to try to resist this imagined natural law of enmity. If someone had said to me then: "The Germans should try to make friends with the Poles, or the Slovenes, or the French," I should have smiled sympathetically at this dreamer and answered: "Should we not try to get rid of winter, seeing how much better life is in summer?"

I have no idea where you are living now or how much you keep up with the political life of the country which has (I hope) become your home. At all events you will no doubt follow me if I say that in some senses it is easier to live in a state in which all spheres of life are 'ideologically regimented'. But believe me the fact that I can now believe that peaceful coexistence between neighbouring nations is a practical possibility — however painfully far from realization this remains as far as the East is concerned — feels to me like release from an evil curse. It is torment to live in a world of ideas where hate and enmity between nations are the *ultima ratio* and the only solution.

In making the inner *volte face* I am speaking of, I discovered how much more happily we can live if we are prepared to take the Utopian commandment, 'Love thy neighbour', seriously, and in the rivalry between nations as well.

I believe now that the shock I experienced at the Slovenian farm was intended as a sharp warning to me, just at the moment when I was about to start interfering in the lives of people who were threatened by the same plight as that peasant woman.

But when I was watching the Poles — who often left their farms with faces of stone, often wept or cursed loudly — I never once thought of her.

~ 12 ~

There was one neighbouring village where I felt particularly close ties with the new settlers. The fact that they were, in a special sense, my protégés had to do with the circumstances of their arrival.

People were normally brought to their new farms by S.S. officers from the Resettlement Office. One day I was told that a village, which had long ago been vacated by the Poles and made ready by us for the arrival of the Germans, would be taken over by its new occupants that afternoon.

The caravan we were waiting for did not arrive until after midnight, and on this occasion it was not accompanied by a contingent from the Resettlement Office. The people had simply found their own way to their village by asking along the road. The S.S. officer did not appear until noon the next day, pleading that his car had broken down.

My girls had wanted to stay and help, but when it got near to midnight we went home and I sent them to bed. Then I cycled back to the village. By now it had started to pour with rain. The darkness was so impenetrable that one could scarcely make out the road. I was already in the village when I saw the German settlers' carts. Their hurricane lanterns gave off a feeble circle of light. The people were standing on the street talking in whispers. Here and there one could hear a woman weeping. The new arrivals were alarmed by the silence of the empty farms and the strangeness of the dark, rainswept countryside. As I went from group to group the reason for their uncertainty and caution became clear. In the camp where they had been living for over a year wild rumours had gone the rounds about alleged acts of revenge by the expelled Poles. It was whispered that on the morning after their first night in a new village whole families had been found with their throats cut. Despite the rain, it was more than an hour before I could persuade one of the peasants to go into his new house with me. After that the other families let me take them into theirs. I do not remember exactly, but by this time I had probably fetched the girls from the camp out of bed again, so that for the rest of the first night most of the settlers had someone with them who could help to banish this mood of apprehension.

I myself stayed with a woman who had eight children and whose husband was at the front. She was in a particularly bad way because the house which had been allotted to her was completely empty. Its previous occupants had sold or hidden almost all their property in time, so that when they were moved out they possessed no more than they were allowed to take with them. That night we made a great bed of straw in the living room and then I carried the children in from the street. Each time I carefully felt my way over the threshold in the dark with one of these drowsy, whimpering bundles I blessed it mentally: May you grow up in this house to be a good, healthy, happy person. May this country be your home.

Later on, when the essential things had been done, I sat down beside the young countrywoman on the straw couch and we chatted like old friends.

She was a brave and — as I was to learn in the coming weeks — an industrious woman, but this start in an empty house with empty barns and stables frightened her. Her husband had volunteered for the army because he could not stand the idleness of life in the camp. Now, alone with her eight children, she faced a great mountain of work, worry and responsibility beyond which she could not see. Would she get a good farmhand to work for her? Would her neighbours help her, as they had promised?

As she cried softly to herself there was a noise from the mare and the foal in the room next door. She had not allowed them to be put in the stable for fear of Polish thieves.

A thick brown candle burned smokily on a chest.

That night I promised to give the woman every help I could. I wanted, above all, to ensure that she got some basic furniture soon. In cases like hers, so called 'N.S. National Welfare furniture' was generally supplied. (This was mass produced for needy people in vast quantities.) When I gave her my promise, I could not foresee that there was to be a long delay in deliveries just at that time. Four weeks later the house was almost as empty as it had been on the first day. It was then that I decided to help her on my own initiative. I still had a lot of sheets of headed notepaper from my old Hitler Youth Office in my possession. To the uninitiated they were hard to distinguish from the letterheads of the 'Gau' and 'Kreis' administrative offices of the Nazi Party.

On one of these sheets I wrote out a forged order from the local Kreisleiter and Landrat specifying that every Polish householder within the commune of XY was obliged to surrender a small part of his furniture and kitchen equipment. Then one morning I borrowed a big haycart from one of our farmers, who had by then been established for some time, giving out that I was going to fetch some furniture for the new arrivals from the chief town of the Kreis.

I drove with this cart to a distant part of the Kreis where — as I knew — resettlement had hardly begun. Here I collected everything my farmer's wife needed. I went into the houses that looked reasonably prosperous, showed the frightened occupants my 'order from the Kreisleiter', read it out and then indicated to the people by gestures which objects they must put on the cart.

They certainly cannot have understood what the 'letter from the Kreisleiter' was all about. I could tell from their terror that they feared I had come to inform them of their forthcoming expulsion, and so they were relieved when I only went to the kitchen cupboard and took three of their seven or eight spoons. The beds were the most important items for me. I had them loaded up with mattresses and bedclothes, though I never took more than one from the same house. This was the greatest loss to those I robbed.

My 'Master Race' act doubtless indicated to the poor people that I was not prepared to argue. Only if everything went off at top speed did I stand the chance that none of them would meanwhile have gone to his village elder — who might be a German or a Pole — to discuss the matter with him. My only escort was Ferdl, an Alsatian with a long shaggy coat who looked like a savage wolf. Only people who lived near my camp knew that he was as mild as a lamb — a goose could put him to flight. Now he followed on my heels and made my job much easier. In case of emergency I carried in the pocket of my windcheater the little pistol that was issued to every leader of an 'Eastern Venture' camp, but I might just as well have carried a potato round with me. I did not know how to use the weapon; I merely wanted to be able to show it in case of trouble. Fortunately I never had occasion to do so.

If I remember rightly, I made two journeys with the cart, and although I only brought shabby old tables, chairs, chests of drawers and beds, the farmer's wife was still pleased to have been provided with the bare essentials.

I had to keep this operation secret from my girls and Ferdl was the only companion I could take with me. This was not only because he looked fierce, but also because he would not talk. I knew very well that amongst other things I was guilty of exceeding my authority and falsifying documents. If the affair had become known I might have been dismissed from the Labour Service and tried by a Party tribunal or perhaps even an ordinary court of law. It was therefore a risk in every sense. But I pushed all these considerations aside. The disillusionment of the farmer's wife who was waiting vainly from week to week for the promised furniture to be delivered was gradually beginning to poison her faith in National Socialist Germany. This I wanted to prevent — even at the cost of such a risk.

If I try now to imagine the situation in the Polish houses, the feeling grows on me that I must have acted in a kind of trance. This dubious adventure created a kind of inner tension which caused everything to pass me by like a phantom. I naturally suppressed any kind of sympathy for the Poles whom I was robbing. Armed with moral blinkers which prevented me from noticing anything likely to worry me or arouse my sympathy, I made straight for my objective in order to achieve it quickly with the minimum of obstacles. Not until I had left the 'raided' village behind did I relax. Then I experienced, in addition, even a certain satisfaction at the risk I had taken. I must not tell you how I feel now about those pirate expeditions. When I look back on the years in the Wartheland I am overcome with shame and regret that I allowed my feelings and actions to be so completely dominated by a demon of hostility towards the nation that is our neighbour.

Six or seven years after the end of the war I told the person who had been my superior in the Labour Service about this adventure, and even then my account horrified her.

In the autumn of 1942 I was transferred to the western Wartheland to establish a new and, this time, a large camp there.

It was located in an old and rather dilapidated country house which stood in an overgrown park. I liked it there. Safe behind the fine oak doors or in enchanted corners of the park one could be living in the midst of that time, and yet feel protected as if by an old ivy mantle which muffled its shrill cacophony. The house did have one disadvantage: we were never wholly able to rid it of bugs and fleas.

My work was very different here. The instructional side of it now came to the fore. The farmers for whom the girls worked were partly long established there and partly settlers who had moved in some considerable time before. Many of them lived on big, well tended farms and their community was an orderly one. I no longer had to play maid-of-all-work and could devote myself to my duties within the camp.

These I enjoyed, although they presented me with new kinds of difficulties. The girls were a rare mixture. The three most distinctive groups were the *Volksdeutsch* German girls who came from homes somewhere in eastern Europe, the school leavers from the Reich and two or three girls who had taken their Abitur at German schools in the Wartheland. I was convinced that the latter only made a show of being German. They had probably attended German schools because it was the only way to continue their studies. I took them for Polish girls from educated families, whose parents had found a way to side nominally with the Germans in the struggle to maintain their social and cultural standard of living under altered political circumstances.

Although they may have found themselves in a difficult situation, these girls were excellent to work with. They were intelligent, industrious, ready to help and accustomed by their special situation to exercising a self discipline which benefited our community.

We never talked together openly about their problems. I never tried to start a conversation on the subject because I knew these girls would have no choice but to lie to me. But I wrestled indirectly for their souls in a very naïve manner. I was convinced that German culture was vastly superior to that of Poland and that these alert young people would have turned towards things German one day almost of their own accord, because they were sensitive to the values with which they came into contact here.

We occasionally argued about whether Bach or Chopin was the greater musical genius, but I generally did no more than unpolemically introduce these girls — and all the others who were interested — to the precious things which I particularly loved myself, whether in the field of literature or the visual arts, or in singing old songs together in their original settings. In all this I was helped by a very gifted deputy of very great character. In general I told myself: We can only win these girls' inner allegiance to the German way of life by making them feel at home in this most German of institutions.

In retrospect, admittedly, I feel that there was always an element of estrangement between the girls and myself which was not overcome. It was rooted in the uncertainties of the political situation. But I should like to think that on a personal level we liked and respected one another.

The educational task presented by the *Volksdeutsch* German girls was considerably harder. Most of them came from Volhynia, and displayed all the characteristics one finds where families in the lowest social orders have for generations been shunted back and forth between two nations. They were, above all, reserved and mistrustful. They had little self confidence and they found it difficult to stand by an opinion. This made it easier to suspect them of bad faith than the others, although they were not by nature deceitful. Most of them could neither read nor write German and their educational level was about zero. I set up a kind of elementary school for them which took up much more time and energy than was allowed for in the programme of work. The girls were extremely keen to learn and some of the school leavers from the Reich made excellent teachers.

When I think back to that first summer at F. I believe I hardly lost my temper with the girls once. At all events I never had to tick any of them off. The community had developed its own nucleus of leaders — responsible girls who made sure that the more unstable ones kept up to the mark. I was particularly grateful to learn that there were always a few of my girls who were determined 'not to let Maschi' (that was my nickname) 'lose her temper'.

A few years ago I met a Hamburg girl from that camp. She had been recommended to me as a particularly gifted youth leader and was one of the driving forces in the community. She has since become a doctor. When we met years later I discovered that already in 1942 she was in contact with a resistance group to which her parents belonged. So this girl would hardly be disposed to find wonderful everything which the Labour Service had to offer. On the contrary: she viewed it with a very critical eye. I was therefore all the more delighted when at our reunion she spoke about her time at the camp with exuberant pleasure. I tell you this because today, when I look back, I sometimes wonder if I was the only person who enjoyed that time.

This young doctor told me something else which surprised me: "When you were giving us ideological training about the racial question, for example, we often said to one another: 'Of course Maschi doesn't believe in all that stuff she spouts. She's too sensible for that.'"

Well, I was far from being too sensible to believe what I said in those classes. I am surprised that my own inner conviction did not have a more convincing effect. Perhaps it is because I was often bored myself by the routine ideological training which was required in the programme.

But I must add this: I could not have been a camp leader if I had not believed wholeheartedly in the things I was supposed to tell the girls in those classes.

As at many stages in this account, I am troubled to know if you will believe what I have written. Will you not suspect me of whitewashing the past? To someone like yourself, who was an enemy of National Socialism and who is, over and above this, opposed temperamentally to any such collective movement, it must, of course, be irritating that I have had so many positive things to say about my time in the Labour Service.

I keep wondering, too, whether in my report to you I should still approve of the things which seemed good to us in the Labour Service at that time. You will certainly agree with me that a truthful report should equally not suppress the memories of things I believe to be good.

Of the six months I must describe now, I can only say that what happened was everything but positive. My new camp personnel was almost entirely composed of west German working girls. Far from having volunteered to go to the east, these girls were furious to be sent so far from their homes. They had been earning good money in the armaments industry and now they were supposed to do a job for which they had not the slightest inclination, in return for pocket money consisting — I believe — of thirty pfennigs a day. In addition they had to put up with never being allowed to do what they wanted after work in the evenings, and only rarely at weekends.

They were bored by every kind of instruction. Most of them thought our folk dances and the songs we sang with them were ridiculous. What they wanted were pop songs and American dances. Their conversation revolved round sex, and despite their youth some of them had already considerable experience in this field. They mostly came from very poor homes and from problem families. A young person who has always been used to belonging to a socially neglected group will find it almost impossible — particularly if he has himself absorbed a certain antisocial feeling — one day to start looking after other people. "Why should I be doing rich farmers' dirty work," many of these girls must have asked themselves, "without being properly paid for it?"

Our honourably intended rhetoric — to the effect that once in his lifetime every young German must learn what it is to do hard manual labour — must have fallen on stony ground. I never discovered any point at which these girls might have been accessible to any of our idealistic arguments, although there must surely have been one.

I could only be certain of their unreserved interest when I discussed the so called facts of life with them. These talks formed a part of the official programme. Although these girls never became a community, a discussion created a good atmosphere. No one had ever before tried to talk to them about these things factually and quite openly but without crudity. Because, in contrast to the schoolgirls, they were already partly concerned in these problems, they approached these talks with a seriousness which gave them a general educational value: after these evenings they would come to me individually for advice about their worries, and I could be sure that for a day or two they would make an effort to behave themselves. But these spurts would quickly flag: there would be fights in the dormitories once more, the farmers would complain about the carelessness of many of the girls, and the 'daredevils' would start trying to climb out of the windows at night to go and meet the airmen who were stationed nearby.

I do not know if you have ever heard anything about the women's Labour Service where you are living now. When I was interned by the Americans in 1945 a junior officer, who as a political investigator had to interrogate me, said to me: "But the women's Labour Service was only set up so that every work maiden should present the Führer with an S.S. man's child. These camps were just whore-houses."

I had the impression that my interrogator believed this statement himself, and replied: "You accuse me of swallowing National Socialist propaganda uncritically. Perhaps you are right. But evidently not even your American public opinion is always capable of distinguishing between truth and falsehood, for you believe the lies which have been circulated abroad about the women's Labour Service."

In case you have heard similar stories I must beg you to believe that I hated spying on my girls at night, and was very unhappy to have to make a long appeal to the conscience of the airman who had been meeting one of my girls before he would admit to his paternity. I can see that girl before me now: she had been orphaned early, a slight, inconspicuous, withdrawn person whose fatalistic outlook on life horrified me.

That summer I realized how spoilt I had been by the fact that my earlier camps had been made up of volunteers, and after all my appeals had fallen on deaf ears, I resigned myself to directing my educational efforts towards the attainment of more lowly ideals. The girls should learn to be punctual, to keep their lockers tidy, to wash themselves thoroughly, to have good table manners and the like.

In doing this I unfortunately acted the sergeant major, and while I had formerly enjoyed the pleasure of never having to tell the girls off, I now had to do it the whole time. But my exhortations went in one ear and out the other.

Finally I sacrificed the essential prerequisite for success in any teacher — my affection for my charges. One day a girl said to me: "There's only one person you like in this camp and that's your dog!"

It was true. Ferdl had had blood poisoning and then shortly afterwards he broke one of his front paws. Both times the vet said he would die and both times I managed to save him. But the time and energy and affection I lavished on him made it clear that the animal meant more to me than the girls.

Then I realized that it was I who had failed, not the girls. I was all the more disheartened because when I first became a youth leader in the National Socialist movement, fellowship with the young working class was the one thing I had romantically yearned for.

I can see in retrospect that the job was simply beyond my capabilities, because I had never had sufficient training as a teacher. Now when I sometimes hear women saying how unhappy they were during their time in the Labour Service I only have to think of that summer of 1943 to imagine the kind of reasons there might have been for their unhappy experience. Naturally there could have been countless others.

In the autumn of 1943 I left the Labour Service. When I had given up work in the head office of the Hitler Youth I had promised to return to the press section after two voluntary years of practical experience as a Labour Service leader. The two years were up and the press department of the Reich Youth Leadership reminded me of my promise. I was now to take over responsibility at this office for the 'female sector'. That is to say, I was to run all the press and propaganda activities concerned with the interests and tasks of German female youth.

Had I not just then been undergoing a period of bitter disillusionment with my own powers of leadership, I would hardly have answered the summons to Berlin. But my old friends in the Hitler Youth appealed to my conscience. I had been deplorably self indulgent in sneaking off to a village in the east just because I enjoyed it, instead of doing a job which was far more important to the war effort, and for which no one more suitable had been available for some time.

At length I applied to be released from the Labour Service and went to Berlin.

~ 13 ~

I dreamed of you last night for the first time since I have been working on this report. I woke up with a terrible feeling of anguish. I lay still because I know that dreams disappear faster the more I move about, and I wanted to hold onto this dream at any cost, although it oppressed me. Little enough of it remained clear in my mind. We were going to school together, as we used to twenty-five years ago. You were pushing your old bicycle along beside me once more. I could not catch a glimpse of your face but I could hear your voice all the time. You kept repeating the same thing over and over again in a dismal monotone which made me sad. I cannot remember what you were saying.

Gradually all my attention became focused on your feet. You were wearing an old pair of sandals *(did* you ever wear sandals?). I was alarmed to see that they were falling to pieces. It seemed to take years before they had come off completely and you were walking barefoot through the sand. I could see the sand spilling over the rims of your bicycle wheels, yellow and powdery.

I walked beside you much more easily, almost without effort, but I wept for your stumbling. As I strive to continue my report I am constantly aware of your nearness, and it makes my heart heavy.

From the autumn of 1943 onwards I had a responsible post at the head office of the Reich Youth Leadership of the Nazi Party. The staff was divided into departments, each of which corresponded to a particular field of work. Within each department there was a female head of department who was responsible for the women's side. Their exact legal position was never made clear, so far as I am aware. The Hitler Youth leaders considered that the B.D.M. leaders were subordinate to them; the B.D.M. took the view that they were solely responsible to their highest superiors, the head of the B.D.M. and the Reich Youth Leader. How authority was exerted in specific instances depended in each case on the personalities of those who had to work together.

I was appointed female head of department in the press and propaganda division of the Reich Youth Leadership, and I was lucky. The male head of department was a shrewd, broadminded, likeable Swabian who felt no need to belittle me.

At this point it is necessary to make one or two general observations about the Hitler Youth. It was only when I joined the Reich Youth Leadership that I gained a complete view of its structure and function within the Party, although I had by then belonged to it for ten years.

Before 1933 the Hitler Youth was a tool in the Party's struggle for political power. When this had been won, the membership of the Hitler Youth was multiplied by thirty within two years. In December 1936 the 'Hitler Youth Law' was proclaimed. This made it the state youth movement which claimed sole responsibility (apart from the home and the school) for the complete physical, mental and moral education of German youth. The diverse political, church and independent youth movements were soon completely defunct. Only minute groups continued to exist illegally, subject to ruthless persecution.

It was not until 1940 that the law about the state youth movement became fully effective. From then on all boys and girls of ten automatically joined the *Deutsche Jungvolk* (German young people) and the *Deutsche Jungmädel* (German young girls) and swore allegiance to Hitler on the Führer's birthday. In this way national service for all young people was established.

It had become analogous with the Labour Service and military conscription.

As the Hitler Youth's monopoly spread to every field of education and youth work, a gigantic apparatus had to be built up within a very few years in order to establish and maintain it.

The Reich Youth Leadership, when I began to work there in 1943, was an organization which rivalled one of the national ministries in the extent and complexity of its machinery.

At the risk of boring you, I must enumerate the various main fields of activity so that you may have some sort of picture of the scope of the office.

At the head of it stood Arthur Axmann, the Reich Youth Leader. He had taken over this post in 1940, at the age of twenty-seven, from Baldur von Schirach. Theoretically his two deputies, the *Stabsführer* and the Reich head of the B.D.M., had equal authority. The staff of the Reich Youth Leadership was divided, as I mentioned, into departments, the most important being: the personnel division, the administrative division, the organizational division, the health division, the accommodation division, the social division, the physical (and pre-military) training division, the ideological training division, the cultural division, the frontier and foreign division and the press and propaganda division.

Each of these divisions was represented on the staff of the regional Hitler Youth and B.D.M. administrations. The regions *(Gebiete),* of which there were ultimately thirty-five in 'Greater Germany', corresponded in the youth section to the district *(Gau)* administrations of the Nazi Party.

Thus — to show how this structure worked — from the late autumn of 1939 until summer 1941 I was in charge of the press and propaganda sections of the regional Hitler Youth and B.D.M. in the Wartheland. In this I had the support of all the press and propaganda sections of the Hitler Youth and B.D.M. area units *(Banne)* within the Wartheland, which corresponded to the area divisions *(Kreise)* of the Party.

Within each field of activity the Hitler Youth was organized on strictly hierarchical lines. Press work started at the lowest level with the area unit press offices, manned by unpaid volunteers. It was continued in the regional press sections by regional headquarters staff and was planned, coordinated and directed by the Press and Propaganda Division of the Reich Youth Leadership. In practice it might, for example, look like this: At the suggestion of the Red Cross it was decided in the Reich Youth Leadership that the B.D.M. and the Jungmädel should undertake work comforting the wounded in the hospitals in Germany. Plans were made for community singing with the patients, choral and instrumental performances and the presentation of plays and improvisations. The older girls were to help the convalescent soldiers with occupational therapy.

This 'operation' began with the Reich head of the B.D.M. writing a directive to all her colleagues for our journal *Das Deutsche Mädel.* Meanwhile we passed articles about the hospitals project to the daily papers in the course of our own regular press work. Whenever possible we placed special features about this subject in the *Völksche Beobachter* or the other big papers. The regional press sections were similarly active within their own districts, as were the press offices of the area units within their areas.

A little later the first stories about this hospital work appeared in our journals and again in the daily press. There were the inevitable statistical boasts of success: '5,780 Thuringian girls in military hospitals venture' or 'B.D.M. visits 370 Bavarian military hospitals'. I always hated these because they were certainly often faked. We collected pictures and copy for the Hitler Youth display cases, pestered the newsreels until they came to a hospital and filmed our girls visiting the wounded, and organized a broadcast from a hospital where the little girls of the Jungmädel were acting folk stories for the soldiers.

One or two more explanations about the general working methods of the Press and Propaganda Division of the Reich Youth Leadership. After 1933 the Hitler Youth had soon won itself a monopoly of the propaganda organs aimed at young people. Not in competition with the other youth movements, of course, but simply because all other publications for young people were banned. The chief Hitler Youth journals were *Der Pimpf (The Lad,* for the Jungvolk), *Das Deutsche Mädel (The German Girl), Junge Welt (Young World), Die Hitler-Jugend, Wille und Macht (Will and Might* — the organ of the leadership), *Das Junge Deutschland (Young Germany,* for social and political topics), *Junge Dorfgemeinschaft (The Young Village Community,* for rural youth), and so on. In addition the Press and Propaganda Division published a daily news sheet, *Der Reichsjugend-Pressedienst (The Reich Youth Press Service)* — though not right up to the end of the war — which supplied the daily press with news and articles which concerned the problems of youth in the broadest sense. Apart from this, we collaborated directly with the editorial offices of the biggest German newspapers.

The regional press sections had their own periodical publications, which might, for example, take the form of regular youth supplements to the daily papers.

Publications intended for use in ideological training were produced in the Ideological Training Division and not by us. They were also legion. The basic aim of the work of our division was to give the public an account of what young people were doing, and in addition to stimulate their understanding of and interest in the problems of National Socialist youth education and youth leadership. The parents of our young people were to be won over to help us.

For all these reasons it was essential for people working in our division to have a knowledge of the activities of almost all the other divisions. For the broad field of youth leadership, for which we had to supply propaganda, was shared between the various divisions. So I had to know, for example, precisely what the training plans of, say, the B.D.M. homecraft schools were, how our country service worked, or how successful the B.D.M. group in Tokyo had been in collecting money for the Winter Relief Fund, so that I could write reports on these things either for our own journals or for newspaper articles.

We also had jobs to do which were not in the strictest sense propagandist, such as publishing diaries for the various age groups of boys and girls. Our division also produced the posters advertising Hitler Youth events and in general any posters aimed particularly at young people. I remember a poster which was supposed to warn girls against associating with 'foreign workers' or prisoners of war. It cost me a lot of trouble because every draft looked either too feeble or too crude, and in view of the delicacy of the subject I was more concerned about the literary style than the Administrative Division, who were paying for the poster, considered necessary. A leaflet, on which the poster was reproduced with a corresponding text, was printed in large numbers and put in the pay packets of the young working girls at all the factories.

Film work was also centred on the Press and Propaganda Division. A series of cultural films were produced there. Shortly before the war I helped to make a film on *B.D.M. Work, Faith and Beauty* which was supposed to show the variety of possibilities for worthwhile evening activities which girls of seventeen to twenty-one could find in this section of the Hitler Youth. Later on the film could only be shown in a mutilated version, because the shots of girls riding, playing tennis and roasting geese were out of date in wartime.

During the last years our division produced a monthly youth film, *Junges Europa (Young Europe),* similar to the weekly newsreels. In 1944 we made a feature film, *Young Eagles:* this would hardly be shown in cinemas today.

The scope of our special work corresponded to equivalent ramifications in the work of all the other divisions of the Reich Youth Leadership. One has to bear in mind that almost every piece of planning involved huge numbers of people. For instance, 7,000,000 young people took part in the Reich sports contest in 1939.

I will give you, if I may, a brief survey of the 'war work' of the Hitler Youth. In the last years this occupied the most important place in our activities. I will quote now a historical publication of 1957. It mentions, amongst other things, Party tasks — the dispatch, guard and propaganda services; tasks for the state and the communes — messenger and firewatching services (to which I would add: service digging trenches for fortifications and tank traps for the 'Third Force of the *Volkssturm*' or Home Guard); the so called 'Technical emergency aid' to the post office, the police and the railways; tasks for the army (messenger, goods loading, nursing and telephone service, etc.); factory and labour squads; collecting salvage and old clothes; farm and harvest work; National Socialist National Welfare service and cultural work. A great number of these tasks were performed by girls. The effect of this Hitler Youth work on the war economy should not be underestimated: in 1942, for example, 600,000 boys and 1,400,000 girls helped with the harvest...

You yourself never belonged to any youth movement, but I know that through your brothers and sisters you were in close contact with one group which was run on the lines of the later youth movements. From all I have written in the last few pages one thing will have emerged very clearly: although the Hitler Youth formally adopted many of the features of the youth movements, it was itself something radically different.

Whatever one thinks of the youth movements today, nobody can dispute that they showed a tremendous vitality, spontaneity and originality in their search for new forms and purposes for a communal life which would be particularly suited to young people. Unfortunately — yes, unfortunately — one can observe none of this when one tries to define the typical characteristics of the Hitler Youth.

We truly have no cause to lament the fact that the Hitler Youth has ceased to exist. But one may legitimately regret that in that period when the young people of Germany were more intensely involved in the life of their nation than at any other time, they were forced into a mould which to a great extent destroyed the specific magic of adolescence — by which I mean all those elements which I mentioned as being typical of the youth movements.

Apart from its beginnings during the 'years of struggle', the Hitler Youth was not a youth movement at all: it became more and more the 'state youth organization' — that is to say, it became more and more institutionalized, and finally became the instrument which the National Socialist régime used to run its ideological training of young people and the war work for certain age groups.

The reasons for this development can be found in the external pressure of events, for the increased membership which the Hitler Youth had to absorb after 1935 was such that any healthy growth was impossible. The influx of masses of new members had to be kept under control, and they could not be slowly won round and introduced to the community by a selection of qualified youth leaders, on the principle of the other youth movements. The most that could be achieved was to recruit them for the organization and to give them a primitive ideological 'orientation' according to Scheme F. By the outbreak of war this process of absorption was still not completed (it was held up by events like the 'Return Home' of Austria), and now there was a new compulsion to abandon the truly communal life of a youth movement: the practical task of war work which completely swamped all other Hitler Youth activities as the years went by.

I believe that the Hitler Youth contained the seeds of a genuine youth movement which were prevented from developing by the unfavourable turn of history — but it is more than doubtful whether they would have been allowed to grow, even without this interference. The character of the 'state youth organization' which moulded the form and content of the work ever more markedly, naturally tended to make use of the available apparatus.

And yet — the Hitler Youth was a youth organization. Its members may have allowed themselves to be dressed in uniforms and regimented, but they were still young people and they behaved like young people. Their characteristic surplus of energy and thirst for action found great scope in their programme of activities, which constantly required great feats to be performed. It was part of the method of the National Socialist Youth leadership to arrange almost everything in the form of competitions. It was not only in sports and in one's profession that one competed. Every unit wanted to have the best group 'home', the most interesting expedition log, the biggest collection for the Winter Relief Fund, and so forth — or at least they were supposed to want it. In the musical competitions Hitler Youth choirs, fife and drum bands, chamber orchestras and amateur theatrical groups competed as did young singers, instrumentalists, sculptors, painters and poets for the glory of the most brilliant performance. There were even story telling competitions to see which boys and girls out of all their contemporaries were best at telling folk stories.

This constant competition introduced an element of unrest and forced activity into the life of the groups even in peacetime. It did not merely channel young people's drive for action; it also inflamed it, where it would have been wiser and better to give the individual within the group and the group as a whole periods when they could mature and develop in tranquillity.

There was certainly a great deal of good and ambitious education in the Hitler Youth. There were groups who learned to act in a masterly way. People told stories, danced and practised handicrafts, and in these fields the regimentation was fortunately often less strict. But the idea of a competition (behind which lay the glorification of the fighter and the heroic) often enough banished the element of meditation even from musical activities, and the playful development of the creative imagination, free of any purpose, was sadly stunted.

The leaders of a youth movement so drilled to activity and performance gradually created a style of their own as 'managers'. They were themselves driven from one activity to the next, and so they drove their charges on in the same manner. Even the young men and women in the Reich Youth Leadership who initiated all this activity were subject to the same restless compulsive drive. The constantly turning wheel of incessant activity continually created a fresh momentum and carried along everyone who came into its sphere of influence.

Compared with the Hitler Youth projects, which always set millions of boys and girls in motion together, the work of the old youth movements seemed like a romantic idyll. Our slogans claimed that the Hitler Youth was a state within a state — as we recalled the activities of the old movements, we felt ourselves the leaders of a 'politically conscious youth' looking back on frivolous children's games — and when had a nation's youth been more self confident than that of the Third Reich? But at that very moment, when our young people believed that they had fully emancipated themselves, they succumbed to the fateful domination of the technological era. The national leadership made no attempt to protect them from the effect of this. The rulers of the state might have proclaimed a culture of 'blood and soil', and they made spasmodic efforts to restore the ethical values of the age of the Nibelungen, but they were blind to the particular threat to us all of the domination of technology. Something of the dehumanization — of the victory of technology over the soul, if I may use this oldfashioned word — which was expressed in the institution of apparatuses for mass murder (the concentration camps), could also be seen in the way the National Socialist state over-organized its young people.

People within the machine, even at the top, were only dimly aware of this dehumanization. Perhaps it caused one unhappiness. But who could stop for such worries in wartime? I remember I sometimes thought of the lost romanticism of the time of the old movements (although I only knew of it by hearsay: when I was very young I had always longed to belong to one of them), and I consoled myself by thinking: After the war the reins will be loosened, then the young people will be released from this quasi-military compulsion and they will be able to enjoy their own lives again in all their diversity.

Anyone who looks today at the training schemes, plans of action or performance reports of the Hitler Youth will gain an impression of a tremendous rigidity, uniformity and energy channelled into physical activity. To some extent this is correct, but it is not the whole picture. These documents do not tell him that although the young people let themselves be moulded into a rigidly organized movement, there were many girls and boys who remained fully alive in the process. They fulfilled with joy and tenacity the tasks that were required of them, proud of their successes and eager to prove themselves in a service which was no child's play but bitter necessity.

Of course they learned to obey too often and too unhesitatingly — they learned too little about thinking for themselves and acting on their own initiative. But this obedience had for them the moral value of a soldier's obedience, rightly understood. They did not wish to spare themselves: they would stand their ground wherever the command summoned them to do so — and it was expected that this would be given in a responsible manner. The fact that it led them into a fight for a bad cause was a misfortune with which many of them have still not been able to come to terms.

When I worked with the Labour Service I was able to establish time and time again, and particularly in the case of the girls who had volunteered for the 'Eastern Venture' and who were all members of the Hitler Youth, that all the regimentation and institutionalization had not destroyed the individual's joy in being of service and willingness to make sacrifices. This is certainly not true of all young people in those years, but it is true of many. When I joined the Reich Youth Leadership in the late autumn of 1943 I at first almost totally lost contact with the smaller units; that is to say with the young people themselves. Only now was I completely swallowed up by the machine.

I took on my job in Berlin out of a sense of duty, without any pleasure, that is; and I felt really unhappy in it until the end of the war. There were basically two main reasons for this. In the first place it became progressively more obvious to me that I was not a born propagandist and I therefore had doubts about the point of my work. In the second place I felt that I did not belong in an office, in which life is reduced to the manipulation of documents.

The conditions under which I started work in Berlin were just about as adverse as one could imagine. The department had recently been bombed: three-quarters of the files concerned with my work had been destroyed and the remaining quarter succumbed to another air raid a few weeks later. Hence I had not even a list of the addresses of my principal colleagues and voluntary workers — neither those in Berlin nor those in the rest of the Reich. Nor was there anyone who could give me a full enough outline of my job. The post to which I had been appointed had been vacant for some time.

Although the last year and a half of the war are nearer to me in time, I remember them less well than the years which preceded them. This may be because those last eighteen months before the collapse were so grim that one is only too glad to lock them away deep in the recesses of one's memory. Furthermore, being continually subjected to danger, one lived through them at times in a mental state of emergency which hindered the accumulation of continuous memories. Finally, too, the fact that I did not like my work must have something to do with it. There was little of that time which I wanted to remember.

I am not even sure how many times my office was bombed out. I can remember four moves but I think there were more than that.

During the first few months I had to hold meetings all over Germany in order to get to know my colleagues in the various regions, to find new ones and to discuss the lines of our future work. Apart from this the male head of our division had given me the job of cultivating the rising generation of editorial talent. Selection camps for young journalists were to be set up in all parts of Germany in collaboration with the Reich Union of Journalists. The young talent of the profession was to be sifted and given technical and political training.

I remember the train journeys better now than the meetings: crowded, barely heated, dawdling trains which one had to keep leaving to take cover in the fields because low flying planes were coming over. Countless nights spent in stations, on chairs at inns or on benches in offices. Long treks, hungry and weary, when a stretch of line had been bombed.

It was no more cosy in Berlin itself. After many raids one had to spend six or seven hours trailing round the city to arrange a piece of work which would normally have taken one telephone call. I only came to know the feeling of having a good night's sleep again, when I was interned after the war. The nights in Berlin were disturbed more and more by alerts. For part of the time I lived in a half-bombed out ground floor flat which anyone could have walked into from the street straight to my bedside over some rubble. Nobody ever tried it because from the outside it looked as if no one could still be living in these ruins. As all the sirens in the immediate vicinity were out of action I could only go to sleep with one eye. Otherwise I should never have heard the faint warning wail from outside my neighbourhood and I should have had no time to run to the nearest shelter, which took me eight minutes.

From the very first day in my new job I had the feeling: You are not at the dynamic centre of the National Socialist Leadership here — you are in a swollen bureaucratic ministerial apparatus. Its formal machinery went on functioning well enough but one had the impression that the wheels were spinning in a void. Then all that we were doing took on an air of shadowy unreality.

Every one of us worked with hectic energy. Countless projects were started up, knocked out by the effects of the war, abandoned, taken up again, cancelled, altered, rejected once again and so on. During the last months of this, the feeling crept over us that all this feverish activity on the part of the Reich Youth Leadership was hardly producing the slightest response in the country.

Our office was like a termites' nest, gradually pervaded by a sense of the coming collapse without a single person daring to breathe a syllable about it. (When the Reich Youth Leader, Arthur Axmann, made a pessimistic remark about the outcome of the war in a speech at Easter 1945, he was reprimanded by the Party Secretariat.) At that time the Western Allies were already in central Germany. All the cells of the termites' nest were filled with a fanatical activity. Our brains gave birth to plans and still more plans, lest we should have a moment to stop and think and

181

then to have to recognize that all this bustle was already beginning to resemble the convulsions of a dance of death.

Disputes about competence between the departments of the Reich Youth Leadership flourished with their old vitality, as befits a ministry. The men gaily continued to battle for their supremacy, although the female element was gaining ground considerably: from week to week the departments were combed for men fit for military service and women youth leaders had to take over where their male comrades had gone to the army.

The heads of department contended with peacetime fervour for precedence in the eyes of the Reich Youth Leader. The one who was his favourite and chief confidant strove to consolidate his position. The others strove to pull him down.

One was generally fighting against ambitious takeover bids from other sections of the Party, for example the S.S. in the field of pre-military training. Or one was fighting with the Party Treasurer and his officials for salaried workers, houses, cars, the financing of journals, films and the like.

The motto of the head of the Press and Propaganda Division at that time was: 'We hold on and we help to conquer.' I understood. The most important thing for us was that the young people — from the young soldiers to the ten-year-old girls collecting medicinal herbs for the chemists — were helping to win the war. But I hated beating the big drum for their achievements and making propaganda capital out of them.

On the personal level I was not happy at my new office. I saw men and women there whom I considered to be ambitious, crude intriguers and I was disillusioned that such worthless people could have risen to the highest ranks of the German Youth Leadership. I accepted the excuse that the war had prevented the creation of a true élite here and I put my faith in the postwar period.

There was certainly a dominant strain of solid workers and there were some excellent people amongst my colleagues, but I made friends with no one. I had no time for personal conversations; I suppose there were circles where people shared a friendly social life out of hours, but I myself had no contact with any such circle.

There is one exception to this which must be mentioned, although I do not relish the memory of it. It must have been in the early autumn of 1944 that I was instructed to accompany the Reich Youth Leader, Arthur Axmann, on an official journey to West Germany, in order to report on it in the press. I believe he spoke in Saarbrücken and at youth rallies in several other towns (perhaps in connection with the Reich Vocational Competition). During one of these rallies the approach of enemy bomber formations was announced and it now emerged that the organizers of the meeting had not made the necessary provision for this eventuality. Axmann was so infuriated at the danger his young audience had been subjected to by this oversight that he wanted to abandon his whole programme and go straight back to Berlin.

I knew the leader of the 'Westmark' region B.D.M. and I also had good relations with the regional head of the Hitler Youth there. For these reasons I strove to pacify the embittered 'chief', and finally Axmann stayed on. In the course of this tour, which lasted several days, I got to know the Reich Youth Leader quite well.

He came from so called humble beginnings. He was in a certain sense the proletarian showpiece of the youth leadership corps: he was proof to us that every German boy had a field marshal's baton in his knapsack. One was always hearing how he and his brothers had been brought up by the widow of a factory worker who had had to earn her living during the depression by taking in washing. He had probably had a deprived youth. So far as I know he made his name in the Berlin Wedding district. At all events he started and ran units of the Hitler Youth there amongst the young working class boys. After 1933, at the age of twenty, he took on the task of building up the Social Welfare Division of the Reich Youth Leadership. One sometimes saw his mother at meetings, an old woman dressed in black who looked simple and likeable, and who gave the impression that she detested being displayed in public.

Axmann personified the socialist pathos which continued to play a part in the Hitler Youth for longer after 1933 than in the other Party organs — with the exception of the Labour Front. For this reason I had welcomed his appointment as Reich Youth Leader. But I was also distressed that this office should be held by a man who clearly had no connection at all with the world of the intellect.

With Baldur von Schirach, I had been attracted by his intellectual interests and the relatively high linguistic level of his speeches in which he often discussed artistic or educational topics (and in a much less primitive and bombastic fashion than Goebbels). In 1937 I was delighted when he acknowledged himself to be indebted to and inspired by Goethe, at a time when Goethe was widely being denigrated in a most stupid manner on account of his 'world citizenship'.

During the last years of the war when Schirach was Gauleiter of Vienna, however, I had been told by worried Austrian friends that his style of life had become that of a complete Party boss. I regarded this as a betrayal of the youth leader's mission. Until the end of the war Schirach was still the 'Reich Leader for the training of Youth' and in this capacity he was still above the Reich Youth Leader. It was painful that the man who had created the Hitler Youth and who was now, as ever, the final authority in matters of youth leadership, should not have been able to resist the temptations of an ostentatious, pleasure seeking, prodigal existence. I never witnessed this way of life myself, however, and I am only repeating what I heard from friends whose word I believe.

During the last months of the war I experienced the same painful disillusionment with regard to Axmann, although his personal extravagance was on a more modest scale. After that tour with him in the west he got his personal assistant Dr. X to invite me to a social evening at the Reich Youth Leadership's inn at Gatow. I asked Dr. X, who was commonly alleged not to be a member of the Hitler Youth at all (I never saw him in uniform) and to be the epitome of intrigue, whether this invitation was to be taken as an order. The answer was yes. Nothing could have been more untimely than this summons. I had to hire a party dress and waste precious hours at the hairdresser's. When the head of the B.D.M. heard I had been invited to Gatow she became noticeably more distant. She found the goings on there distasteful, for two reasons. She herself lived very modestly and she knew that the people who met at the tavern maligned her as a 'narrow minded prude'. She also knew that a good many plots about official matters were hatched out there over her head between Axmann and his favourites in the B.D.M. administration.

I had no desire at all to become one of these. Particularly not after I had been through the first social evening at Gatow.

The inn stood in a garden by the lake and was built and furnished in very good taste. Everything there had an aura of peace and bore witness to an abundance which was in jarring contrast to our normal wartime existence. Compared with our accustomed way of life, the eating and drinking there was often sheer gluttony. The head waiter moved about like one in a luxury hotel, and when the whisper went round that bomber formations were approaching Berlin nobody looked as if it spoilt their pleasure.

In my judgement the assembled Hitler Youth and B.D.M. leaders were a classically unrepresentative selection. In private Axmann seemed to prefer to associate with those of his colleagues whom I considered to be charlatans and self important egoists. You can imagine how unhappy I felt in this circle. At intervals Axmann appeared at my side, slapped my back with his artificial hand (he had lost a forearm as a lieutenant in the Campaign in the west) and asked me jovially if I was enjoying myself. When I replied: "Not at all, *Reichjugendführer"*, he laughed and strolled away.

On my second or third visit to Gatow I heard a conversation between several film starlets who were sarcastically arranging who was to entertain 'the old man' (meaning Axmann) and at what times, so that they could each of them have a rest, for the following morning the girls had to be back in the studio at least half awake. Axmann had invited them personally, which was clearly a frequent occurrence, presumably because he and his friends got bored with having no one but the B.D.M. leaders.

I had probably only been to Gatow three or, at most, four times when I refused a further invitation. When Axmann stopped me one day on the so called 'Marble floor' where the heads of the Reich Youth Leadership had their rooms and asked me why I did not come any more, I replied: "Because I find it indecent to dance and get drunk there while bombs are falling elsewhere."

He looked taken aback for a moment and then passed on without a word. At that moment my thought was: 'The betrayal of socialism.' Apart from being intellectually ill equipped for his political career, Axmann had not had the strength of character for it.

In the regular business meetings of heads of department of the B.D.M., which were presided over by its Reich leader, there were sometimes general discussions about fundamental problems. There was the question of illegitimate children, for example. One of the heads of department of the Hitler Youth had been openly making out a case for legalized bigamy. His argument was that the biological bloodletting which the war was inflicting on the German nation should be countered, amongst other ways, by letting a man beget children with several women. (This would naturally be subject to certain principles in the selection of mates, which would ensure the continuation of the 'substance of the nordic race'.) Such liaisons should be legalized as temporary or morganatic marriages.

The proposal was similar to ideas which were current in the S.S. So far as I know there was not a single one of the senior B.D.M. leaders in our office who did not reject it absolutely. We women were quickly united in the view that the family should be the only place for children to grow up in and that the destruction of the basic principle of monogamy must be prevented by women. At one meeting the Reich head of the B.D.M. declared that any unmarried B.D.M. leader who became pregnant must resign her office, because an exemplary personal life was an indispensable part of every youth leader's vocation. The fact that we could nevertheless treat unmarried mothers humanely in so far as they deserved it, was a different matter.

There was very probably a good deal of flirting during youth group activities, especially when boys and girls were working together. The Hitler Youth was a mass organization and, as I have mentioned, it had not had the time to train up a good corps of leaders.

I should like to dwell on the matter of illegitimate children and legalized bigamy for a moment more, at the risk of giving you the impression that it was particularly important to us. It was not, in fact, but there is an episode from my own working experience which fits in here and which may help me, better than any other example, to give you a clear picture of my activities of that period.

For a time there was a lively discussion of this question in public. It was a part of my job as a propagandist to make sure that the views of the B.D.M. in this dispute were given a hearing. I therefore asked the Reich head of the B.D.M. (herself no inspired propagandist, which was why I liked her) to put forward our views from the most prominent public platform available. A rally of 'young working girls' at one of the biggest German industrial works afforded an opportunity for this. I had proposed to her the way our approach to the problem should be formulated and she approved. Before we left Berlin I had already written reports for the biggest newspapers and agencies, which only awaited transmission. They contained a rejection by the women's youth leadership of the tendencies within the S.S. towards a 'population policy'.

My chief was short sighted. Without her glasses she could not read, but at rallies she could not be seen wearing glasses because of the impression it created. She was an academic and she did not want to look like a bluestocking. She therefore always learned her speeches by heart, being no good at improvising. On the drive from Berlin to the town in West Germany where the rally was to be held she tried to imprint the proposed text on her memory. Probably she was too tired to do it, but perhaps she also had second thoughts. During the rally I waited in vain for the 'fighting words' which had meanwhile been sent to the agencies and the press. Some of the papers printed them without her having said them.

During the last weeks of the war one sometimes heard sharp criticisms of the leading members of the Party and the Government being made in our office. They were naturally only voiced behind locked doors. I remember one of the heads of department of the Reich Youth Leadership declaring one day in a despairing outburst that it was now proven that Bormann, the head of the Party Secretariat, was leading Germany to ruin. He was omitting to give Hitler the necessary information or else he was informing him falsely.

I myself never had any insight into high politics, and the Hitler Youth leaders avoided involving us in arguments on the subject.

I answered the head of department's complaints about Bormann with a question: "If you can really prove that, why don't you make sure that Bormann disappears?"

"To do that we should have to go over his head to Hitler," he replied, "and that is just what Bormann would stop us doing by every means in his power."

"All right," I said, "so you are convinced that this man is digging Germany's grave, are you?"

"Yes!"

"Then why have you not got rid of him long ago? You can go to see him every day. What do you carry that great pistol around for? I only know one answer to this question: you are too cowardly to sacrifice yourself for such a deed, although you believe it to be necessary."

In conversations of this kind one was always 'pacified' with the assurance that after the war the young people and the soldiers from the front, together with the Führer, would bring about a revolution within the Party. The 'peacocks' would be swept away to the devil with a broom of steel.

I too allowed myself to be fuddled by this music of the future in order to drown the inner voice which was repeating, more and more insistently: "There is no future any more."

14

In September 1944 my parents died in a night bombing attack by the British which destroyed seventy-eight per cent of my mother's home town and killed twelve to fifteen thousand people. I had been staying with them for two days, to help them move house. So far as I know, I was the only person to emerge alive from a cellar in which some thirty people, including my parents, were either suffocated or burned to death.

I would rather not describe to you the events of that night. I wonder if you can ever have experienced anything similar. When I think of you, I am only too willing to imagine you in pleasant surroundings, and I picture you as one of those who were able to escape to England or America before Hitler's political police gained control of the whole continent. "Perhaps she is no longer what they call a 'German refugee' in those countries," I tell myself; "perhaps she has married an Englishman or an American and has long since come to feel at home in this new country."

But suppose my picture is completely wrong? There cannot be many Jews of German origin in the world today whose lives have been easy.

So who can say if you too do not wake up in the night with a start, or hold your hand when you are about to put a piece of food in your mouth more often than I do? Suddenly one mistrusts peace, the quiet of the night, the festiveness of a richly covered table, the beauty of a landscape or the illuminating power of a good idea. 'Is all this real?' one wonders. 'Or am I simply dreaming before waking again to grim reality?'

In the days following my parents' death I and my comrades from the training college for youth leaders set up welfare centres in the ruined town. At that time I formed the resolve to abandon my work in the Berlin office and to do practical war work, in whatever capacity.

When I look back on those days I think I can detect a profound change, which must have taken place in me then without my knowing it.

Out of the dim haze of half forgotten memories there emerges a moment which perhaps had decisive significance. On the morning after the raid I stood alone in a broad square. The acrid smoke from the burning houses had left me almost blinded for several hours. But on the outskirts of the town someone had treated them with boracic lotion so that I could make compresses, and now I could see again. The square seemed to me infinitely broad and bleak. Round it there were nothing but ruins, still smoking. As I walked slowly across it I kept passing corpses. In the middle of the square there was a heap of dead, piled up in confusion, like the tipped out contents of a timber lorry.

I stood still. The house in which my parents had died was in this square. Perhaps they had escaped from the cellar after all, but then collapsed in the fire storm. Perhaps I should find them in this heap of bodies. I took hold of the khaki yellow coat of a dead prisoner of war and was seized with such horror that I turned about on the spot. I wanted to run, but I had collapsed on the ground and no longer had the strength to get up. I crawled across the square on all fours like a child. In the middle, between the heap of corpses and a row of dead, who had been laid out neatly side by side, I stopped and sat up. Only now did I see the sun. As if behind clouds, it hung behind the smoke from the fires, large and red in the dawn sky which held the promise of a clear blue September day.

As I stood up with an effort I had the feeling that I was the only person left alive on the whole earth.

Perhaps it was at that moment that I lost hope.

While still almost a child I was chosen to improve the world. I wanted there to be not a single one of our people left who was poor or despised. Everything I did was based on the hope that Germany would become the happiest country in the world. For the sake of this end I reacted to all difficulties by increasing my efforts.

That morning I gave way at the knees not only physically but psychologically. I understood, though indeed barely consciously, that this terrible mass death could no longer be regarded as a meaningful sacrifice. Something senseless was happening, not merely that — something insane. Surely now the worst was bound to happen, which would prevent a recovery. But what could this worst be? The stranglehold of Germany's enemies grew tighter every day. The worst could only be...

Perhaps I did not dare to feel as far as that. I certainly did not think as far as that. But from now on I was no longer ruled by hope but by a gloomy fatalism. Outwardly nothing in my life changed. I went on trying to lend a hand wherever I was needed and I still did not admit for a long time that the war was lost. But my inward and outward activity was now no more than a running fight. I can see an indication of this altered situation, the significance of which only became clear to me very much later, in the fact that from now on I was silent if someone abused Hitler or National Socialism in my presence. In the old days I should have made a passionate attempt to alter the views of critics and doubters. Henceforth I let them talk and was content if they did what the moment required.

Please do not conclude from all this that from the death of my parents I might possibly have begun to view National Socialism with a critical eye. An estrangement of this kind would have to have been fully conscious. There was to be no question of this for a long time. The fact that I had to wait so many years for this to happen was chiefly connected with my internment. But I must not anticipate. It was still September 1944.

I travelled back to Berlin with an almost empty briefcase as my only luggage. I arrived at night. Enemy bombers were circling over the city. After the all-clear I drove to the hostel where I had been living for the past few weeks. When I stood in front of it I suddenly saw that this building had also become a ruin.

I sat down on the kerb with a feeling of mental confusion. It was dark and cold and the air smelt of fires which would not be put out for a long time yet. Gradually thoughts formed themselves clearly again in my mind. I said to myself: So now all you possess is the clothes on your body and what you have in this briefcase! This realization gave me a sense of release — but the freedom I felt made my blood run cold.

A few yards away from me rats were scuttling backwards and forwards between a cellar window and a crack in the wall. There is nothing I loathe more than rats, but now I watched them with an indifferent attentiveness.

In that hour of the night, when I sat amongst the bombed ruins of a burnt-out Berlin street, the sense of property died in me. It took almost seven years to acquire it again. For the time being I refused to buy myself more than two sets of underwear and two nightdresses. With these possessions I got through several months: then they were further reduced without my being troubled. The Reich head of the B.D.M. scolded me on account of my unbecoming conduct. I wore ski trousers, and two sweaters one on top of the other: I no longer possessed a coat, dress or jacket. (Later I was given a coat.)

She turned a deaf ear to my plea to be allowed to give up the press work. I was needed more, she told me, at headquarters: besides, I was too unstable for active service as a leader. When I asked her what she meant by 'unstable', she replied: "You have an artistic temperament and you are therefore unsuited to lead a group."

I did not share this view but I had to bow to it. However, I soon found a way to avoid open disobedience but to do what I thought right. From now on I only made star appearances at my office. About two days a week sufficed to answer the post and keep the work in hand going through. During the remaining time I found my own work. In this way I was almost always able during the last months of the war to do what seemed the most important thing at any given moment, which at that time was the most tolerable mode of existence.

I cannot list all the forms my 'war work' took: it would make this report too long. But I will mention some of them. I twice led columns of refugees from the Wartheland from Lusatia to central Germany. One of them was shot at by low flying aircraft near an autobahn bridge. I remember taking refuge with a family of peasants under their cart. A young sheepdog had stayed in the cart. It was tied to the handle of a basket. Prompted by its mournful howling, a fourteen-year-old boy, the peasant's son, left our shelter to go to it. A second later he was lying dead beside the cart. His father who had stayed holding the horses was wounded.

Some of the Germans who had fled from the Wartheland were crowded together in Lusatia. Many of these refugees could find nowhere to live, and for a long time they felt the after effects of their panic flight from the Russian tanks.

I remember, too, a winter morning when, for reasons that I never discovered, the air raid sirens in Kottbus wailed for five minutes solid. The rumour spread like a brush fire that Russian paratroops had landed, and suddenly panic broke out amongst the refugees, whose carts had already blocked the narrow streets of the town. The men lost their heads and whipped up their horses. The carts crashed against one another, became entangled, overturned. People fell beneath them and were crushed against the walls of houses.

I worked in Kottbus at a depot for children who had lost their families on the flight from the east. We picked them up and sent them to central Germany in transports via the headquarters of the children's evacuation service in Dresden. Time and again I cannot help remembering how I sent these children to Dresden at the very moment when the most terrible bombing attacks of the Second World War were descending on that city. We had wanted to save them, and we sent them into the middle of one of the most ghastly massacres in German history.

I did not make my westward escape out of some of the little towns in Lusatia until the first Russian tanks were already entering them from the east. I left one town pulling a cart containing a dozen small children. The staff of a home which had left had not been able to take them. A boy of perhaps fourteen or fifteen helped me. He had the energy and composure of a grown man. We kept blocking the path of the fleeing cars and wagons, forcing them to stop and handing children at random into the vehicles. There were two brothers amongst the children, one about seven and the other a little boy of two. The elder brother fought for the little one like a mother for her child. I came across the two of them again later in a refugee camp. I watched the elder brother stealing a sausage from a sack, biting it into pieces and pushing it bit by bit into his brother's mouth. Believe me, I saw more people helping one another during the last months of the war than ever before or since. Everywhere I met people who had left all they had behind them because the war had taken away their homes, their belongings and often their families as well. Now they were free to step in wherever they were needed. There were people among them who had been rich or poor; there were old people and young people; some were National Socialists and others made no bones about the fact that they were violently opposed to the régime.

I shall never forget my encounters with the youngest of them, still half children, who did what they believed to be their duty until they were literally ready to drop. They had been fed on legends of heroism for as long as they could remember. For them the call to the 'ultimate sacrifice' was no empty phrase. It went straight to their hearts and they felt that now their hour had come, the moment when they really counted and were no longer dismissed because they were still too young. They shovelled away day and night on the East wall or the West wall — the system of earthworks and tank traps which was built along all the frontiers during the last months. They looked after refugees, they helped the wounded. During air raids they fought the fires and strove to rescue sick and wounded people. Finally they went in against the Russians with 'panzer-fists'[12], which were given out by the *Volkssturm*.

In one suburb of Berlin I saw a row of dead anti-aircraft auxiliaries lying side by side. It was just after an air raid. The anti-aircraft base where these schoolboys were serving had received several direct hits: I went into a barrack room where the survivors were gathered. They sat on the floor along one wall, and the white faces they turned towards me were distorted with fear. Many of them were weeping.

In another room lay the wounded. One of them, a boy with a soft round childish face, held himself rigid when the officer I was with asked him if he was in pain. "Yes, but it doesn't matter. Germany must triumph."

At his trial at Nuremburg the Reich Youth Leader, Arthur Axmann, had to answer the charge that on Hitler's orders he sent out a battalion of about 600 boys of fifteen and sixteen as late as April 23 1945 to defend the Pichelsdorf Bridge in Berlin. "I shall never cease to regret the losses which were suffered then by my young comrades," said Axmann, or words to that effect.

Unlike him I did not have to witness this terrible children's war, the last and most senseless sacrifice of youth when the issue of victory or defeat had long since been decided, but I can see the angel faces beneath the steel helmets and I know what went on in those boys' hearts. They had sung countless times:

"Germany, look on us, we dedicate our death to thee, as the least we can give. When death comes to our ranks we will become the great seed."

I am sure that fear kept clutching at their throats, but they burned with the desire to prove themselves as soldiers. They wanted to stand by the promises made in their songs.

But I dread to think what despair and misery must have overcome them as they saw their comrades bleeding to death

---

[12] Anti-tank hand weapons. *Translator's note.*

beside them and when their own intoxication gave way to sober consciousness.

None of us who led those young people can remember, without feelings of guilt and horror, how they were smashed at the war fronts. In the state of blind frenzy to which they had been incited, how could they have recognized the contradiction between those human values (patriotism, loyalty, courage, obedience) to which they believed they were sacrificing themselves, and the inhumanity of the 'Führer' they worshipped? Drunk with power, he cynically let whole hecatombs of young people bleed to death.

If there is anything that forces us to examine the principles on which we operated as leaders in the Hitler Youth and in the Labour Service, it is this senseless sacrifice of young people.

It cannot be overlooked that in these organizations there were astonishing achievements in individual fields. I have mentioned many examples — but they do not alter the basic fact. If Axmann had not learnt to idolize the German nation he would not have sent out those fifteen- and sixteen-year-olds to defend Berlin on April 23 1945. He was these boys' supreme leader — but their lives and wellbeing meant less to him than National Socialist Germany, which was even then in its death throes.

This worship of our own nation, the obverse of which was our contempt for foreign nations, was the central driving force in our training of young people. In the name of this religion we demanded and ourselves offered blind obedience. This certainly enabled us to foster real virtues such as courage and self sacrifice. But these were devalued by the suppression of all education for that central virtue which could alone have made full sense of acts of courage and self sacrifice: no one made us think for ourselves or develop the ability to make moral decisions on our own responsibility. Our motto was: The Führer orders, we follow!

I have interrupted the chronological report briefly here because it seemed important to make that point at this stage.

During the last months of the war I was also given official war work by the Reich Youth Leadership. The Gauleiter of Berlin,

Goebbels, had asked Axmann if the Hitler Youth would take over the work of the station commandants at the biggest Berlin main line railway termini. The former commandants had been appointed from the National Socialist National Welfare Service, but they had failed. Utter chaos reigned at the stations: he, the Gauleiter, no longer had anyone available who could restore order.

Axmann was in a similar position to Goebbels — he had already had to give up all his qualified youth leaders. He therefore proposed that the senior B.D.M. leaders should take on the job. I was allotted to a station in the eastern part of the city. After a very short time I failed in this task, like my predecessor.

Overcrowded transport trains filled with refugees would arrive there unscheduled and without my receiving prior notice. They descended in thousands from the unheated trains, with children, old and sick people, the bodies of those who had died on the way, bundles of bedding and shapeless luggage in tow. Families lost one another in the confusion, mothers shouted for their children, children for their mothers.

No one knew where to go or where to find shelter. I had not been told where the refugees were to go, and with the twelve- and thirteen-year-old boys who had been made available to me as 'auxiliaries' I could only try to move the people along slowly out of the station premises and into the city to make room for fresh transport trains.

There were no air raid shelters near the station. We could only guide the people to a few cellars, but there was hardly room for a small part of the refugees. When the enemy bombers came over Berlin the people stampeded into every corner of a room or shed which would offer them the thinnest pasteboard roof over their heads.

One night a raid came when the station buildings were packed with refugees. I could hear people shouting, cursing and praying in the darkness round me, and I was waiting for the moment when a real panic would break out. Then there would be people killed, I knew, without a single bomb hitting the station. When the enemy aircraft had turned back a deathly silence of complete exhaustion fell over the station. Men, women and children collapsed onto their luggage or huddled close together to try to keep a little warm.

I lay down on my work table and tried to go to sleep. But my nerves were too strained. Towards morning I heard an abruptly stifled cry from a nearby hall, which was followed by a brief scuffle. I sprang to the door and flashed my torch across the room. A man and a woman were carrying someone past me. "Let us past," said the man. "He's dead. He's been dead for four days but his wife won't be parted from him. We can't lug him round with us till Judgement Day. We'll put him down somewhere. Perhaps someone will bury him."

I went back to my table. Underneath it were sleeping the boys who were on duty. One of them had told me he had carried a basket with the body of a dead child in it. Next morning, if I remember rightly, I reported that the job was beyond me.

A short time later I was told to go to Frankfurt-an-der-Oder. Operating from there I was to help to set up soldiers' hostels in the vicinity of the front line.

The civilian population had been evacuated from Frankfurt and the town had been proclaimed a fortress. I found the Hitler Youth headquarters in the cellar of a corner house by the great old bridge across the Oder. There I was told in which section of the front I had to set up the hostels. I was supplied with a pass, which would give me freedom of movement in the front area, and I made my way through as far as Seelow. As far as I remember, the headquarters of a recently posted division was located there.

This section of the front had been stable for weeks, and they seemed to believe that it would not be in motion for the time being. At all events the commander wanted as many homes as possible set up so that his N.C.O.s and the most deserving of his soldiers could have two or three days of rest and recuperation.

The running of the homes was to be taken over by senior B.D.M. leaders who had lost the areas they had been in charge of through the withdrawal of the front.

My new job was neither difficult nor dangerous. I went through the evacuated villages which lay immediately behind the front, searched out suitable houses, and with the help of soldiers fitted them out for my purpose within a few hours. I had everything I needed in the way of beds, linen, radios, chairs, card tables and so on, collected from the other houses. The nearest company undertook the provision of a temporary delousing station in the cellar and a latrine in the garden. Houses which I had found in the morning could be taken over the same evening by the B.D.M. leaders, and the soldiers could move into them.

One day the officers, with whom I had frequent dealings, asked me if the Hitler Youth would be prepared to do something to boost the morale of the troops. They thought that groups of instrumentalists or singers might be brought right into the trenches during the night to make music with the soldiers. The fate of Berlin depended on the steadiness of these soldiers, and if Berlin could not be held, the base would be lost for the use of that last, saving weapon to which Hitler would only turn at the hour of greatest danger. Nothing would do more to put heart into the soldiers than for them to meet boys and girls who still believed in a German victory.

When I asked about the danger to which the group of musicians would be exposed, the officers banished all my fears. I was assured that a Russian attack on this front, which had been static for weeks, would not get under way so quickly that the young people could not be taken back to Berlin first. Apart from that the idea was only to bring them up at night. They would be protected in the trenches from the Russian snipers, who presented the only real danger.

After this conversation I sent for two musical groups from the Hitler Youth of the Western Mark of Brandenburg.

As you can imagine, it was my duty to let my superiors in Berlin decide if this dangerous special action was to be undertaken or not. But I avoided asking them because I presumed that they would forbid me to take the boys and girls into the front line. If the fighting morale of the troops could be strengthened by an encounter with these children, I thought (and who was a better judge of that than their own officers?), then the operation must be risked. But I knew in advance that I would never get away with this view in Berlin.

I picked up the musical groups at Seelow and went on through the night with a small group of boys and girls to the soldiers in the trenches. One or two officers went with us. They carried the sweets and tobacco we were allowed to distribute to the soldiers. I think I know what thoughts will cross your mind as you read this. It was the same idolization of Germany which made the Reich Youth Leader send out a battalion of children into the last, hopeless battle for Berlin, that made me arrange this adventure with the musical groups at the front.

In the Nuremburg proceedings against Axmann the word 'blindness' was frequently used. It is probably the only expression which adequately describes our state of mind at that time. An eye which gazes fascinated at one point which seems to be the source of all the light in the world must be dazzled by this abundance of light, and at the same time be blinded to everything that is not illuminated by this light. The mystery which seemed to lie behind the words 'Greater Germany' blinded us with the force of a spell.

Fate was more merciful than I deserved, and none of the children I took to the soldiers by night came to any harm. The boys and girls regarded these 'outings' as a wonderful adventure. When they had finished singing or playing we sometimes heard shouts of applause coming over from the Russian trenches. But on occasions they also tried to create a disturbance: they bellowed through our songs with the loudspeakers which they used to call upon the German soldiers to desert.

While I took good care that the boys and girls never left the protection of the trenches, I used to walk along the top edge of the trench myself. This was less laborious, for there were long sections in the trenches where one had to wade through loose sand. The Russian snipers did not disturb me. Nor did I bother to dodge the Russian artillery which during the daytime kept certain crossroads and level crossings under fire. As for the two or three Russian planes (like the soldiers we called them 'the day's sewing machines') which unloaded a quota of bombs in our area every day, they made us laugh. Compared with the air forces of the Western powers they were as effective as Stone Age weapons.

When I was crossing a field with a soldier one day at noon I suddenly realized that I had got used to risking my life quite frivolously. For the first time I asked myself: Why? Why are you not careful? Could it be that you don't believe in the future?

Although I had heard the whistle of an approaching shell I had not flung myself down like my companion, and he scolded me for this.

From all those weeks which immediately preceded the collapse of Germany, I cannot remember a single conversation in which the probability of our defeat was mentioned. You might think we would have had no other subject of conversation. But believe me when I say that our gaze was fixed, as if by hypnosis, on what was immediately in front of us. The next step, and the one after that, might take us over the brink. But that was something we did not wish to see or hear or think about.

In the course of the years we had sealed ourselves off with a thick layer of cement against the attempts to disturb us which popped up from our subconscious. If I think back now to those weeks, I can perceive, better than I could then, what had happened inside me without my being aware of it.

I was firmly convinced that I would not outlive the 'Third Reich'. If it was condemned to go under, then so was I. The one thing would automatically follow the other without my having to do anything about it. I did not picture my death as a last sacrifice which I should have to make. Nor did I think of suicide. I was filled with a shadowy impression that 'my world' would be flung off its course, like a constellation in a cosmic catastrophe, and would drag me with it — like a tiny speck of dust — into outer darkness.

I must sometimes have been disturbed by the vague fear that I would miss the end which was intended for me and would then be forced to outlive my 'world'. Perhaps I was also secretly afraid that when the crucial moment came I should cling to life like a coward. This, I could see, would condemn me to a life of bitter self contempt — indeed worse, to an existence robbed of all inner possibilities of life.

This I dreaded, and it is certainly the reason for my 'frivolous' behaviour in the face of danger. I did not wish to dodge the bullet that was meant for me.

At night I sometimes came across farmers ploughing between the trenches. They must have obtained special permission to return to the evacuated area, and worked in places where they were out of range of the Russian snipers. The freshly turned soil already smelt of spring. As the lone ploughmen moved in the moonlit mist their action moved me so much that I had to weep. I found comfort in the earthly immortality of this action, which will not go under, though empires may collapse. But in almost the same moment I put myself on my guard against accepting this comfort. It was a part of our blindness that one did not want anything to outlive the Third Reich. It must have been the subterranean despair of such a feeling that gave birth to the gruesome idea of a 'scorched earth' policy — of which you must certainly have heard.

Towards the middle of April I had been to my Berlin office for a day and a night, as I often did, and I was returning to the front in the evening in a military vehicle. When we got near to Seelow I saw unusual fireworks of tracer bullets over the Russian trenches. I asked the field ambulance driver who was taking me what he thought of it, and he replied: "It generally looks like that before an attack comes off."

This remark made me prick up my ears. I decided at once to make my way through to R. The soldiers' rest home there was in particular danger because it was located in a 'peninsula' held by German troops which projected into Russian occupied territory. When I reached R. my B.D.M. colleagues there were just celebrating the birthday of a Viennese captain of artillery whose detachment was nearby. I told the officers present what I had seen. At the same moment the bombs began to fall round about with an intensity that was generally confined to the Western raids.

The officers rushed off to their battle headquarters, and the captain of artillery took my briefcase with him by mistake, so that from now on I was relieved of even this 'burdensome possession'.

After the planes had turned back, the regimental commander, a major from Munich, sent his car for us and had us brought to his battle headquarters.

He would have been acting more responsibly if he had sent us back to the west straight away. Perhaps he could still cherish the illusion that such a bombardment would not be followed by further enemy action: at all events he was unwilling to be parted from the company of my two comrades who had looked after the hostel.

I am surprised that I did not have us sent back to the west straight away myself. My energy was sapped by a stomach and bowel upset which had been troubling me for several days, and my comrades would not take orders from me: in the face of a threatened collapse of the world, differences of rank play no part. So I went with them to the battle headquarters, although it seemed senseless to me, for I did not want to be thought a coward. You must have experienced situations yourself in which you have acted unreasonably because you felt too miserable to make a rational decision. We spent the night at the headquarters, an underground bunker in a stubble field. There were several two tiered bunks in this dugout, and the major had had an open fireplace built into it. I do not know if it was ever used. At that time a small iron stove was giving out a considerable heat.

I was so tired that I quickly fell asleep, wrapped in a fur-lined top coat, although there was noise all around me.

Shortly before dawn I woke up with a start: the air was filled with a noise that sounded like a pot of peas as big as a mountain on the boil. Without ever having heard a description of it I knew at once that this was a barrage.

The major was sitting on the bed on my right, and looked at me in alarm. "As soon as the barrage stops the Russian tanks will come," he said. "Do you know how to use panzer-fists? All we can do now is sell our skins as dearly as possible."

During the last few months I had had some training in pistol shooting at the Reich Youth Leadership, and we had also had to learn how to use panzer-fists. But I had only fired two or three trial shots. I hated the noise the weapons made. As I listened to the barrage, which made the bunker vibrate slightly the whole time, I wondered if the B.D.M. leaders in the other soldiers' hostels would manage to escape to safety. Fortunately their chances were much better than ours. And thank heaven, most of all, that all the boys and girls from the musical groups had been sent home.

Although in the past year I had several times been in situations in which my chances of survival were almost nil, I still could not help my knees shaking now. But beneath this physical fear, or perhaps above it, there was a level at which I was not afraid of death. I had gone into the war prepared to die, and this I was still ready to do.

Listening to the barrage, I considered whether we ought to try to escape or if we should defend the bunker with the men until none of us was left alive. In case of need, I had a small pistol. It gave me a feeling of security.

I decided that I would not try to escape. I do not remember how long the barrage lasted. Suddenly the concentration of fire moved round and we found ourselves more on the edge of the target area. Now the first runners from the trenches arrived, pale men smeared with blood and dirt, whose faces were marked with horror. One of them, a thin, oldish soldier with a head like a skull, sank sobbing against a wooden pile. His report was: "Apart from myself, there are only two men left alive!"

I forget how big his unit had been. He stumbled to his feet. As he left the battle headquarters I followed him to the exit. The horizon all round was red with burning villages. At the first light of dawn the target area switched once more, and this was our salvation. The shells no longer fell on us like hail: now individual shots could be distinguished.

"Try to get through to the regimental aid post," the major advised us. "From there my car can take you a few miles to the west. After that you'll be out of reach of the tanks."

We started out. The soldier who was detailed to accompany us stayed put in the first foxhole that was out of sight of the battle headquarters. He squeezed with me into the same hole for one person. I could feel his whole body trembling. The night under the barrage had got into his bones.

As we made our way along the road, the gunfire drove us from one piece of cover to the next. In almost every bomb crater or foxhole I had to resist the impulse to use my pistol. I was so exhausted that all I wanted was peace.

We found out in Seelow during the course of the morning that none of my B.D.M. colleagues had suffered a scratch. They had all left their soldiers' rest homes at the last minute — but in time.

I felt as if a miracle had happened. But from that day on I knew that Germany would lose the war. The same afternoon I had myself taken to a field hospital which was temporarily installed in a beautiful country house. Here I would stay as an auxiliary nurse and wait for the end of the war. Some of my colleagues had the same plan. We lost sight of one another when shortly afterwards I went to Berlin and then to another hospital, where I remained.

Here, too, the doctors worked day and night without ever gaining control of the influx of wounded. The fighters of the Western allies circled over the house and the thunder of the front drew steadily closer. Every party of wounded brought news of fresh breakthroughs by the Russians.

What would become of the wounded when they fell into their hands? In the end the soldiers lay closely packed together, even in the corridors of the house. The stretcher bearers never stopped bringing groaning bundles of mangled human flesh up the outside staircase and unloading them where a gap occurred. There were only gaps when one of the men had died.

During those days and nights I simply tried to continue existing physically. For hours at a time I sometimes managed to be aware of the sights and sounds of horror only with my outward senses. Then my hands could work smoothly and quickly.

One morning we had to move in a great hurry. We put the wounded into lorries and took them to Fürstenwalde, where I believe a school had been made available to us for the field hospital. From there I drove to Berlin for the last time. My office had already been largely vacated and transferred to Bavaria. I was ordered to report to Garmisch for 'Werewolf' training[13], but I paid no attention to this.

On April 19 the ceremonial induction of ten-year-old boys and girls into the Hitler Youth was held as it was every year. It took place in the domed hall at the Reich Sports Ground in Berlin. While the distant thunder of battle could already be heard in the eastern suburbs, the Reich Youth Leader called upon his 'youngest comrades' to fight for the victory of Greater Germany. The next day, the Führer's birthday, there were six air raids on Berlin. A few days later the Russian artillery began to bombard the city. On April 20 I left Berlin for the last time. I set out once again for Fürstenwalde in order to find the doctors and medical orderlies with whom I had recently been working and to stay with them.

---

[13] Sabotage training organized by the S.S. *Translator's note.*

An ambulance pulled up beside me at the edge of the town. One of our doctors helped me up into the driver's cabin. "Come with me," he said. "We have to move again."

I had no plans for the future. For days I had been living in a hazy state in which I did what the moment required, but my mind was clouded with impenetrable fog.

At the moment when the doctor pulled me up into the lorry I suddenly realized that I wanted to wait for the end of the war on the 'Eastern Front'. I could not have given any rational motive for this; I just had the feeling that it would be cowardice to leave this area now.

"Where are we going?" I asked the doctor.

"To southern Germany," he replied. "We are going to break through."

"Then stop the lorry, I want to stay here."

"Why?"

The argument that began with this exchange ended with my thrashing about and the doctor gripping me by the hands to stop me forcing my way out.

After he had talked to me for a long time he released his grip. I made no further attempt to leave the lorry. But for years afterwards I was ashamed that I had not.

15

I cannot remember where I left the ambulance. I got a lift from friends to Innsbruck. There I tried vainly to obtain work in a military hospital. Everywhere there were more trained nurses than could be used. No one was interested in untrained helpers.

I finally got a job from the Labour Exchange working for a nursery that was planting spruce firs in the northern hills above the town. We clung to the steep mountain slopes and dug the roots of the young trees into the thin layer of earth which covered the rock. The work was exhausting, but I did it lovingly and with great care. Nothing I could have done now would have made more sense to me. These little trees would outlive the ruin of my world. Nihilistic despair, which had sometimes made me wish that nothing should survive this ruin, had given way at the sight of the landscape which surrounded me.

But the bombs were still falling all the time: the sound of their deathdealing explosions reached us from the city, magnified by the echoes from the mountains.

My last meetings with the leaders of the Tyrolean Hitler Youth took place under the aegis of the so called 'Werewolf' training, in which S.S. officers schooled us in sabotage techniques.

We all looked towards a dark future with the helplessness of children. Only one thing seemed certain to us: that no power on earth would succeed in destroying our community, the fellowship of the corps of Hitler Youth Leaders. Many of my Tyrolean friends had had experience of illegal youth work from the period before the union of their country with Germany. With them I sought salvation in the idea that now a new period of illegal activity would begin, although no one knew what its political purpose would be.

So we adjusted ourselves to the idea of 'fighting on'. We deliberately overlooked the fact that all was already lost. I cannot remember a single one of us lamenting the disaster which had overtaken us. This was due less to our heroism than to our blindness about the finality of the disaster.

I remember one idea which I permitted myself to indulge in at that time. I thought bitterly: "So it *was* wrong after all to make National Socialism into a mass produced article which anyone could buy. It should have remained a small, strictly selected élite group of leaders — then it would not have been watered down and betrayed a thousand times over by the army of opportunists."

During my first years in the Hitler Youth I had often crossed swords with my superiors because I argued that it was necessary to build up an élite. Did not the collapse now prove that I had been right at that time, although I was only a child? Now, I believed, the German defeat would force us to accept the principle of forming an 'order'. The vast mass of fellow travellers in the Party would in any case openly turn traitor within the shortest possible time: only those who were serious in their convictions would be left. I had no doubt that a considerable section of the senior Hitler Youth leadership would continue their work illegally in a new way, and in the midst of our impasse I took comfort from the thought that they would form a fighting political association which would be more worthy of the name than the ill organized, flabby structure of the Hitler Youth at that time.

On April 30, after I had spent several days planting fir trees on the northern range, I met an S.S. officer who introduced himself as the leader of a so called 'hunting commando group' *(Jagdkommando).*

His men were located in a remote mountain valley, he explained, and had no one to cook for them and look after their washing. I was ready to undertake this straight away, and three

B.D.M. colleagues were willing to go with me. On the night of May 1 (the day before the Americans occupied Innsbruck) we drove through a snowstorm in an army amphibious craft to the valley where we were to find refuge during the first months of peace.

I do not remember now the rank of our detachment chief. He was a Knight of the Iron Gross and was subordinate to Skorzeny — 'Mussolini's liberator' — who was in hiding with his staff in another valley.

Our detachment was divided up into groups of twelve men in different hiding places in the mountains. They had been busy for days hiding supplies of food, civilian and military clothing, arms and sabotage equipment, which had been stored in the valley, all round the mountains. Every group set up its stores dump. The leading group, which was commanded by the Knight of the Iron Cross himself, constructed a base in the woods which was lit by electric light and where one could go down into a kind of cellar.

The men had already had experience of dangerous sabotage operations. Several of them told of how they had been dropped behind the Russian lines dressed as American paratroops to work as military agents.

This may sound like a fairy story, but they now seemed to be planning something similar for the future. They outlined to one another in conversation how they could carry on sabotage operations in the occupied zone. Later on a great counter attack would be launched from the so called 'Alpine fortress', with the intention of driving the enemies back out of Germany.

Despite these conversations, however, I had the impression that most of the men were really only concerned to be in safety during the first dangerous weeks after the war.

We had abundant equipment and a hiding place which the Americans would probably not find very quickly. The fact that we were able to humbug ourselves with the idea of this politico-military 'mission' helped us to retain our mental stability for a time after the defeat of Germany. Four weeks after the ceasefire we were still living in our familiar world of military procedure and Nazi ideas. The utterly unreal hope that we could one day re-establish this world from our funkhole protected us from the annihilating realization that it had already ceased to exist.

Shortly after the Americans had occupied the valley, the Knight of the Iron Cross appeared at our group's hideout and showed us with childish pleasure a haul of precious jewels, which were supposed to be a part of the Hungarian crown jewels. By now we had left our military Utopia behind and began to consider more 'practical' aims. The capital from these jewels, which had apparently been brought by one of Skorzeny's runners, would, so he told us, finance the illegal establishment of a new Nazi Party in Austria.

The jewels obsessed the minds of our men in a most ominous way. I heard more than one of them saying that they should make the chief divide the valuables between them. And if he refused to do so, they had pistols enough.

You can no doubt imagine that the weeks I spent living in a tiny hut with ten or twelve men were not exactly boring. I had to cook for them on an improvised hearth, and we had only damp wood for fuel. The smoke stung our eyes, but if we let the fire go out we froze wretchedly.

The hut was not meant for living in — it was only a tool shed — and the wind whistled through the countless cracks in it. On one wall was an unglazed picture of the Virgin Mary in a wooden frame. The damp made the paper crinkle, and the men watched its progress. "Our Madonna is getting more and more wrinkles from worry," they said. "We'll soon be for the high jump."

At night the entire contents of the hut, which consisted of the hearth, a table and a few benches, had to be put out in the snow, so that there could be room for everyone to sleep on the floor. Even then we would lie packed close together like sardines. This was no bad thing, however, for although we slept in fur lined top coats, we should certainly have frozen without contact with the animal warmth of our neighbours.

Our supplies unfortunately included brandy and even champagne. The men had hidden the alcoholic drinks somewhere in the vicinity where I never found them. They had taken this precaution after I threatened to break all their bottles of booze the first evening they got drunk. You can imagine that my situation as the only girl amongst these men was not easy, especially at a time when all that had previously held good was now being called into question. But I was fortunate: not once did I get into real difficulties. When we knew one another better, my comrades occasionally told me that it was a slight to their manly honour that I had not struck up an amorous liaison with any of them. Did not a single one of them please me?

When the men drank more than they needed to quench their thirst I would creep onto a pile of coats in the farthest corner of the hut and pretend to be asleep. Often that did not work because they did not like me to withdraw from their circle.

On some evenings we suddenly felt a yearning for intellectual satisfaction. Then we embarked on conversations about philosophical topics which contrasted grotesquely with our physical situation. The few discussion leaders — myself amongst them — would rack their brains to remember the fragments of philosophy they had learned at school, while the less 'intellectual' types imbibed the spirit in more fluid form. On one occasion Niko — who was a teacher in civilian life — surprised us by reciting long speeches from classical plays, and sometimes the men persuaded me to read to them from the two books I carried in my pack, *Hyperion* by Hölderlin and *Adel und Untergang* (Nobility and Decline) by J. Weinheber. The title of this anthology of poems summarized my own view of our situation. We ourselves, I felt — carried away as I was by my own pathos — were the aristocratic leaders of our nation, which was doomed to decline.

The situation was romantic: down below in the valley burned the watch fires which the Americans maintained on hidden landmarks, while up above we sat wrapped in fur coats listening to the poems of Hölderlin by the light of a candle. Perhaps we should be discovered the next day by one of the occupying power's aircraft, which were searching the more inaccessible regions for suspicious signs. What would face us then nobody knew.

I have never met any of those men since and have had no news of them. I doubt if I should recognize any of them if I met him unexpectedly. What you would probably like to ask me now is what I have often asked myself since then: What kind of men were they, with whom you spent those weeks after the war? What was their past? These questions forced themselves upon me when I learned about the part played by the S.S. in the extermination of the Jews. I have since realized that I shall never be able to supply the answers. I learned from the diary of one of the camp commandants of Auschwitz that this man was both a mass murderer and a kindly father, a lover of animals and a keen gardener.

Sometimes, since I made this discovery, something comes over me when I am talking to a friendly bank employee or a florist's assistant who is telling me about how he loves Italian opera. Suddenly the question springs to my mind and drives every other thought out of my head: Where were you during the war? What did you do then?... You cannot tell by looking at people. Generally you can tell nothing by looking at them. If I think back to my comrades in the hut I should say they were rough but decent fellows. I would not suspect them of being the ones who... But you know what I mean. I had no unpleasant experiences with them myself. That is all I can say.

After about four weeks an attack of flu forced me to go down into the valley and seek refuge for a few days in a comfortable winter sports hostel where there were beds. I found two of my B.D.M. comrades there as well. They had left their groups and passed themselves off to the Americans as the owners of the hostel. A secret field hospital for members of our commando groups who fell sick was to be set up here.

On my second day there six or seven of my comrades came to visit me disguised as farm workers. An American sentry became suspicious, and within a quarter of an hour the house was surrounded. The men still managed to throw the pistols — without which, apparently, some of them could not even go for a walk — into my bed. I pushed them under the mattress. While the American sergeant who searched the house was poking round my bed with a riding whip I was coughing like someone gravely ill. One of my friends made it clear to the sergeant that I was suffering from diphtheria. My bed was the only place in the house that was not thoroughly inspected.

Meanwhile my comrades of the S.S. had been arrested. The next day they were released again. The sergeant detailed two soldiers to protect us, as he said — but naturally, in fact, to watch us.

They made a second raid, and this time discovered a box containing brandy from the S.S. stores. One of the two was a Mexican, almost as black as a negro. He got drunk very quickly and then became so wild that his fair skinned comrade fled the house. The drunken man suddenly flung open the door of my room and lay down beside me with his gun almost in one bound. The fact that I nevertheless managed to escape by jumping through the window so enraged him that he went round the house shooting blindly. For a full hour this fellow kept us in fear and trembling while he repeatedly tried to force one of us onto a bed. He would aim his gun at us at point blank range and switch the barrel up into the air at the last minute, so that the shot went into the ceiling. Fortunately we spoke enough English to be able always to distract and pacify him. A few days after this turbulent contact with the occupying forces we three women decided to leave the valley.

Before I describe my further 'adventures', however, I must first mention an experience which happened round about May 10. It was then I learned that Hitler had planned his own death.

I remember the moment very clearly. One of the farmers who lived in an out-of-the-way part of the valley had given me permission to do the washing for my group at his farm. One evening I went into his living room and found a wireless set there.

I was alone, and switched it on. Suddenly a triumphant voice announced that a few days before Hitler had taken his own life in his Berlin command bunker. As I listened with bated breath, I looked through a latticed window at a wall of rock on the other side of the valley, which glowed red in the evening sun.

Suddenly a rainstorm lashed against the window panes. I flung open the window and looked across to the mountains. At that moment, with a certainty which left no room for the slightest shadow of doubt, I expected the wall of rock to rear up and plunge into the valley below. Hitler was dead!

But nothing happened. The glow on the mountain faded. The peaks turned violet, almost black, and then the rain fell steady and cold.

With a feeling of inner emptiness that made me feel giddy I climbed back up to the men. When I opened the door of the hut the candle on the table went out. Then I said in the darkness: "Hitler is dead! He's committed suicide in his bunker in Berlin!"

I heard the men leap to their feet. Then for a long time there was silence. That night they got drunk almost without speaking a word. Meanwhile I lay as if stunned in my corner. I could not even weep.

Towards morning the quietest member of our group, a peasant lad from Mecklenburg who was not yet twenty, had a delirious attack. Shouting, he went for his friend with an open knife. The men who were sober forced him back with a bench into the corner where the picture of the Virgin Mary hung. Suddenly he stopped yelling and slashed the picture to pieces with small, swift jabs.

It did not occur to me at the time, but I believe now that he was venting on the picture his desperate fury at Hitler having left us in the lurch.

You may perhaps be surprised at how little I have said so far about Hitler. I never saw him close to, probably because I never bothered to try to do so. It was not that I lacked the interest, but I considered that taking part in official functions was a waste of time so long as the Third Reich was still not built or the war still not won...

I never had much use for the parades or cordons of honour when one saw the Führer's car driving past at top speed. After being bored by two or three of these, I avoided this 'duty' in future.

I certainly heard him speak several times at youth rallies, amongst others on the Reich Party Day in 1938 in Nuremburg. But I was always so busy with my press work there that I could not permit myself the 'debauchery' of ecstatic rapture. Nor did any one of these meetings remain in my memory as particularly impressive.

To conclude from this that I did not love the Führer and was not inspired by him would be false. I was happy that a 'man of the people', the son of a customs official, should have succeeded in rising to be head of the Reich. This symbolized my highest ideal — the National Community. I ascribed to the political genius of the Führer all the successes which the Third Reich had achieved: the elimination of the postwar misery and of the disunity our people had suffered in a multi-party state; the liquidation of the dictated peace of Versailles and the effacing of the 'dishonour' inflicted upon us by our former enemies; the 'bringing home' of the lost frontier territories, and of the *Volksdeutsch* Germans from the Diaspora. And finally, had he not given meaning to my own life by calling upon me to serve my nation?

When I came home on the evening of July 20 1944, switched on my radio and heard the news of the attempt to assassinate Hitler, I sagged at the knees as if struck by an invisible fist. But then came the next comforting sentence: the attempt had been a failure. Hitler lived.

'Providence' had preserved him. During the last months of the war I always had to fight back tears when I heard Hitler's voice on the radio or saw him on the newsreels. One's conscious mind might refuse to recognize the signs of an imminent collapse, which were becoming more and more obvious, but the immediate impressions one received through one's eyes and ears could not be falsified, and one's heart was gripped with fear at the appalling truth: the newsreels showed an ageing man, who walked with a stoop and glanced anxiously about him. His voice sounded shrill with despair. Was he, then, destined to fail? For us he embodied the unprecedented effort which had made the German nation take over the government of the continent. In looking at him one saw the sum total of all the countless sacrifices of lives, health and property which that effort had demanded. Had all this been in vain?

Though it may scarcely sound credible, the four weeks between my leaving the S.S. valley and my arrest have remained in my memory as a particularly happy time. If I was not completely happy then, it was only because I was not spared contact with the misfortunes of other people.

In those weeks I managed to switch off my knowledge of the defeat and its grim consequences. I clung to the feeling of happiness which came from my awareness that the war was over and the killing had stopped. I did not choose to consider the fate which awaited the people in the Russian occupied zone.

I had lived in a hell during the last half year of the war. The sight of horribly disfigured corpses and smoking ruins had become a daily experience. Everywhere one encountered desperate people whose minds were disturbed and whose souls were numb with pain. One was almost constantly threatened by annihilation. There was no corner where one could feel safe from the bombs. Time fuses lurked in peaceful gardens in the suburbs and low flying aircraft attacked the farmers in the fields.

One could only resist such an excess of horror and danger without succumbing to despair as long as one was upheld by the belief that this suffering had a point, and would lead to a victory that would justify all the sacrifices. The night my parents died I lost that inner faith. I was not aware of the loss, but I felt its effects.

My efforts to fight against despair and misery, wherever I happened to be at the time, came to have something mechanical about them. My head and hands went on working, kept in motion by force of habit. My soul was numb with fear and horror.

In the hut I had already begun to relax from this paralysed state. I awoke from it fully only at the moment when I became aware with my whole being that the war was over. This moment would not have engraved itself on my memory with such intensity if a particular piece of music, which I had loved for many years, had not played a decisive role in it.

I was lying under a bush, which was filled with humming bees, watching children at play on the edge of a village. They were throwing a turnip to one another like a ball and shaking with laughter. Suddenly a window in the house behind them opened and I heard, faintly at first and then more clearly, the great *Ricercare* from the *Musical Offering.* As I absorbed the music, along with the scent of the flowering bush and the children's laughter, I felt as if I had awoken from an evil enchantment, in which I had been tormented by terrible phantoms and demons of hell. Now I should begin to live like a human being again.

I find it hard to recapture my mood at that time. Perhaps you have experienced something similar on some occasion — a period of complete release, just when it would have been 'natural' and even, perhaps, 'reasonable' to allow your head and heart to be tormented by worries and problems.

For four weeks I rambled through the Tyrolean and Salzburg alps with my rucksack. During the first few days I had a friend with me: after that I was alone. I knew I only had a short reprieve before I lost my freedom. Somewhere, at some time, I should be arrested and who could say if it might not be ten years before I could walk through woods again. I would have thought it wrong to avoid arrest for any length of time, but for the moment I enjoyed as a gift every day's grace in this incomparably beautiful country.

Although the Americans had ordered that nobody was to travel a distance of more than six kilometers without a pass, one did not have to worry about this. One got sufficient warning when approaching a sentry. If I could not avoid him, I would put my rucksack on a farm cart and stride past the soldier smiling, with a rake on my shoulder. Or I would crawl between the flour sacks of a mill lorry.

Later I was able to forge every kind of American pass on a typewriter. After that I no longer had to crawl between flour sacks.

The fact that I was so happy then was due to the intensity with which I lived for the moment. I was free of all responsibility and I avoided considering the past or the future.

I would lie for hours in a field of gentians if I felt like it, or sit and talk to a cowman. Sometimes I helped farmers with their haymaking and earned myself a midday meal or wrote out an application to the local commandant for them, in exchange for bread and a night's rest in the barn.

I was in a village in the Pinzgau when a Luftwaffe hospital was being handed over to the Americans, and stole several blankets which I later exchanged for bread and bacon.

When I had almost climbed to the top of the Gerlos Pass, between Salzburg and the Ziller valley, I was picked up by a horsedrawn carriage whose driver was a gipsy. I sat between him and his master, a former officer of the Imperial Hungarian air force, while we began a breakneck journey down the mountain. In the evening I strolled with the gipsy through a village that was overflowing with refugees.

He had a Hungarian-German dictionary with him and declared his love for me, looking up the words one by one. Although I disappointed him bitterly because I would not spend the night with him in the barn, he gave me, as a parting gift, a huge hunk of beautiful white bread and a piece of ham.

I spent that night in a schoolroom, where a layer of straw had been put down for the homeless. There I met the wife of a local government official from southern Austria with her three small children. She was in despair, because although she was not short of money, she could not scrape together enough food for the children anywhere. The commune was no longer giving out ration cards to refugees, and the local farmers were deaf to all pleas if they were not offered anything sufficiently attractive in return. In the middle of the night an American officer came to fetch her. "Keep on eye on my children," she said. "I'll be back in the morning."

When dawn broke she came back in tears. She had no reason to be ashamed in front of me, but she said: "I only do it for my children. In any case, I can't stand much more of it."

Before I left the school I gave the woman what the gipsy had given me. It was still early in the morning. I saw the Hungarian carriage standing near the edge of the village. The gipsy was lying asleep amidst boxes and bags. I woke him up and made him understand by signs that I had given away his bread and ham. Still half asleep, he cut me more bread and ham and put it in my rucksack. He was much more open handed than I. At the bottom of my rucksack were concentrated foodstuffs, which I regarded as iron rations and only intended to touch in an emergency. I am not sure if I gave any of them to the children.

~ 16 ~

At the end of June I spent a few days in the S.S. valley once more, in order to replenish my stocks of food. The few men who had not yet tried to smuggle themselves into army demobilization camps or to make their way home were hiding together in a remote alpine pasture, each as the illegal 'subtenant' of an alpine dairywoman. But we were even driven from there during my short visit. The Austrian Resistance had discovered the hiding place, and several men were arrested. There were finally only two of them, one of my B.D.M. comrades and myself left. The four of us hid in the woods during the day and crept into the hut which had been used by the leading group at night. After the remaining two men had been arrested on a visit to the alpine pasture, we girls decided to leave for good. This was all the more urgent because the Resistance were also after my friend.

I was arrested in Bad Reichenhall on July 13 with three women comrades from the Reich Youth Leadership, including the Reich head of the B.D.M. The three of them had taken refuge on farms near Zell am See, and I had gone to visit them when I chanced to hear where they were living. They wanted to avoid being arrested by the Austrian Resistance, and as I had some experience of crossing frontiers illegally, they asked me to take them to Reichenhall. Just as we were ready to start, a former employee of the Personnel Department of the Reich Youth Leadership suddenly appeared and offered to drive us to Reichenhall in his car. I did not even know him by sight, but my colleagues had worked with him. Getting past the sentry at the frontier, a negro soldier, was so easy that, looking back, I realize we should have guessed he was expecting us. When we got out by the hospital in Bad Reichenhall the American detectives were already waiting to receive us. The 'helpful' comrade had deliberately driven us into a trap. At least that is how we interpreted what happened.

We were taken into Munich in a jeep the same night. On the way I tore up my forged passes with tiny movements of my hands, so that our guard did not notice, and scattered them to the night winds.

Immediately after our arrival at a Munich villa, which was said to have been Hitler's private residence, our interrogations began. The officer, who called me into his office first, spoke good German without a trace of accent and was so pleasant that I found it hard to lie to him. I told him that I had been a Labour Service leader. I did not tell him about my service in the Reich Youth Leadership. I wanted to avoid any hint from which they might have deduced that one of my companions was the head of the B.D.M. I attempted this deception because we could not be sure whether our comrade had really led us into a trap and if the Americans consequently knew with whom they were dealing.

My comrades also tried to deceive the interrogator. For a time he played along with this deception with charm and humour. Then he suddenly produced a photograph of the B.D.M. head from a file and showed it with a grin.

We had all four of us lied with little conviction, and we felt relieved to be able to tell the truth.

After my interrogation an N.C.O. took me onto a gallery above the hall of the house where my friends awaited their turn. He offered me a chair and put a finger to his lips to indicate that I was not to talk. When he had disappeared into a room I heard my companions softly calling up to me: "What was it like? How did they treat you?"

I leaned forward over the railings and replied, just as softly: "Objectively and courteously."

At that moment the N.C.O. flung open the door he had just gone through and slapped my face hard twice. I fell back into the chair. The man's blows were no love pats, but the situation struck me as so comic that I had to laugh out loud.

When the interrogating officer later took his leave of us, he said: "Don't worry about what will happen to you. The Americans are gentlemen."

"Not all," I interrupted, looking at the N.C.O. who had slapped my face. But he put on such a pathetic expression that I refrained from telling tales about him to his chief.

The two slaps I had to thank him for were the only physical punishment I received as long as I enjoyed the hospitality of the Americans.

My first weeks under arrest were spent in a small civil prison in Friedburg near Augsburg. Later on I was moved with a party to the old gaol in Heidelberg.

The man in charge of our party had already vainly tried to get rid of us at several prisons. The governor of the Heidelberg gaol also wrung his hands when he saw us getting out of the van. His prison was long since overcrowded.

While my friends were housed on the women's side, as many as eight to a cell in cells designed for one (the other prisoners were a mixture of political prisoners, criminals and prostitutes), I was put in a cell by myself on the men's side.

The first day there was the worst of my imprisonment; the only time I was really wretched. I was overwhelmed with horror and despair at our situation, and I was sufficiently inexperienced to give way to these feelings. For the first time I faced the truth: the Third Reich, to which millions of Germans had sacrificed their lives, their health and their property, had burst like a soap bubble.

From the morning until late into the night I lay on the floor of my cell and wept until I had no more tears left. When I woke up next day I knew that I was faced with a choice. On the one hand I had it in my power to destroy myself by continuing to yield to despair and horror; and if I did not succeed in killing myself in this way I should end up in a lunatic asylum — of that I was certain.

But I could also resist the onslaught of misery with all my strength. Then I should survive the collapse of the world in which I had been happy. This was only possible, of course, so long as I kept my thoughts and feelings under strict control. There were frontiers which they must never cross again: beyond loomed self destruction.

I did not cross these frontiers again during my internment, and I seldom came dangerously near to them.

My solitary confinement only lasted a few days. One morning the wardress announced that I was to have a cell mate whom I should have to keep an eye on discreetly. She had attacks of frenzy, I was told, in which she ran her head against the wall and smashed everything to pieces.

Frau O. said she had worked as an agent in Spain. I got on with her because I never contradicted her, neither when she served me up with tall stories, nor when she did things I disliked. In protest against the August heat she ran about naked most of the day. Sometimes she climbed onto the toilet bucket and up the bars of the window and perched, blithely naked, on the sloping window sill. From this position she could flirt with the negro soldier who stood on guard outside the prison gate. Their conversations were complicated, for Frau O. spoke no English and had to get me to say every sentence first.

"How do you say: I love you?"

"How do you say: give me a cigarette...?"

Thanks to her simulated fits she had managed to be allowed to have her bag with her in the cell. Amongst her possessions was a reel of thread, with the help of which she could fish for the sentry's gifts of cigarettes.

When one night the poor fellow wanted to collect the thanks for his love offerings, he was put to flight by a phalanx of angry wardresses.

In the so called 'Party bosses' camp' at Mannheim-Seckenheim, where I spent the next stage of my internment, my room mate was a fifty-year-old Frenchwoman, whose statements about her past varied as constantly as those of Frau O. Jeannette was entertaining and charming. She often wept to think that I should have to 'languish' for many years in American prisons. She 'loved' me because I gave her all of my daily cigarette ration. When an American officer appeared, she showered him with curses which she got me to repeat to her first.

Her liking for the other ranks, however, knew no bounds, and in the course of time this made trouble between us.

When we lay in bed at night she always wanted to hear German songs or poems. Her favourite song was *Der Mond ist aufgegangen* (The moon has risen). She learned it from me and we sang it together before wishing one another good night. Then she would say: "Now you go to sleep and don't pay any attention to me."

That was easier said than done, for quite often one of the sentries would soon appear and climb into bed with Jeannette. The men were often drunk, and my bed was nearest the door. It took quite an effort to make them understand that they had come to the wrong number.

In the late autumn of 1945 I entered the Ludwigsburg camp for women, which sometimes held 3,000 inmates. From now on one lived in a swarming ant heap, slept in the same room with thirty to 150 people, was subject to endless roll calls (even at night) and had to queue up on every possible occasion.

When I meet women who were interned there with me, I am often surprised at how differently that time has engraved itself on their memories. For me the essential significance of this period of my life lay in the fact that it was a time of enforced mental and physical idleness, such as I had lacked since my childhood and which I needed more than almost everything else I had had to do without in those years. I myself did not suffer in the camp, but there were women amongst my companions there who had been arrested in the street and who had gone for months without hearing what had become of their children or their elderly parents.

This uncertainty was hard to bear. There were also old and sick women in the camp.

If such people are inclined to wax heroic in retrospect about those years, this may be because of the great effort it cost them to endure their sufferings in the camp. But there are also men and women who indulge in lamentations about hardships they never suffered.

I feel angry and ashamed when I hear them speaking of their years of internment in West Germany as their 'time in the concentration camp', and I never let such misuse of language go uncorrected. We, my comrades and I, were not in a concentration camp. We were not subjected to cynical torture by our interrogators. We never had to fear the deadly injections of the camp doctors or the gas chambers. In comparison with what the inmates of the National Socialist concentration camps had to suffer, we lived extremely comfortably. The fact that on occasions we were cold and hungry may have been due, here and there, to the personal animosity of members of the camp staff. But at that time almost everyone in Germany went cold and hungry and I heartily despised those who were better off. They could only have escaped the general hardships by dishonest means.

I myself had good nerves, and apart from an attack of jaundice my health was good. It was also lucky for me that for once, at last, I did not have to work. For some women the idleness was a hardship. For me it was a precious gift. For ten years I had of my own free will worked myself quite unreasonably hard and had carried the burden of more and more oppressive responsibilities.

Now I enjoyed lying somewhere on the sand every day for hours at a time, dreaming or losing myself in a poem. Amongst the women there I was particularly friendly with the former musical director of the Reich Youth Leadership. She preferred ancient music and rehearsed four- and five-part pieces with a carefully selected choir. Although I could not join in the singing myself, I learnt a lot from this.

From time to time I also amused myself by compiling a synoptic historical chart. I went my rounds from the historian to the economist, thence to the architect and the musical historian, until I had collected all the data I needed.

All this happened at a more leisurely pace than I had ever before in my life been able to allow myself. Naturally there were days when one bitterly missed solitude or when one longed very much to walk through the woods. But in the healing idleness which the inventors of 'automatic arrest' had imposed upon me, it was possible for the psychological after effects of the horror, the fear and ten years of overstrain to begin to pass off slowly — even if this meant postponing any real attempt to come to grips with our experience. One also had the opportunity to summon up one's inner strength for this attempt when it came to be made. For a while, at least, I regained that most basic feeling of my existence, which I had lost — the feeling of being at home in this world.

Politically, I believe it was unnecessary and even in many respects a blunder to put us behind bars. Perhaps a tiny percentage of the women and girls who were interned might have been prepared to carry on some kind of underground resistance activities after 1945 if they had been left at liberty, but it would certainly have been of no consequence. If the imprisonment of many women for two, three and four years was intended to re-educate them for democracy, then in my view the effort was wasted.

Both during my internment and later I have heard repeatedly of women who only became 'proper National Socialists' in the camp, and I have observed that 'converts' from this period cling to their new 'religion' with startling intolerance. They were mostly women who should not, by rights, have been in the camp at all: they had been mistaken for someone else, or something of the kind.

The number of such people is small. What is more significant is the fact that very many women who were interned as National Socialists came out more Nazi than before.

The American and German authorities who confined us cheerfully left us to stew in our own juice and gave us next to no help in reaching a critical assessment of what had been going on in Germany for the past fifteen years.

Only a very few of us were interned because a specific, clearcut charge had been made against them. For example, that of denouncing neighbours who listened to enemy radio broadcasts. (One avoided these people in the camp because they were by nature suspicious.) Most of the women had been brought in when it was decided to extend automatic arrest to a large proportion of Party officials. This section included the B.D.M. and *Frauenschaft* (Women's Nazi Party) leaders from the middle ranks upwards.

There were amongst us, naturally, some who had sought office from motives of ambition and self aggrandizement. But I believe they were in the minority — a very tiny minority. The majority of the youth leaders had been attracted to the Hitler Youth by the same impulse as myself. Most numerous amongst the women were those who had sought an opening for social work. They were generally women with families, so that for many of them, especially during the war, their Party office had been a burden which could only be borne at great personal sacrifice. Now they were being punished for this sacrifice by being deprived of their freedom. Were they not bound to feel that they were unjustly treated?

But when has a judge, whose own impartiality is open to doubt, ever induced in an accused man a readiness to criticize himself? With few exceptions the instructors who were sent to the camp at intervals to 're-educate' us for democracy seemed to me lamentable. Even on their own special subjects they were on occasion bested by more skilled specialists amongst us.

I can hear you objecting that the German authorities had other preoccupations at that time, apart from our re-education. That is certainly true, but it is nevertheless a pity that we had to waste the years of our internment instead of using them for a period of radical rethinking under the guidance of mature and intelligent people who had not been dazzled by the madness of the Thousand Year Reich. With the exception of the political criminals, the men and women who were under arrest at that time, though they were by no means an intellectual élite of the nation, were particularly active, responsive and enterprising citizens. If events had made it possible for them to leave the camps with an increased faculty for self criticism, the problem of our unassimilated past would be less pressing for our nation today.

Instead of this, our time in the camps served to fortify our feelings of selfrighteousness. That is why it would have been cleverer to let us out of our 'Nazi reservation' as soon as possible and throw us straight into the hurlyburly of coming to grips with the newly forming democratic way of life.

Even the interrogations by the American Counter Intelligence Corps officers, which dragged on for years, only effected a change in someone's ideas in very exceptional cases.

My first interrogator was acting as an instructor for his young colleagues. I sat surrounded by a circle of lieutenants of twenty to twenty-five, who were to learn from my case how to deal with a pigheaded Nazi. Although I understand English very well, I had told them I did not know the language. This caused the students to discuss me all the more freely and increased my contempt for them, which made them abuse me heartily.

One day the chief interrogator asked me: "What would you do if we made you sleep with a Jew?"

My reply was instantaneous: "I should strangle him."

The circle of students roared with laughter. I had not intended to make a joke.

Even at the start of the interrogations, when I was inexperienced, I was never afraid of the Americans. Their manner convinced me at once that I need expect no cruel treatment. I was glad of this, but in a certain respect it annoyed me: it would have given me satisfaction to find them brutal.

To begin with I was locked up several times with a pencil and a piece of paper and told I would not be given food until I had made a list of the names and addresses of certain of my colleagues in the Reich Youth Leadership. When I returned the paper blank, my interrogator resorted to more menacing weapons. "If you continue to be so stubborn we shall hand you over to the Russians. You worked in the east for years. You know what that would mean."

As I did not doubt for a second that this threat was only bluff, I was scarcely being heroic when I returned the paper blank once more.

On occasion I had an interrogator with whom I had long conversations about art. One could easily tell that he felt unhappy in his role of investigator, and I liked him for that reason. Sometimes I tried to comfort him: "It's not your fault that you have been ordered to do this unpleasant job."

One day he told me he had been present at the 'capture of D.' (my mother's home town).

"Indeed?" I said. "Well, all you had to capture was a heap of ruins. I suppose you thought that was very heroic of you?"

The American looked at me uncertainly for a moment and then replied: "You Germans are always thinking about heroic deeds. As if that was what mattered. What we want is to be as happy as possible. Isn't that more important?"

The conversation would scarcely have stuck in my memory if it had not made me think. This interrogator was a Jew, by the way, as indeed were most of his colleagues.

At Ludwigsburg we often had to wait in a hall until it was our turn to go in. The walls were covered with posters which showed horrific photographs of mountains of corpses in concentration camps or dying concentration camp prisoners. You probably know these posters. At that time they were used to broadcast our shame almost everywhere in the world. While we were waiting, we had to stand in front of these posters and look at them.

One day I saw an American sentry deliberately push over an internee with only one leg, who was leaning against the wall without his crutch. After seeing this I exclaimed in rage to my interrogator that I could not believe a German soldier would ever have treated a prisoner as meanly as this. Furthermore I questioned the documentary authenticity of the concentration camp posters. They were all faked photographs, designed to defame us Nazis as subhuman. The C.I.C. officer caught his breath and then shouted at me. It was the only time that any one of these men ever did so. Almost at once his voice became quiet again and he spoke to me as one speaks to a backward child, but with a perceptible undertone of resignation.

We considered what these posters and our interrogators said about the concentration camps to be fantastically exaggerated, if not simply invented. But the question kept posing itself: Where do these mountains of starved corpses come from? That kind of thing cannot be faked.

It was said at the camp that the Dachau photographs had been produced by digging up the mass graves of the victims of the Munich air raids and transporting their terrible contents to Dachau. I regarded this theory with scepticism. I knew what the victims of air raids looked like. They looked quite different from the corpses of starved people. Another version claimed that the posters had been made with photographs from famine areas in Asia. But there were reasons to doubt this as well. The question was not a comfortable one to answer, so one had to be all the more careful not to go into it seriously.

There were amongst the women internees a number of ex-concentration camp overseers. Most of them were coarse and aggressive people, but one or two of them did not make a bad impression on me, and I believed them when they assured me that there had been no apparatus of extermination in the concentration camps.

There were also several former concentration camp inmates interned with us. They were young foreign women who acted as prostitutes for our sentries. Why these girls had been kept in

German concentration camps and why the Americans shut them up again with us I never discovered. They told us that they had left their women's concentration camp voluntarily in order to 'work' in the brothels in the men's camps, and that they had been very well treated there.

I have never been able to verify if these girls were lying to us. Probably the 'pretty little brothels on the edge of the woods' of which they babbled were in big labour camps and not in the concentration camps. But we were not capable of making such distinctions at that time. We thought the installation of brothels for the prisoners in wartime was a waste of money. But if even this need of the prisoners was catered for, did not everything speak against the plausibility of the 'horror stories' the Americans wanted to make us believe?

During the Nuremberg trial in May 1946 we heard a relay of the closing speeches of the chief defendants. Baldur von Schirach, who had built up the Hitler Youth and was their supreme chief until the last, said, amongst other things: "My guilt consists in having organized the youth of our nation for mass murder."

This admission hit many of us like an underhand blow. I had crept away out of the hall and sat in a dark corner behind the platform, but even there I still felt as ashamed of what I considered to be my former supreme chief's weakness as if hundreds of pairs of triumphant eyes had been focused upon me. Near me I could hear stifled sobbing. When I got up a voice I did not recognize said beside me: "What do you expect? He had become a typical Party boss years ago. People like that can't stand the strain of prison."

At that time we could have no idea that at Nuremberg Schirach had been confronted with evidence that Hitler really had murdered millions of people.

You will be expecting to hear now how we gradually became suspicious and began to think things over. But in fact — and this is something I still do not understand today — the leaders of the women's youth movement lived there for years in close proximity, together with the senior leaders of the *Frauenschaft* and the Labour Service, and yet I cannot remember a single conversation in which an attempt was made at an objective analysis of our National Socialist beliefs and their practical application. We talked endlessly, for we were not short of time. The past was chewed over and the present was deplored. This or that part of our work now seemed to us a wretched blunder and we wrote off many Party officials, but we never touched the basic questions. In my presence nobody ever thought of asking: "What if the American allegations about the concentration camps are true after all? What conclusions should we draw from that?"

Or: What are we to make of the fact that Hitler, Himmler and Goebbels abandoned their responsibility, leaving seventeen-year-old girl youth leaders to be hauled up here before a court?

There probably were women amongst us who asked questions of this kind. But the fateful isolation, which one had already experienced during the war as an exposed 'top official', must have continued on into the camp — there can be no other explanation for the fact that these problems were never mentioned in our presence.

The thought often half crossed my mind that I ought to equip myself, for future arguments, with a clear idea of what it was I sought to defend as my National Socialist philosophy. But as soon as I began to consider this, everything I tried to catch hold of slipped through my fingers. Horror crept over me. Could it perhaps be that the imposing intellectual edifice of our philosophy had never really existed at all? I had never read Rosenberg's[14] books or any of the theoretical literature of the Party apart from *Mein Kampf.* I had left the philosophical and scientific basis of National Socialism to the 'intellectual leaders' of the movement. To occupy oneself deeply with such things during the war would have seemed to me a criminal waste of

---

[14] Alfred Rosenberg, author of *The Myth of the Twentieth Century,* which expounded the idea of the superiority of the nordic race. *Translator's note.*

time. Now it seemed as if I must make up for all this. But where were they, then, those great, deep ideas and certain truths which had been our foundations for the new world we had sought to build? A barely audible voice within me said: "Nowhere. They never existed." In this answer lay hidden the force of a deadly disillusionment. I had only one defence against it: to stop thinking. One could instead take heart from the old slogans, which did not force one to think. One was also afforded the pleasant illusion of facing up to our situation if one busily noted these slogans in one's diary.

Amongst my notes there is the following sentence: 'There is no doubt that National Socialism as the idea of racial renewal, the Greater German Reich and a united Europe, has foundered. Now all the envious and revengeful enemies of Germany have made it their whipping boy. But one day history will show that it was one of the greatest political conceptions of modern times...'

Even in the hour of its ruin, this 'great conception' still lent glory to those who had subscribed to it. We felt we were the only loyalists in the land, holding fast to our beliefs and redeeming the honour of our nation 'at a time when opportunists and informers ruled the day'. In this we were certainly not free from self pity, but our feeling was genuine.

After all this you will no longer be in any doubt about our attitude to 'denazification'. We denied our judges any kind of right to this office. What sort of Germans must they be, we asked ourselves, who were prepared to act as the stooges of the occupying powers and sit in judgement on fellow countrymen, whose only crime was that they had striven to realize a political ideal?

I so despised these courts that I should not have hesitated to use every kind of lie and deception against them if it had seemed necessary. But when I was called before one of them for the first time it just did not seem worth the trouble to consider whether it would be advisable to tell a lie about this point or that. It takes an effort to lie consistently, and I did not feel these judges were worth the effort.

I was prosecuted amongst the number of the 'principal accused', and my only concern was to avoid being written off as a 'fellow-traveller'.

The hearing lasted nine hours. Soon after the beginning of the battle of words an uncomfortable feeling crept over me, which it would be hard to define. I suddenly could not help sensing that the judges (none of whom was a trained lawyer) were taking their task very seriously.

Even the public prosecutor, who was said to be a joiner by trade, seemed to be genuinely convinced that he owed it to Germany and the world to have me imprisoned for several years to do penance for my political crimes.

In the instant I realized this, my arrogance melted away and I experienced a kind of community of feeling between my judges and myself. What bound us together was a sense of shame. In a frenzy of nationalistic passion, the nation to which they and I belonged had sought to appropriate the leadership of the continent. Whatever one thought about it, the fact could not be denied. It had unleashed a world war which had finally brought about its own downfall. It would be years before the millions who had died all over the world had all been accounted for. We, the survivors, bore the mark of hellish experience. And now this same nation, with the anxious, bureaucratic manner of a narrowminded village magistrate, was going about the business of solemnly and ingenuously sitting in judgement on the role each one of us had played in the terrible theatre of the world during the past ten years. Did this nation think it could write off the catastrophe in this way?

In the midst of the proceedings I wanted to leap up and say: "Don't trouble yourselves: you can condemn me as the chief culprit, as far as I'm concerned, but for heaven's sake realize that what we are engaged in here together is madness. We are responding to a volcanic eruption, which has set half the world on fire, by reciting moralistic verses for children."

After the hearing one of the jurors, an old man whose mental powers must have been on the wane, embraced me in tears. I took him for a Communist. He first asked me if my mother had never told me that Horst Wessel had been a pimp — to which I replied: "My mother never in her life knew what a pimp was."

After that his behaviour towards me became tinged with the accents of the class struggle, which were directed against my bourgeois origins. This man had risked his life to help his son to desert by keeping him hidden. On the day when the Americans marched in, joyfully welcomed by both father and son, the boy was killed by a stray bullet from the weapon of a negro soldier.

As I tried to comfort the old man with useless words, I was aware of the whole misery of the political indecision into which our nation had been plunged.

Although the judgement on me stated in black and white that through my press and propaganda work I had 'poisoned' the youth of Germany with National Socialism, I got off more lightly than my friend, who had only been director of music and had important points in her favour. Simply through lack of eloquence, she had failed to succeed, as I had done without intending to, in winning the judges' sympathy. These men and women, who lacked the professional judge's experience in looking at things objectively, found it impossible to disregard their personal feelings.

~ 17 ~

We found the world into which we were released a hostile one. To begin with, it obliged us to join in the struggle for existence, which we had so far been spared, though hardly under the most pleasant conditions. Apart from the old American soldier's uniform I was wearing I possessed nothing, and I was forced to spend months vainly battling to be accepted onto the roll of residents in my mother's home town, where the rest of my family had come to live after the war. As this acceptance was refused me, the authorities also gave me no ration cards. The then head of the housing office, to whom I had finally struggled after days of standing in queues, said to me, when he heard I had been a Labour Service leader near Lodz for a time: "Well, go to Russia then. If the Nazis had won you'd be a big *Gauführerin* there by now."

So I understood that I had to live off what my brothers and sisters could spare for me from their own meagre rations. All the unpleasantness of these circumstances was relatively easy to bear because my 'fight against democracy' maintained my inner tension. The fact that I had been released from the camp did not mean I had left the community of the internees. As far as I was able, I used my freedom of movement to help some of those who had had to stay in prison. I tried to help their political trials along, stole up to the camp fence for secret conversations until the sentries drove me away with stones, and found ways of smuggling news into the camp. I did all this with the feeling that democracy was something despicable and hateful, an opponent worthy of no honourable enmity.

As my efforts to gain admission to the town and to obtain ration cards remained fruitless, I finally went to a little farm in the Vogelborg, which belonged to the parents of a friend of mine. The food shortage was less of an insoluble problem in the country.

After my return to the town where I had spent the last part of my internment, I undertook to look after the most prominent of the political prisoners, who was still in the men's camp there. I had meanwhile obtained a job as a reporter on a daily paper, thanks to the help of the understanding juror at my second trial. At least for the time being my employers were not to be told about my political past.

The following story may give you some idea of the risks I was prepared to take at that time for the sake of my 'convictions'. One day I drove to see the chief of the Hessian Denazification Authorities and explained to him that I had been sent by my office to interview him. This official willingly answered my questions, and I managed to winkle out of him some important information about the forthcoming trial of the prominent prisoner I was looking after. Naturally he asked me to regard some of what he told me as 'off the record'.

Fortunately this man never subsequently bothered to find out why the interview had not appeared in the paper.

I should never have embarked upon an adventure of this kind if I had not felt utterly convinced that it was unjust for my friends and myself to be treated as an inferior breed.

Out of my revolt against this and my consciousness of belonging to a community which no enemy decree could destroy, I fashioned for myself the support I needed in order to keep going at that time. The community had become 'invisible' but its effects were felt in my daily existence for many years. For example, long years after I could have afforded to eat butter on my bread instead of margarine I continued to live very frugally. There were so many families of former comrades in which the children had to go hungry because the breadwinners were dead or in prisons. I should have forced myself to forget them and learned to indulge myself — by spending something, whether on clothes, food or other comforts. But former National Socialists were always turning up unexpectedly, people I had not known before, who asked me for money to provide for families who had to live in hiding, or who were in need for some other reason. I was happy to be able to help them and I sometimes gave away more than half my earnings, although my income was still small.

I am not telling you all this in order to boast of my generosity. My actions cost me no effort, thanks, no doubt, to the fact that I had completely lost all feeling for material possessions during the last year of the war. It took a long time to acquire it again. I merely want to explain how real my ties with the now invisible community of my old friends were to me — and certainly to many people in the same position.

Amongst the former Hitler Youth members I saw from time to time there was much whispering of illegal associations, but I never became involved in any of this. Indeed, I never made any attempt to be admitted to any group of former members. One reason may have been that I never came across anyone whose personality was such that they could win me over to these activities.

One day a woman comrade, whom I had known only slightly, called on me and subjected me to a surreptitious 'examination', which was, I now believe, designed to determine whether a particular group of former Party members would seek closer contact with me. From my visitor's veiled remarks I gathered that this group tried to help National Socialists in difficulties. I learned how tangible this help could be a few days later when I heard on the news that a certain leading National Socialist had escaped from prison. My visitor had told me, in passing, that this man expected to be transferred to Dachau in a few days' time, where he would have to undergo a very gruelling trial. "We shall have to make sure he disappears before then."

I did not do well in my 'examination', otherwise I should have heard more from these people at some time. There were no basic differences of opinion between us, and they were doing as a group what I was doing as an individual.

But although I yearned for the community I had lived in for so many years, I felt an inner resistance to joining any kind of group. The crucial point was that I did not wish to subordinate myself again. I must have been unconsciously afraid of submitting myself to authority for a second time. I approved of such groups in principle, but I did not want to be hindered in reaching my own solutions to the problems which faced me.

During the first two years after my internment I found my life physically hard but psychologically not too difficult. Germany, I thought, was under the sway of the victorious enemies and their stooges. I was in honour bound to despise these people. I must survive this wretched period and help my friends as best I could.

This attitude was still nourished by the pathetic selfrighteousness which we had acquired during our time in the camp. After my release, I had tried to express our feelings about life in a sonnet cycle. Today I can recognize in this the tense hostility with which I faced a changed world. But this inner tension had to give and the pathos gradually to peel away.

I was left with a crushing disillusionment.

The despair which had overtaken me on the first day of my solitary confinement in Heidelberg prison was now to become my dominant mood for years. I was no longer able to suppress the realization that all the sacrifices had been in vain. Millions of people had willingly given their lives for Germany, for which I too had been ready to die. Millions had thrown their loved ones, their health and their possessions into the scales but it had failed to tip them: they had been cynically and unjustly manipulated — or so it seemed to me. When had every class and age group of our nation ever overcome their native laziness and selfishness to such an extent as during the last war? And now what was their reward?

To keep thinking these thoughts over and over again began to endanger my life. In my sonnet sequence I had still been able to intoxicate myself with my own pathos. In it I had sworn to my friends that I would live each day in the sight of our dead. I meant it sincerely, but it was only one of those rhetorical attempts to escape the terrible truth which many poets — and people who think they are poets — make at such times.

Now the dead were forcing me to live with them. I struggled with the images of my memory in grim nightmares. But the things vomited up by my subconscious surpassed even my experience. A vast army of ghosts, cripples and monsters inhabited my dream landscapes, where cities burned and forests were mown down by a hail of bombs.

Sometimes the ghosts crossed the frontier of my waking consciousness and met me in the street or came through the walls of my room to my table.

I had refused to make room inside me for fear until almost the last days of the war. Now it filled me constantly. Even in broad daylight I could not venture a hundred yards out of a village into the open country without feeling afraid. Evening walks when one was overtaken by nightfall became torture to me, even in company. I remember suddenly breaking into a run in the well lit corridor of the Law Courts, which I used to visit every day, because I felt there was something uncanny and menacing behind me.

It could happen to me in a street that I did not dare to go any farther because I was convinced that at the next step I took the houses to left and right of me would plunge backwards into space. Such situations, in which I was afraid of something specific, were admittedly only rare, but for years I experienced an unspecific, aimless fear, which only gradually lost intensity.

My fear was bound up with despair at the apparent pointlessness of all our experience. During the period of the Third Reich we were spoilt by a sense of the significance of our existence which affected almost every activity. If we ate a piece of bread we could believe we were strengthening ourselves for the fight for a German victory. If we decided not to eat the bread we could believe that it would fortify for the struggle someone else whose need was greater than ours. Now both things seemed equally pointless — to eat the bread or not to eat it.

But there must be someone to blame for all this. I was looking for him. The idea that the mass murders of the war could be blamed onto men seemed to me absurd. The power for such monstrous madness could only lie in God's hand. In my naivety it was He I named as the secret patron of the Third Reich, though without ever putting it in quite those terms. Now I believed I could recognize His true face — that of an evil, bloodthirsty God, who rewarded love and sacrifice with annihilation — and I hated Him passionately.

At this point in my report you may object: "But what if Hitler's Germany had won the war? Would the mass murders still have caused you to lose faith in the patron God?"

One cannot answer such questions directly. I could say that if Germany had won, the sacrifice of German blood would not have caused me to lose faith in the justice of the historical process, because it would no longer have seemed pointless. But how I should have reacted if I had known of the monstrous sufferings of the Jews and of their extent from personal experience and not merely in theory, I would not dare to judge.

The feeling that we were the victims of a final piece of cynical cruelty called one's own existence into question. Only a titan or a wholly irreligious person, faced with such a God and with this knowledge, could have affirmed that the course of history had no purpose without wishing for his own death at the same time.

I was far removed from such titanic defiance. I reacted to my new knowledge of the world by repeatedly falling into a state of mental and physical paralysis for days on end, during which I was unable to move hand or foot and in which my one thought was: If only you could die!

I never tried to put this wish into effect. This may have been because for as long as I was in a state of the deepest depression, I was also physically as if bound. But apart from this, I felt certain that death was not the end, but only a gate. Escape into Nirvana was barred to me. The first time I realized this, I regarded it as the most merciless truth I could have been forced to accept. About a year after my release from camp I began to be interested in contemporary philosophy. Sartre fascinated me (I felt I was well and truly 'condemned to freedom'). Later Heidegger meant more to me. I experienced 'alienation' as my own situation.

After all my experiences complete freedom from ties of any kind seemed the only proper attitude, and I found it was a test of a person's stature to see who would succeed in remaining steadfastly independent. The only fixed point amid this 'nihilism' was my firm hatred of the supreme being.

Metaphysically I had by then reached absolute zero. This situation fully corresponded with the nadir of my material fortunes. When I look back on it now, I must say that the fact of being plunged into utter poverty, when I was young enough to venture on a new start in life, is one of the providential turns of fate for which I should be very grateful.

I seldom meet former National Socialists of whom I should say that they have lived solely in the past since 1945. They will say, for example: "Yes, the economic growth of West Germany is a great achievement; it would not be possible without America's help." Then come the 'buts'. "But what a disintegration of our cultural life! What a lack of national consciousness! What a racial decline!" and so on. The next sentence always runs: "How much better it all was in Hitler's day!"

These people I am talking about had the greatest time of their lives during the Third Reich. By this I do not mean because they may have held an office which flattered them or because they had power, but because in those days they 'believed in something', that roused them out of the narrowness of their humble existence and gave them a service to perform which extended them.

After 1945 these people's misfortune was their fear of poverty, and nothing since then has altered in this: it is hard to have to give up the fragment of a 'great age' one has experienced oneself. Perhaps one can only do it if one is subconsciously aware that one's spiritual powers are still sufficient to seek out a new meaning for one's emptied existence. But that, in my experience, is largely a question of age. Those of my earlier companions who had passed their mid twenties by the end of the war generally, it seems to me, no longer felt strong enough to give way to healing despair. Even today they still cling to the past and live the joyless lives of the 'bereaved'.

I hope you do not expect me to describe the stages of my inner journey, up to the point where I stand today, in so much detail that you can see which one led to the next and so on. All this is still too near to me, and such inner processes take place on many levels in a manner which it is hard to be aware of. But I will tell you as best I can. It may surprise or horrify you that it took me a good dozen years to complete my inner break with National Socialism. Other people from my former circle of friends are still in the middle of the process today. An Austrian friend of mine, who played a leading role in the Hitler Youth both before and after her country was annexed to the Reich, got through the process in half a year, and I have had the opportunity to verify that her change of heart has been radical. During the summer of 1945 she spent every spare moment reading Goethe and Shakespeare, and when she had put this intellectual and spiritual cleansing cure behind her she was 'healed'.

In saying that I lived for a time at an absolute nadir, I have simplified more than I should have done. Already during my internment there were points of contact with my future which already put me beyond zero.

Amongst the representatives of democracy with whom I came into close contact there were two people with great powers of persuasion, both personal and practical. Both of them later became close friends of mine, and I owe it to the two of them that I did not stay stuck fast in the intellectual confusion and immature defiance of nihilism. The first thing that impressed me about these people was the breadth of their mental horizon, the clarity of their thought and their basic culture. Both had been resolute opponents of National Socialism, but this had not prevented them approaching us with an openness and a lack of personal prejudice which cleared the way for objective and enlightening discussions.

I am referring here to Hermann Schafft, a well known Evangelical theologian who was a Christian Socialist before 1933 and had been an intellectual leader in the movement for youth and now held an important post in the educational field. He died in 1959, at the age of fifty-seven.

The second 'democrat' who became my mentor was a woman who had arrived at an intensive interest in the philosophy of Martin Heidegger, via the study of mathematics, physics and, later, ethnology, and had found in it her intellectual centre.

When I got to know both of them better I asked myself: "How is it possible for such outstanding people to have been opponents of National Socialism? Evidently even people of this intellectual calibre could be mistaken in their political judgements."

The National Socialist principle, 'Youth must be led by youth', which was applied in the Hitler Youth, meant that the rising generation was fatally lacking in contacts with more mature people.

I was always vaguely aware of this lack. It gives me food for thought now, when I realize that all the older men and women who had a certain fascination for me also disappointed me. They were not 'real National Socialists'. It proved impossible to become friends with them, although I felt a desperate need for a mentor of this kind.

The reason for it is illuminating: my choice fell instinctively on people who, thanks to their quality of character and intellectual eminence, were too perceptive to identify themselves with National Socialism. The other adults, who were as much under the spell of Nazism as we were, had not the stature of true teachers. Although I naturally did not recognize it at the time, the very fact that they were in thrall to National Socialism proved that though they might be older than me, they had not the personal and intellectual maturity that I sought. Nothing about them made me want them for my friends. Over the years one built up a feeling of resentment, nourished by chagrin and defiance — 'the older generation [that is, the ones I cared about] leave us alone!'

I am not ashamed to admit that I did not again experience a friendship which one might call really fruitful in the broadest sense until after I was thirty. And then I was happy to enjoy rewarding friendships as a comforting complement to a tough process of re-education.

There are quite a number of friends from that time whom I remember with gratitude. I named Hermann Schafft because he is now dead. The others, fortunately, are still alive. There was the abbess of an Evangelical convent on Lüneburg Heath, where I took part in a (secular) choral week with some Hitler Youth friends shortly after my release. I was then a real 'outsider'. I avoided people if I did not know them to have been National Socialists. I expected them to despise and hate me.

On the evening of the second day of Whitsuntide I met the abbess in her garden, a paradise of flowers filled with the glory of tumbling blossom. I surprised myself by asking her if she had the time and the inclination for a walk. She was watering the flowers. She took off her gardening apron without a word and held the little gate open for me. We ranged through the woods until long after midnight, and when we got back home she fetched a bottle of wine from the cellar — in those days it was a rarity — and later brewed up some coffee.

That night I probably talked nonstop. When I walked through the long, dim corridors next day I was surprised to feel that something important had changed. Was it something in the world around me or something in me?

Amidst the fine antique furniture, beneath the centuries-old portraits of the abbesses, or in front of their memorials at the entrance to the little church, I had felt as if I were on a Utopian island. This peace, this timelessness and feeling of being unhurt could not be a part of my own reality. It was impossible that the inhabitants of this house should have taken part in the horror, the destruction, the hate and the despair of the war.

Their 'dream world' had been incorporated into my real world overnight, and nowhere had it been necessary to cross even the shallowest of ditches. Had I not feared an abyss of estrangement — indeed, of hostility?

At that time I still did not myself feel any guilt with regard to my political past. But I was aware of the compulsion that the 'others' had to regard me as a kind of criminal, as an unalterable fact. Now one of these 'others' had accepted me, though I must be absolutely unacceptable to her.

Because this woman was a Christian (in my eyes, at that time, a rather dubious category of people, who were the victims of religious autosuggestion), she had offered me friendship, and I felt that this had made me 'good' in her eyes. The guilt which I (in their view) had objectively taken on myself was wiped out, and it was as if it had never been.

The experience made me feel both more and less certain of myself. More certain, because it had been proved that the 'others' were not *a priori* my enemies, but less certain because I must gradually learn to distinguish amongst the 'others' between potential friends and potential enemies.

Hermann Schafft was asked by one of the internees to visit us at the Darmstadt women's camp. He gave a talk to those who wanted to hear him: I no longer remember the subject. But two things stuck in my memory. The man who sat before us in the small camp office, and who was said to be an important official of the Hessian Education Authority, wore an almost shabby black suit with a big patch on the right knee which did not quite match the trousers — and he had the face to declare that the Jews and the Germans had more in common than any other two peoples.

The shabby suit must have impressed me, because I was annoyed that one of the 'bigwigs of the new régime' should have such an unassuming appearance. During the war the ostentation of some of the leading men in the Party had embittered me. Now I was meeting one of the new men and he — to my exasperation — looked just as I would have wished my former Party comrades in top posts to have looked. The thesis that Jews and Germans had a fundamental kinship shocked me so violently that I wrestled with it for years. I can only summarize his arguments in favour of it. Hermann Schafft mentioned both peoples' restless search for God, their unpopularity with other nations, generally on account of their particular achievements or their ambition, and finally their notions of being a chosen race.

I got into conversation with him while I was still at the camp. What won me over to him was that he neither treated us as an inferior kind of person, nor strove to win our sympathy, although he pitied us and was indulgent about our views.

He wanted to give us practical help, and in this he displayed a sixth sense for the particular needs of every individual — and not just their intellectual and spiritual needs.

I do not know what may have induced him to intervene in one case or another on behalf of the followers of the régime of violence he had so hated. He was certainly not one of those who went round indiscriminately at that time declaring everyone to be washed whiter than white.

I was always meeting people later on who owed to him the fact that they were able to start a new life after 1945. He cut down the period of starvation for many families by helping politically suspect fathers or mothers to get jobs. Where he smoothed someone's path towards starting a new life, he intended — but without saying so explicitly — that it should be a totally new existence. He trusted people to recognize and accept practical assistance as a long term capital investment for the provision of moral assistance. A former Hitler Youth leader whom Hermann Schafft had helped back into his profession told me (I think in 1951): "This man stopped me going back into the Church. Despite my beliefs, I had made up my mind to do it for career reasons, because I could not bear to stand by and see the plight of my family any longer." Our new friend had warned him against this dishonourable step.

My memories of the first months after my internment are focused, so far as encounters with Hermann Schafft are concerned, on liver sausage and cakes. He sometimes appeared suddenly in my room and put some such treasure on my desk with a laugh. One of the farmers in the village where he was the local pastor had killed a pig, and he was glad to be able to pass on his share. His sausage was not 'a sprat to catch a mackerel'. He did not bring it because hungry people are less receptive to lessons in democracy and Christianity. Indeed, there was very rarely time for long conversations. But the feeling of encouragement he left behind him after a fifteen minute visit lasted a long time.

We faced one another as if on opposite sides of a frontier. Although he was so much older, he stood in the country of the future, while I stood in the country of the past. His elements were hope, the will to build, renewal. Mine were disillusionment, grief, stubbornness. Each time he came, he drew me a little further towards his side — even if this step by step tug of war was left unspoken.

At my second hearing in the court of appeal, where I was again prosecuted as one of the 'chief criminals', he came forward as a witness for the defence.

He had only known me for a few months. I remember clearly how very embarrassed I was when the president of the court of appeal asked him what he had to say. In point of fact there were no facts he could advance in my defence. He said roughly the following: "I am convinced that the accused, if she can only be given time to come to grips with the past, will become a reliable citizen of a democratic state. To send her now to a labour camp would achieve nothing. She would then only shut herself off completely from everything new."

To some extent, therefore, he stood surety for me — and in good faith. I found the obligation that this implied to be a disturbing problem, for I was by no means certain that I should become a good democrat. For the moment I despised democracy. When I voiced my doubts Hermann Schafft nodded with a smile. "What I have said I must answer for, not you. And I think I can."

It was only later that I gained the impression that he had considered the appeal boards to be an extremely abortive proceeding from the first, but he had tried not to let me notice this attitude. He probably knew cases where such proceedings — despite their inadequacy — had given people the stimulus to reflection and a change of heart. He did not wish to reduce the chance of this through his criticisms. When he saw that I only regarded the court with a mixture of contempt and pity, he tried to save the day for me, and to some extent he succeeded. He said: "Look at this independently of the institution and the verdict. It is only important for you to recognize the fact: 'I have been judged; that is to say, I have been give a new direction.'"

What he meant by this new direction only became clear to me by degrees. For the moment he left me wondering what he meant. This was part of his 'method'. Readymade answers would probably have gone in one ear and out the other. But such questions lodged in us with barbed hooks.

After the hearing Hermann Schafft took two of my comrades from the camp and myself by car to the village in Upper Hesse where he was the pastor (in addition to his work as director of the education authority). There we experienced what we later jokingly referred to as our 'confirmation classes'. We were allowed to stay for a few days, and we were blissfully happy. The garden, the comfortable and roomy rectory, the satisfying meals, the record library (which ranged from the Gregorian Chant to the *Threepenny Opera)* and finally the nightly conversations with our host — all these were almost fabulous delights, the first pleasant experiences of peacetime.

Those evening conversations! The notes I made at the time remind me that Hermann Schafft described our complete secession from the Church years before as 'cheap'. No other word of criticism could have had such a shock effect on us. We should have taken it in our stride if he had scolded us either superficially or solemnly, but this crushing verdict on our intellectual and spiritual sense of style hit us hard. No doubt it was intended to. He thought it 'cheap', if I interpret him correctly in retrospect, for us to believe we could opt out, by means of a signature, of the 2,000-year-old tradition of western Christian thought. In his explanation he used a mocking phrase, something like: 'To every ant its own Renaissance!'

I will not go into more detail here about what he tried to bring nearer to us as the essence of his own Christian faith, but I must say that now, for the first time, I encountered the Christian teaching in a form which made it seem to me a desirable prize. I felt clearly that it would satisfy me if I could believe.

The fact that I nevertheless could not re-enter the Church (although I went to his services often, and not without feeling moved) never caused him to complain or reproach me. He knew that we had dedicated ourselves to National Socialism with religious fervour and were now on the threshold of a dangerous crisis, in which at first only release from bondage could be found. Nevertheless, the fact that so resolute a witness of the Christian teaching commanded my affection and respect tore a great breach in the wall of my prejudice. Perhaps, I said to myself, it was not just a political error that made a man like this hostile to National Socialism.

One of the phrases Hermann Schafft often used at that time was 'confident despair'. I hated it and made no bones about it. It betrayed a lack of intellectual honesty, I declared. Despair was very modern and I could understand why Christians who wanted to be up to date should inscribe it on their banners, but anyone who had really known despair could not speak of 'confident' despair. (I probably believed that despair had been the monopoly of people like myself at that time.) In any case I quoted a counter slogan, which I had found in one of Rilke's letters. There he spoke of an attitude of 'honestly being able to forgo all comfort'.

"Try to live according to your counter slogan," replied Hermann Schafft. "But don't be afraid to seek comfort when one day you understand that it is beyond our strength. Such an attitude always contains the risk of bad faith and personal hubris."

Later he would listen to my enthusiastic tirades about Sartre or Gottfried Benn's obscure nihilistic-aesthetic 'metaphysics', and argued amiably with me about Heidegger. He had striven to ensure that we did not miss the 'grace of the point of zero'. Now that he knew our minds were in motion, he watched our excursions into the intellectual world unperturbed.

At that time I was devouring from choice the literature which had been banned from the Third Reich. I read American and French authors, but also Benn, Kafka and Thomas Mann. Meanwhile I was also encountering 'degenerate art' for the first time (with the exception of the Barlach exhibition previously mentioned) outside the context of a presentation which sought to revile it.

I went to every available exhibition, and often listened to modern music. At first I did it in order to examine the trash that was pouring into our cultural life again, so that I could quote specific examples to defend my point of view in argument. But what I found there — in literature, the plastic arts and music — only baffled me for a short time. Soon it fascinated me; at any rate individual works in all the media did so. The fact that it moved me so directly is probably due to the nihilistic element, the discords, the expression of a disturbed continuum in modern art. Here I believed I was encountering the expression of my own experiences.

I accepted everything greedily, though critically. Nor was I irritated at having to give my approval to the new art quite against my will. At that time I found myself in the midst of a turbulence in which there were many contradictory tendencies. It was not possible to think or react logically the whole time.

Many things were opposed to the process of inner release from National Socialism. The fear of not being true to the ideals of one's youth, for example. I kept asking myself: 'Are you not just swimming with the tide?' The problem of loyalty, as far as I can see, still plays a decisive role for many of my old friends today. It is always a difficult matter to break a pledge of loyalty only when this breach is demanded or even honoured by the 'new masters'. One suspects oneself of having been influenced by the new régime as soon as one notices that one is moving away from the old ties. But should one be hindered from taking wholly seriously the altered views one arrives at by the uncomfortable feeling that they are moving in the direction dictated by expediency?

Apart from fear of my own 'disloyalty', it was above all the many obvious shortcomings of democracy that made it difficult for me to advance 'backwards'. How many young people were up to their ears in the black market? How many became criminals? How often I had to report for my newspaper on the trials of former members of the denazification authorities, who had turned out to be bogus lawyers or had committed some other crime! What lamentable abuses were brought on by party politics! How uncontrollably materialism was getting the upper hand!

With great patience my new friends taught me to see questions where previously I had seen nothing to question. Despite this I thrust aside the most pressing question of what National Socialism had in fact been for as long as I could. I had good reason to do so. Already during my internment it had sometimes begun to dawn on me that I might be left only with something frighteningly wretched, if I tried to grasp the substance of this thing in my hand. I was afraid of the bitter shame this discovery would cause.

One day I heard a conversation in which a former Party official was trying to incite his son against democracy. I saw the boy's confusion and I suddenly sided with his democratic history teacher, who had obviously been deriding the National Socialist glorification of the peasantry. Had I not myself discovered a great measure of egoism, envy and narrowmindedness amongst the peasants in East Prussia, the Wartheland, Austria and, most recently, the Vogelsburg? Why should they be of more value in the composition of a whole nation than the tradespeople, the urban working class or the so called intelligentsia? Because they are biologically healthier than the other classes, came my own reply. They produce more children. They offer the means for the racial renewal of our nation. But what does that signify? It is remarkable how difficult I found it to give the boy an answer to such questions. I had the clear feeling that the old theories of the nordic race had now become so laughable that I scarcely dared to utter them.

After this conversation I plunged myself into some of the basic texts of National Socialism. I still would not admit that its 'idea' had hardly been more than a dilettante biological materialism, combined with nationalist megalomania, in which the old religious idea of the Reich was replaced by an artificially cooked up Germanic myth.

Since the time when you and I had enthused over Plato at the age of sixteen the mere concept of 'the Idea' had had something numinous and venerable about it for me. This may sound grotesque, but it is true. Up till the end of the war and beyond I lived under the half conscious impression that the 'Idea' of National Socialism which was so often glorified must also possess an intellectual, numinous and venerable quality. After the war, I said to myself, when action no longer takes up my whole energy, I will go into this question thoroughly. Until then I will leave it to the Party theorists to work on the construction of a philosophical system.

I remember how jealous I felt of my mentor, when I later heard her describing her own breach with scientific Marxism. In her youth she had been a convinced and active Communist, and it had cost her profound argument to recognize the weaknesses of this impressive closed system of thought.

By comparison with this, I could only feel ashamed that I had considered something as primitive and woolly as National Socialism to be an 'Idea' to which it seemed worth devoting my whole existence. And how many there had been who fell victims, like myself, to this terrible delusion!

It is noteworthy that all the people whom I asked at that time, what had National Socialism meant to them, gave me different answers. "The defeat of parliamentarianism by the Führer State," said one. "The overcoming of urban influences by means of a healthy peasantry," said another. A third had been a National Socialist because the 'revival of the military spirit' had fascinated him. A fourth had been convinced by 'the sensible policies for the family'; a fifth by the slogan that 'Germany's future lay in the east'. The sixth had been won over to Hitler by his financial measures, and so on.

One day I began to understand that almost every concept and most of the obsessions of my parents' generation, who had dreamed since 1918 of the salvation of Germany, had somewhere been fitted into the confused mosaic of this ideology. How many people had only kept their eyes obsessively fixed on the realization of their own special panacea, whether with satisfaction or with growing disillusionment, and never looked at the whole process at all?

The catastrophic role played by half-education in just this connection one day became clear to me. In the upper school I had enjoyed extremely stimulating lessons in natural science. What we were taught in biology seemed so satisfying because it was based on proven scientific fact and not on opinions. Here, I believed, everything was observable and nothing was ambiguous. I was sure that a progressive, realistic, healthy policy would emerge from a world view that was based on natural laws and scientific facts.

Equipped with the blinkers of this credulous, optimistic attitude, I then also promptly swallowed the most fantastic nonsense. I swallowed it, although at times I laughed at it — for example, the glorification of a type of man who had certain distinctive physical characteristics and who was credited with the particular virtues of the hero. This was the 'Master Race'. But for this racial mystique, the scientific orientation of National Socialism would certainly not have impressed me. For how else, ultimately, could the 'inwardness' of the Germans have created its essential dose of intoxicating poison?

Bound up with the idea of the master race was, for me, the dream of a vocation of leadership which had almost messianic features. The Germans were to bring new wealth to the world. All I knew about the history of the West was what I had picked up at school and, thanks to my idleness, that was not much. The vagueness of my knowledge permitted me, for example, to make Frederick II of Hohenstauffen (he had already fascinated me in my childhood) into the direct ancestor and inspiration of our own epoch.

Or Hölderlin! Before I began to understand a single one of his poems, I was already drunk with the glory of his language. Now I saw him as a prophet of the Reich whose birth I had witnessed. In the ceremonies I conducted as a Labour Service leader no poet was so often quoted as he. Whenever I presented a team of 'work maidens' before the flag for the first time, I quoted the same words from Hölderlin: "No one must judge our future nation by the flag alone: everything must be regenerated; it must be utterly renewed; our joy must be filled with seriousness and our work with gaiety. Nothing, not the smallest or most everyday thing, must be devoid of spirit and the gods."

I was not alone in my veneration of Hölderlin. It was quite typical. In the book from which I took almost all the material for the ceremonies and countless readings by the flag, Hölderlin was quoted just as often as Hitler. This was *Witnesses of the Germans,* published by the Reich Women's Leadership in 1939. The collection ends with an ode by Ludwig Friedrich Barthel, 'On the coming and everlasting Reich'. I often read it aloud, because I was very fond of it. It ends with the line: 'The new Reich must be near to God's garden'.

I believe it was in 1950 that this book came into my hands again, about the same time as I bought a new edition of Hölderlin.

Now when I read the loved and often quoted verses again I can only say that I was overcome with horror. With what invocations had Hölderlin celebrated Germany! 'Holy heart of the nations', or 'Thou land of love'. He had called it 'all-tolerating' and he had praised the work of the German nation as 'a new creation born of love and as good as thou'.

Was it possible that I had read out these verses to my comrades in the morning at the flag ceremony and that an hour later we had been helping to drive the Polish peasants out of their farms?

Yes, and without for a moment being aware of a contradiction.

Something uncanny must have happened there. Not only to us but to countless of our compatriots. We had allowed ourselves to be fascinated by a 'dream of the Germans', without ever having any precise idea of its significance or content. It concealed something mysterious, precious and numinous, which one could only approach with reverence. Was there a greater happiness or a nobler mission than to serve the fulfilment of this dream? Hölderlin had foretold it. We made him our prophet, but we were satisfied to cloak our resentful and ambitious nationalism in his high rhetoric, although the former was only a pitiful caricature of the latter.

None of us had really read Hölderlin. Without lamenting the fact, he had called the Germans 'poor in deeds and full of thoughts'. Now we bore the visions of his superb history aloft before us, proudly — as if their beauty was to our own credit, without noticing that we had become infinitely poor in thoughts, and, in a terrible sense, full of deeds.

'The new Reich must be near to God's garden' — we had dreamed of this and at the same time we had served a reality which, if mainly only in a veiled form, was inspired by satanic impulses.

Old friends of mine often point out to me that Hitler should have aimed to create not merely a Greater German Reich but a united Europe. It is idle to speculate about how this Europe would have looked. At the end of the war, which Hitler clearly regarded as an appropriate means of the realization of his plans, Europe was strewn with corpses and in ruins.

The idea of the leadership vocation of the Race of Heroes had indeed not been intended to find fulfilment in a bloodbath without precedent in history, but that is what it produced.

The individual German who, whether voluntarily or under orders, was the bearer of this idea, was certainly expected to live a life of renunciation and hardship (and ultimately to sacrifice his life), but he was excused having to think for himself and having to develop his own sense of responsibility. The so called 'leadership principle' *(Führerprinzip)* appealed to that spirit of servility which the shortlived Weimar Republic had not been able to replace with a citizen's sense of responsibility.

The people who wanted to lead Europe themselves rushed, with passionate abandon, to assume the role of followers and voluntarily to surrender their rights in a manner which demonstrated their catastrophic political immaturity.

One of my new friends occasionally showed me an album containing reproductions of portraits, statues and photographs of the intellectual leaders of Europe since the Renaissance. We looked at it together. Then it was pressed into my hand with the challenge: "Now, pick out the nordic Master Men."

The fruits of my effort to do so would hardly have lent convincing support to a racial theorist of the old style.

From now on I sought contacts with foreigners, above all those of 'different races'. From now on I wanted to rely only on my own accumulated experience. There was no lack of opportunities. At the house of some of my friends' friends I sometimes met negro students, and I was moved by the detached intensity with which they discussed philosophical questions and the seriousness with which they strove not to debase the Christian commandment of tolerance to the level of a mere chauvinistic slogan in their struggle for the rights of their own race.

When I enrolled as a student at Frankfurt University I belonged to a group in which Americans, French (both white and coloured) and Germans met Asians of very varied nationalities.

The conclusion to which my observations compelled me (I later spent almost a year in France and had a chance to look about amongst this 'racially tainted and degenerate nation') was as follows. The National Socialist racial theory was erroneous, based on fiction and not on fact. For reasons which cannot be gone into here, we as a nation worked ourselves up to a state of self deification, the obverse of which could only be contempt and hatred for the other 'inferior' nations. In so doing we sank into the narrowmindedness of a primitive tribe that believes its own tribal gods to be the most powerful in the world.

How painful for us to have to realize after the event that the great outpouring of positive human qualities we had voluntarily put at the service of our 'idea' had finally been canalized into a mean ditch which devalued them. When we strove to be unselfish, humble, industrious, friendly and ready to help others, all this was only with regard to our own people. We only wanted to behave in a brotherly fashion towards our own compatriots.

You know that I became a National Socialist because the idea of the National Community inspired me. What I had never realized was the number of Germans who were not considered worthy to belong to this community. I will speak of the German Jews in another context, but there were also those pious people who wished to obey God rather than men, all our fellow citizens who suffered from hereditary diseases, the mentally sick, the Marxists, the pacifists, the artists whose consciences forbade them to create 'healthy art'...

For years after the end of the war I derived a feeling of self righteousness from the knowledge that I had become a National Socialist because I wanted to help the socially underprivileged members of our nation — that is, from an impulse of love. The fact that you, for example, were not allowed to belong to the National Community I overlooked for as long as I could.

Only in 1950 or 1951, in the course of conversation with a Japanese Christian, did I suddenly grasp how narrow this love had been — a kind of primitive family selfishness. What good are kindness, self sacrifice, energy and a sense of responsibility, if they are so jealously guarded that only one's brothers and sisters may benefit from them? Not much more than the instinctive reactions which keep a herd of wild animals together.

~ 18 ~

You will no doubt be waiting to hear how I came to grips with my former anti-semitism. I avoided tackling the question for as long as possible. I could well foresee that it would be the hardest one of all.

In 1952 Hermann Schafft took me to Stuttgart. He was going to meet a friend who had gone to the U.S.A. in 1933, and who was now staying in Germany again for the first time.

Looking back, I believe he took me along expressly to be present at this reunion. The American was a lively old man who did not look particularly Jewish. Their conversation contained a great many unfinished sentences. "And what became of XY and his family?"

"His youngest daughter escaped to Palestine via France. All the others — Auschwitz..."

For the first time I was in the presence of someone who bore witness to the violent deaths of Jewish men and women and children. Out of the circle of his relatives and close friends thirty-two people had been murdered, including four children of less than school age.

On the homeward journey my friend spoke of other Jews who had been close friends of his, and I began to believe things coming from him which I had never been willing to believe when either the Americans or the German newspapers said them.

The total of six or seven millions had left me cold. Such an astronomic figure does not come to life on its own. When people spoke of the Germans who were killed in the war or died as refugees the totals of the horror meant something to me.

Amongst these dead there were people one had loved oneself. But what did 6,000,000 dead Jews mean?

Since that journey to Stuttgart their fate has left me no peace. Since that day I have no longer been able to comfort myself with the thought that I myself 'did not hurt the hair of a single Jew's head' for since then I have become better at remembering things which were connected with my own guilt.

This process itself again took years. Anti-semitism had been second nature to me since childhood, as you know. Now I began to believe that it was wrong, but my bad conscience made me avoid Jews more than ever. When I think back again to how I felt at that time, I realize that I was in danger of building up a fresh hatred of the people we had wronged, just because of my growing feelings of guilt. From this experience I can understand the wretched entanglement of those who lack the strength to 'bail out' when their feelings of guilt arouse fresh hatred and the hatred provokes the feelings of guilt which goad them on into an even more tortured state.

Two things helped me. In the first place I had begun really to understand that love (and not the jealous love of the 'National Community' but a broad love embracing all mankind) is greater than hate. Secondly, although I avoided Jews so carefully, there was one I could not help meeting (not before 1955, I believe). She was the wife of a secondary school teacher, and both her parents had died in a concentration camp. She returned from exile with her husband as soon as possible, and they had adopted two war orphans in their teens. The girl had had a junior rank as a Labour Service leader and the boy had been a Luftwaffe auxiliary. When I met the woman she knew about my political past, which made me all the more uneasy. I will never forget the glow of spontaneous kindness in this person's eyes when she first held out her hand to me. It bridged all the gulfs, without denying them.

At that moment I jumped free from the devil's wheel. I was no longer in danger of converting feelings of guilt into fresh hatred. The forgiving love which I had encountered gave me the strength to accept our guilt and my own. Only now did I cease to be a National Socialist.

Up till that day, in all the confusion of my psychological state, I had still been ruled by the feeling that my former companions and I had been wronged. To begin with I sheltered behind the notion that it was democracy, which had locked us up like criminals and tried us, that had wronged us — we who had been willing to make every sacrifice. Later the idea gradually permeated me that it was really Hitler who had wronged us. He had misused our youthful self sacrifice to satisfy his own diseased lust for power. The same thing had befallen most of the immature idealists of those years, whether they were still half children or foolish adults. They had wanted to love and, before they had time to notice, they were involved in a campaign of hate.

These successive insights were steps which I could not miss, but there was still an error in them — one which amounted to a justification of myself. 'It is the fault of the others. You are unstained by guilt.' And not merely unstained, but with an aura of innocent suffering.

I am tempted to invoke the Christian concept of Grace when I think of what happened to me then. A stranger offered me her hand with a smile and in that instant I knew that I shared the guilt for her parents' death.

And not only for that.

In the year of the 'Night of the Broken Glass' I was twenty. You know that long before that I had claimed the independence of an adult in all matters. When I stood before the ghettoes in Lodz and Kutno I was three or four years older and I was in fact used to an extremely independent existence. What right have I, I asked myself now, to claim that I was still too young to perceive what was going on? Only the sham right of a bad conscience afraid of the truth.

I was not too young but too hard hearted, too cowardly and too flattered by the role of leader which I played in the Third Reich to admit that with my whole being I was helping to commit a crime unworthy of mankind.

All the 'honourable idealists', as well as the apathetic people of those years, scorned to be alarmed or to take heed of such warnings as the Nuremberg Laws, the Night of the Broken Glass, or the sudden disappearance without trace of neighbours who were Jews, Marxists or people regarded as enemies of the state for their religious views. Let each one of them ask himself of what he is guilty through his own faint heartedness, and whether he can truthfully claim that he did not himself 'hurt the hair of a single Jew's head'.

After this encounter, which was so shaking for me, I read at length the documentation on the fate of the European Jews during the Third Reich and on the campaign against the other 'elements hostile to the state' under Hitler. I was not free of mistrust as I did this. Paper is long suffering, I told myself. But at the same time I was horrified by the grim statistics of the annihilation machines.

I still sometimes meet Germans today who try to salve their consciences by saying: "All these statements are untrue, or at least they are shamelessly exaggerated."

For a long time there was something of this attitude in me. I privately tried to quibble over the total of five, six or seven million. After all it might have been 'only' two or three million. A murderer's position before the court is very different according to whether he has killed two people or seven... But I had no means of checking the totals given in the statistics. What shattered me was the evidence of the fate of individual people, families or groups. I am thinking here, for example, of the Warsaw ghetto, where 440,000 Jews were starved or burned to death. What I read in a documentary diary report about the death of these men, women and children so overwhelmed me that I lay weeping on the floor of my room for half the night. During the battle of the ghetto I was nearer Warsaw than Berlin. I had been fighting, as if for my own salvation, to get the children of the *Volksdeutsch* settlers into the habit of cleaning their teeth every day. A mere ninety miles away thousands of children were burning and starving — with my consent.

When I read in the newspapers at the time with what stubbornness and 'cheek' the Jews had dared to sell their skins as dearly as possible, I shared the indignation of the author of the article with full conviction. As if our soldiers were not much more urgently needed at the front than for the 'smoking out of this nest of resistance'. Not for one second did my imagination make the effort to conjure up what these words 'smoking out this nest of resistance' really meant: the murder of half starved children, old people and adults. Only now, twelve years later, did I cease warding off the images of horror. After that night numbers became unimportant to me. I have subsequently met many people, Jews, socialists and Christians of the most varied denominations, who have given me evidence — often only in passing — of the violent deaths of their relations and friends.

Again and again I am moved not merely to sorrow and shame but to horror at something uncanny when I think how close behind the façade of the apparently positive, constructive and even humane idea to which I had given all my attention, the cynicism and the murder began. One was only the obverse of the other.

Perhaps you expect me to explain how my 'metaphysical orientation' has taken account of this inner development. I have told you of the hatred of the Supreme Being with which I reacted to the realization that all the sacrifices made for 'Greater Germany' had been in vain. As I came to understand with what insane hubris I had allowed myself to be misused as a tool, so my hate died down. It would have been wrong for this hubris to triumph. Of course the fact that in my changed view the defeat of Germany no longer seemed to me to be the most senseless of all historical stupidities did not bring to life a single one of the dead people who had been sacrificed to an extravagant national dream.

But if I am ready to admit that our hubris carried with it its own terrible punishment, what can assuage my desire for cosmic justice with regard to the fate of the Jews? Must I not hate God once again, for what happened to them?

It says in the Old Testament: 'My thoughts are not your thoughts and my ways are not your ways.'

One must learn to live with questions to which there is no answer, even when this lack leaves the horizon eternally dark.

I have almost reached the end of what I wanted to write to you. Looking back, I ask myself once more the question I have asked repeatedly: How will you take it?

The answer may depend on the amount of suffering which you, your family and all your friends had to endure up to the end of the war. In trying to guess at your reactions I think of some Jewish friends who come from Germany like you and with whom I stayed recently in London.

During the days we spent together we were often gay, but even when we were laughing at my host's stories of Upper Silesia until the tears ran down our faces I continued to wonder silently: 'How can you manage to be friends with a person of my origins, knowing your own past?'

I did not ask this question out loud, and I ask it here now only with a great feeling of diffidence. While I was in London the trial of Eichmann was running in Jerusalem. Sometimes I saw opening up behind my friends the wilderness of horror on the edge of which every adult Jew who is our contemporary lives. At such moments one comprehends that for them every rapprochement with a former National Socialist must be an undertaking fraught with anguish. What kind of behaviour, I wonder, do their dead expect of them? Must it not mean everpresent grief to live one's life accountable to the victims? And would not flight from this accountability lead also into grief?

My friends are kindly people. They must sometimes want to escape into forgetfulness, not out of frivolity but out of the natural kindness of their natures, and from such a distance they would also like to forgive. But I believe that they feel they have no power to grant the *absolvo te* to which their hearts may urge them, to one person or another. The dead at their backs are too powerful because of their awesomely great numbers. What individual could dare to speak on their behalf?

It is this anguish which every Jew must bring with him as his portion wherever he forms a friendship with Germans, and this anguish must be painfully aggravated when the person has a past like mine.

The anguish of the Germans, their dowry, is the burden of guilt which cannot be endured. One can only live with it because human nature, concerned with self preservation, never absorbs more than a part of this guilt, just as water only takes up a specific quantity of salt.

When I was with my friends in London, I was often forced to think that we exist, they and I, where in fact it has become impossible to exist — over an abyss of sorrow and over an abyss of guilt. But we live and, as I said, we have even laughed heartily together. That this is so I take to be a reflection of the basic paradox of human existence. And I dare (though always in the grip of that fear which visits those who behold a miracle), I dare to hope for a lasting dialogue in which sympathy may lead to trust and trust to truthfulness. Only this could establish the mutual 'recognition' (in the biblical sense) which may perhaps enable Jews and Germans, despite everything, to live together and to love one another.

During the trial of Eichmann I frequently talked to the seventeen-year-old daughter of a Hitler Youth comrade of mine who was shot down as a pilot shortly before the end of the war. One day the girl asked me to describe the particular characteristics of her father, whose friend I had been. I gave her an honest picture of a humorous, helpful, somewhat lazy and not exactly tidy but thoroughly decent man who was particularly fond of animals.

"And was he a real Nazi?" asked the girl.

"Yes," I replied, "he was a convinced National Socialist."

"But you said he was helpful and thoroughly decent..."

For the young people who look at their parents, secretly asking: "So you were a National Socialist?" there are contradictions which we should not try to gloss over.

This problem faces me with the following question: Should I have replied to the girl: "You are only looking at one side of the question. National Socialism was not as horrible and deeply evil as, say, the trial of Eichmann shows. It also contained good elements. For example, what attracted your father and myself was, amongst other things, the fact that it sought to realize a National Community or that it taught us to make sacrifices for something beyond our own selfish aims"?

Probably, then, my friend's daughter would have answered: "Then National Socialism wasn't half as bad as they tell us in school and everywhere else."

To arrive at this conclusion from my correction would not only be a hasty and crude oversimplification, it would also open the door to a dangerous error. Would it then have been better to ignore the contradiction which had troubled the girl and which was the starting point of our conversation? No, that too would be wrong.

Because one day it could happen that someone who wants to stir up trouble will come and say to the young people who were only children at the end of the war: "Look at your parents. Do you believe they are villains or fools? No, of course not. But you know that they were National Socialists. Your schools and the so called mass media have been telling you ever since you can remember that National Socialism was the rule of the devil. You yourselves did not experience it, so you cannot check if these statements are true. But you know your parents better than anything else, and you believe they are decent people. Do you believe they would voluntarily have served the rule of the devil? There is something wrong somewhere. In other words it cannot be true that National Socialism was a bad thing. The democrats have been serving you up with that fairy story for long enough..."

Such an argument seems to have a fatal logic about it. One must therefore guard against this by trying to explain to the young people in more detail what happened in the Third Reich. My reply to the seventeen-year-old girl I mentioned just now was something like this: "Your father and I and countless other Germans hoped that Hitler would 'save' our nation. As you know, it was a question of 'saving' us from the postwar economic crisis and from an internal strife that was even more destructive than the one France has suffered during the past decade. We dreamed then of a strong Germany, respected amongst the nations not from fear but from admiration — and Hitler promised to fulfil this dream for us. Dreams are something dangerous in politics. They stop the dreamer from seeing what is really happening. Hitler whipped up our yearning political dream into a fanatical passion. When he had succeeded in doing this we followed him blindly. 'Now you are mine,' he once said. In this state of bondage we had forfeited our freedom of conscience. We were prepared to make any sacrifices for Germany, and your father sacrificed his life, but we did not realize that Hitler had betrayed our dream of the Reich. He was possessed by an insane lust for power, and he dragged us into a brutal war of conquest at the end of which Germany's political and moral greatness had been totally destroyed.

"Your father was a good man. He was good in the same way that many people of all nations are. But he had one weakness which is typically German. He allowed himself to be carried away by romantic ideas of Germany's future and avoided informing himself sufficiently about politics. That is the only reason why Hitler was able to involve him in his own fanaticism. That was the catastrophe. Even a person of particular integrity and kindliness can be induced by fanaticism to do evil, because the fanatic believes that the end justifies the means. He keeps his eyes fixed on a single goal, as if bewitched, and becomes blind and deaf to everything else. The evil done by people like your father, who were in themselves good, resulted from them blinding themselves to the suffering which Hitler's brutal power politics inflicted on his enemies, such as the Jews or the Poles."

If I try to put myself in your place I believe I can see what you will find difficult to accept in my words to this girl, and indeed often in the whole of this report. I must now try to grasp one last important idea. Many of those who suffered under National Socialism perhaps even today build up the inner strength they need to endure the creeping poison of this suffering (which is still active) by regarding Hitler as the incarnation of evil. Nothing could be more understandable.

How often in the history of the West have men who were subjected to terrible suffering by a man of power believed they could see in him the Antichrist. Is the suffering made more bearable by such a view? It certainly does not become more meaningful, but the soul destroying senselessness of it is perhaps mitigated if one can say to oneself: Such profound wickedness can only be the work of Satan, who seeks his victims among the innocent. And whenever the survivors of such periods of suffering look back on their dead, it takes away a little of the annihilating horror from their grief if they can say: "You are not the victims of a catastrophic combination of senseless accidents. The power which crushed you revealed itself thereby as that of ultimate evil, which fights against a more human future for mankind. If there is any meaning at all in history — however hidden it may be — then the witness of your suffering will serve as a guide to those whose task it is to fight for the fulfilment of this meaning."

What is the object of these remarks? I must once again speak of myself in order to explain what I mean. In the course of my report you must have recognized that I, that is someone whose average harmlessness of character you would not dispute, clung with passionate devotion to the man in whom you saw the embodiment of evil. And you have further seen that in the service he commanded I have done many things which — taken in themselves — must be called 'good' rather than 'evil'. And finally you have followed me, in reading this report, into situations in which I displayed a callousness which was alien both to myself and you and therefore terrifying.

271

Why do I emphasize this point so much? Because I believe that here we must recognize something very important: we encounter good and evil, if we look back on these descriptions, interlocking in a way which makes them hard to disentangle.

Perhaps the most important and certainly the most terrifying realization the last decades have forced upon us is that we can no longer distinguish neatly between those who are evil and those who are good. Amongst those who, as the executors of the 'Final Solution to the Jewish Question', allowed themselves to be misused for the routine handling of unspeakable acts of cruelty, there were demonstrably affectionate fathers of families who grew flowers in their spare time and were particularly fond of animals.

The head of the 'Central Authority for the Publication of National Socialist Crimes', a high legal office of the Federal Republic, recently said the following in a press interview about the men against whom his office had brought proceedings (all without exception were cases of murder and other very serious crimes of violence): "Before the court stand carefully dressed fathers of families, apparently harmless citizens, most of whom live respectably and are well thought of by their neighbours. They appear to be fully normal people, who look so utterly different and behave so utterly differently from common murderers."

Or think of certain accounts of the Spanish Civil War. There the sons of the most distinguished families in the country, who called themselves without conscious hypocrisy the defenders of Christian culture, committed the most abominable atrocities. (The deeds of cruelty performed by the other side are not relevant here.)

What I learned about myself and what we all should learn, even those of us who are not forced to such self discovery, is that the frontier between good and evil can run straight through the middle of us without our being aware of this. None of us — not even the most educated, sensitive and cultivated, not even the pious man — should feel immune from the possibility of one day, too, becoming the blind and cold hearted servant of evil. I do not intend with this statement to insult all those who remained aloof during the Third Reich from every kind of collaboration with the evil power. We know of many who gave their lives because they would not become entangled in the guilt. And many — many, thank God! — were able to keep their hands clean without having to make this ultimate sacrifice, though they had to make many others.

Perhaps it is not easy for these guiltless people to understand what I mean. They have not felt themselves shuddering to the marrow with deathly horror at the realization that you too, you yourself, who believed you loved beauty, wanted to help the poor and weak, strove to be a true friend... even you were capable of murder! You learned to look past the half starving Polish children as if they were tree stumps and you did not even permit yourself to be horrified when you looked into the ghettoes. That is just the behaviour of a potential 'ideological murderer'. When one has once experienced that, one trembles for the goodness of good people all over the world. Not only amongst one's own nation. Is there — one asks oneself — any guarantee that evil will not one day conquer them? And wherein would such a guarantee lie?

I did not mention the concentration camp commandant who was in private life a lover of children, animals and flowers because I thought, say, that the dark side of his terrible life was redeemed by these attractive features. And I do not believe that it reduces my own guilt when I can prove that nature has endowed me with a good intelligence, an appreciation of human qualities, a taste for music, and so on. My callousness towards the Polish children is not mitigated by the fact that I was writing lyrical poems then about — for instance — a moonlit night. Quite the reverse.

Do you understand what I am trying to express? The ghastly thing was just the fact that it was not gangsters and roughnecks, but decent, intelligent and moral people who allowed themselves to be induced to acquiesce in something deeply evil and to serve it.

That is what I should like to say to every good person. Not with the implication: 'Your goodness has feet of clay just as much as mine had', but rather to implore him: 'Be on your guard.' Take warning. There is nowhere any good thing — however worthy of respect it may seem — which one may serve with the means of evil (that is of lovelessness).

A few weeks ago someone who was amongst the foremost youth leaders of the Third Reich wrote to me: 'Leave it to posterity to decide the rights and wrongs of it. We are too near to the events to be able to judge objectively.'

There is something tempting about this point of view. But I believe it is wrong. If there is the merest spark of hope that individuals and nations may learn from history, then it is not the dissertations of the historians which are going to give the instructive stimulus in fifty years' time — all the less so as time passes more and more quickly. Those who were there and who have striven for detachment and critical evaluation must now speak. They must point to the mistakes they recognize and their causes, to the confusions and the mesh of guilt. Even if they still cannot manage to master the emotion which accompanies such looking and thinking back, or constantly maintain the tone of balanced objectivity.

For anyone who has once gone astray so disastrously in their political views as I have, to pass judgement — in the sense I have given my remarks here — is a risk. I was recently asked if the thought never occurred to me that I might be erring in my judgement all over again and could therefore be obliged to recant later. I replied: "No one is proof against making political errors at any time, but wherever one is concerned with people living together — and politics also covers this — there is always a simple commandment and with it a yardstick: human kindness. Where it is sinned against callously, the politics are wrong. Anyone who does not endeavour to avoid wars at all costs, anyone who locks up political opponents or tortures them in other ways just because of their opinions, anyone who out of lust for power or frivolity inflicts suffering on members of his own or of foreign nations, however tempting may be the political idea he advocates, I will in future always be opposed to him."

What I have written during the last few pages does not claim to give a complete analysis of National Socialism. This will indeed be left to the historians, and it will be possible to do it more precisely in thirty years' time than today or ten years hence.

Who would dispute this? I certainly would not. Nevertheless I am sorry to see how many of my old friends, whose moral integrity I do not doubt, have entrenched themselves behind the view: 'Let posterity judge'. The tempting argument that contemporaries can never reach an objective judgement soothes them if they are afraid of the effort and the risk of coming to grips with the past wholeheartedly.

As I have been writing to you I have been worried lest the motives which make me write to you may perhaps, without my being aware of it myself, contain some impulse towards self justification. Efforts of this kind plunge a person into a state of schizophrenia. While he is condemning himself with genuine remorse, he suddenly hears a voice saying to him: "But all that is nonsense. After all, you did your best. Look round in the world. The struggle for power leads to dehumanization everywhere."

If you have felt now and again, as you were reading, that an impulse towards self justification had crept in, I beg you to reflect that I have striven to describe to you a painful process of inner reorientation which has taken many years. In the course of such a development there is progress and retreat and then more progress. Perhaps this report is itself a final element of the process; perhaps you may consider that there are some areas onto which I must throw more light and realize that my reorientation is not fully successful there. I consider it possible that the process I have spoken of may have to be taken still further. But let me assure you once more: the thought that I might (consciously or unconsciously) have attempted to justify myself in your eyes fills me with shame.

Afterword

by Marianne Schweitzer Burkenroad with Helen Epstein

Melita Maschmann's account of why she became a Nazi is addressed to a Jewish friend and classmate who left Germany in 1939. Readers have speculated whether this was a literary device or perhaps a composite of several girls. For me, there has never been a question because I was that Jewish friend. Melita and I met in April of 1933 in Berlin's Hohenzollern Oberlyzeum when we were both 15 years old and I was Marianne Schweitzer.

For a very long time after the war I didn't think about our relationship. I left Germany in 1939, went to college and graduate school in the U.S., married, and had three children. But now, with the republication of Melita's book, my friendship with the idealistic friend of my adolescence has caused me to reflect.

Marianne's parents, Ernst and Franziska in 1938
(courtesy Marianne Schweitzer Burkenroad)

In January of 1933, when Hitler came to power, I was living with my parents Ernst and Franziska Körte Schweitzer, my older

276

sister Gabriele, and my younger brothers Eike and Christoph in a small house in Westend, Berlin. My sister Rele and I attended the Staatliche Augustaschule Gymnasium where she was a stellar student and I was nearly flunking Latin and math.

In the outside world, there was the burning of the Reichstag in February, followed by mass arrests of opponents of the Nazis, and the first deportations to concentration camps. In my personal world that April, my mother had the good sense to have me transferred to the less demanding Hohenzollern Oberlyzeum where Melita became one of my new classmates.

She soon was my best friend. We did homework together, discussed "Dichter und Denker" (poets and philosophers), wrote each other letters and exchanged confidences in the passionate way of adolescent girls. We both idolized our female literature teacher Dr. Flashar.

We were very different girls. Melita was quick, articulate, and gregarious – a joiner. I was more of a listener and observer. "Marianne is a book locked with seven seals," she once complained to my mother. While we were still in school Melita told me about a failed love relationship she had suffered and chided me for being interested in boys. Was she perhaps jealous? I don't know.

Melita often came to my house after school. Her father was a businessman; mine was a physician. My mother had wide-ranging intellectual and cultural interests and another classmate, Annemarie Meichsner Lancelle, later wrote: "My earlier relationship to modern art was closely linked to my friendship to Marianne S. from my class. The outstanding pictures in her parents' cultivated, half-Jewish house had a greater impact on me than museum visits."

I think that Melita was bored by her conventional and conservative parents, and that Nazism provided a way for her to rebel but still conform to their nationalist views. She believed — as did many others at the time — that Hitler would remedy the shame of the Versailles Treaty and restore pride to Germany. He said he would unify the many political parties, and provide jobs for everyone, in part by getting rid of the "foreign" Jewish element and Melita saw Jews as competitors in many fields where Germans were unemployed.

My friend began to attend Nazi rallies and kept trying to persuade me to go with her. Then she joined the League of German Girls, and became what I called a 150% Nazi. I very briefly attended meetings of an anti-Nazi youth group, but I was not by nature drawn to groups. I also thought Hitler was a hysterical fanatic and couldn't understand why Melita was impressed by him or the Nazi Party.

In addition, I looked down on the Nazis for reasons of cultural snobbery. I thought they had betrayed the Germany of "Dichter und Denker" by their ignorance. They burned the books of the best German writers and condemned many great artists and musicians. One of those they accused of creating "degenerate art" was my uncle, the sculptor Gerhard Marcks.

I expressed my disdain in minor acts of defiance. Dr. Zorn, the director of the Lyzeum, accused me of deliberately coming up the back staircase with both hands on my bicycle to avoid performing the obligatory "Heil Hitler" salute. Melita said I couldn't understand Hitler's greatness because of my "Jewish blood."

Until a year earlier, I had no idea I had "Jewish blood." Although we were not a churchgoing family, we observed Christmas and Easter in the traditional ways and belonged to the Lutheran church. My parents, my three siblings and I were all baptized and I took confirmation classes with Martin Niemöller, the former U-boat commander and his brother who substituted when Martin was in prison for anti-Nazi activities.

It was in 1932 that my sister Rele provoked my father to reveal our Jewish ancestry for the first time. She played the violin and had rejected a violin teacher because he "looked too Jewish." Our father had responded in a rather convoluted way by saying

"Don't you know that your grandmother came from the same people as Jesus...?"

Algunde Hollaender, Marianne's grandmother
(courtesy Marianne Schweitzer Burkenroad)

Our mother's side, the Körtes, were "Aryan" by Hitler's standards. But our father's parents, Eugen Schweitzer and Algunde Hollaender, were Jews born in Poland who had been baptized as adults. My father and his two brothers were considered Jews by Hitler's laws. Though all were married to non-Jewish wives, our lives were dramatically changed. The whole family was devastated and worried about our future. My mother's "Aryan" side stood by my father. My Körte grandmother said, "If Hitler is against Ernst, I am against Hitler."

We heard no anti-Jewish remarks at home, but the anti-semitism of that time was so pervasive and the images in periodicals such as Der Stürmer so ugly, that Rele later wrote of her shock at learning her relation to "monsters." She considered herself "the typical German girl with blond, curly hair" and didn't suspect she was "connected in any way with world Jewry." I took the news more in stride. I was happy to be able to stay in school and glad not to be eligible to join the Hitler Youth.

According to Hitler, I was a Mischling: half Aryan; half Jew. I learned that the Jewish teachers that had once taught at the Lyzeum had all been dismissed before my arrival, along with most of the Jewish girls who had once comprised one third of the student body. There were only three of us "with Jewish blood" left. One of the non-Jews, Maria Nietert, who helped me pass my final math exam, told me that except for herself, everyone in our class became a Nazi including Dr. Flashar.

In September of 1935, the Nuremberg Laws were introduced. My "Jewish" father was barred from treating "Aryan" patients, employing "Aryans," attending concerts or the theater, or using public transportation. Rele had passed her Abitur, the certification of completing a high school degree but as a Mischling, was ineligible to attend university. She couldn't marry her "Aryan" boyfriend Hans, a medical student. Both were members of an illegal anti-fascist youth group called "dj 1.11."

In 1936, Melita suddenly disappeared from school. I was very upset that she had left without a word to me, her best friend. When I questioned Dr. Flashar, she was evasive. The Maschmanns, she explained, had decided that Melita needed a more rigorous academic preparation for her Abitur and had transferred her to a boarding school. (In her memoir, Melita writes that they sent her away to curtail her Nazi activities).

Marianne in 1937 (courtesy Marianne Schweitzer Burkenroad)

Melita reappeared at our house in the fall of 1937 saying that she wished to renew our friendship. In fact, as she later confessed to me, she had been engaged by the Gestapo to spy on us. In her memoir, she writes that she was summoned by the Gestapo and told that an anti-Nazi organization met at our home. Since Melita had access, it was her duty to find out what was going on.

The Schweitzers' house, at Ebereschenallee 9, Westend, Berlin
(courtesy Marianne Schweitzer Burkenroad)

As I remember it, I was surprised to see her and not very receptive. On the evening of November 1, there was a loud knocking on our door and a contingent of Gestapo men began a search of our house. They had expected to find a secret meeting but found only myself, my mother and my siblings. They arrested Rele and took some books and papers – among them my diary! My mother had the presence of mind to telephone my father and tell him to remain at his office. I asked him to find Melita and warn her that the Gestapo had my diaries in which she appeared.

The next day I went to the police prison on the Alexanderplatz with my sister's nightgown and toothbrush as one would to a patient in a hospital. She was arrested for conspiracy to commit high treason and sent to Lichtenburg prison, near Torgau where she remained until July of 1938. My mother was also arrested but released after a week. I fetched her from prison and will never forget how shabby she looked and how badly she smelled. I still feel ashamed to have been so repelled by her appearance. She was terribly shaken. She had been held in isolation the entire time. The interrogator told her over and over again that her daughter had confessed. She had no idea to what, of course.

It was my mother, not my father, who accomplished the complicated task of getting all the papers together for emigration. She also began to study physical therapy and encouraged me to learn photography and cooking – skills she thought would be useful in other countries.

My father was 50 and deep into his study of Freudian psychoanalysis. Rele did not want to leave without Hans, who was completing his medical studies. My mother wouldn't leave without my younger brother Eike who — although a Mischling — was required to serve in the military or without our younger brother Christoph who she thought was too young to travel alone. I was the only one in the family who wanted to leave, although I was afraid; I had always dreamed of living in California.

Then came Kristallnacht. In November of 1938, my father and his brother Kurt were among the 30,000 Jewish men beaten up, arrested and sent to concentration camps in attacks on Jews throughout Germany. Seven weeks later he was released through the intervention of my mother's brother. His head was shaved. He had a bad cough and a ruptured hernia. He left for England in March of 1939.

I followed him to London in August, saw him a couple of times and then took the train to Liverpool where I boarded the Cunard White Star. Two days later, the ship began to zig-zag. It was September 1. Hitler had invaded Poland and England declared war on Germany. I suddenly realized that I now was completely cut off and on my own. Seeing the lights on the American shore and passing the Statue of Liberty were emotional moments for me. We landed on the fifth of September, 1939.

No one met me in New York but friends had arranged for financial help and a place for me to live. I soon had a part-time job as a waitress at Schrafft's restaurant and was studying

English. An organization helping refugees asked me whether I wanted to go to college. I was not sure what that meant but said "yes" as a matter of course. I was accepted on scholarship at Bryn Mawr, entered after Thanksgiving of 1939, and graduated in three years, part of the class of 1942.

Marianne in September 1939 (courtesy Marianne Schweitzer Burkenroad)

I spent the rest of the war years taking a master's degree in anthropology at Yale. My father arrived in New York in January 1940, became a Jungian analyst and practiced almost to the day of his death in 1981. My mother and Christoph arrived in New York in 1944 after a long sojourn in Cuba. She worked as a physical therapist in New York. My brother Eike died as a German soldier on the Russian front. Rele and Hans remained in Germany and started a family before the war's end.

In 1947, I married Martin David Burkenroad, a marine biologist and secular Jew. I was very busy and no longer thinking about Melita at all when I received a letter from her, via my mother, in October of 1948. Melita obtained her address from my sculptor uncle Gerhard Marcks, who had an exhibit in Darmstadt where Melita was living. My mother passed the letter on to me without comment. "Eleven years of world history have passed," Melita wrote. "Then we were children, now we are people who have been marked by life... Is it possible to go back to the great friendship of our youth?"

In February of 1950, she wrote me another letter, in which she confessed to spying on us.

"Believe me I was shocked about this assignment," Melita wrote. "I refused again and again, protesting that I would not spy on people who had been my friends. The Gestapo man responded that I should sacrifice my personal inclination for higher goals. I did it but with a heavy heart. I was also convinced that I would not be successful.

"Looking back I should have known that there would be a house search and that I had an obligation to warn you. Some days later I met your father who told me that Rele had been arrested; that the Gestapo had confiscated your diaries in which you presumably had written about our conversations, and that I should tell the truth if asked."

She also wrote me: "After 1945 I was in prison and political camps for two and three-quarter years, insisting that I was a convinced and active Nazi until the collapse. I was found guilty because of my activity as a leader in the Hitler youth organization. I knew better and didn't consider myself innocently incarcerated like others. During these five years I realized how we lived under the spell of our ideas and obligations. It is shocking to realize how this being bewitched affects our ethical behavior and leads us to evil action in the belief that it is necessary and correct to act so. I will always remain in your debt. I never stopped to wish you the best."

I did not reply but Melita continued to write to Rele in Germany, and to my mother in New York.

In June 1950 I received another letter via my mother: "I have always been ashamed about what happened in 1937. My parents would have been 71 years old. They suffocated in the cellar. I was the only one of many who escaped."

In August 1950: "I am happy that you are in the U.S. and say nix to all things German while I try to heal the breaks with people and renew our friendship."

In 1954, we moved to Panama where Martin had a job as a shrimp fisheries consultant to the Food and Agriculture Organization of the U.N. My youngest child was five months old. I taught German at the National University of Panama and was active as a volunteer at the National Museum of Anthropology.

Although I never replied, Melita continued to write to me: about her memories of the Schweitzer family, about heart and kidney problems, about attending classes at the University of Frankfurt, and writing newspaper articles. She mentioned a novel she was writing with characters named Peter Schweitzer and Marianne: "Not you but the book deals with my former foolishness and unkindness and break of trust due to political duty." By the 1960s, she was mentioning her interest in visiting India and Afghanistan.

In 1963, I was invited by the Goethe Institute to visit Germany, together with other teachers of German from Latin America. It was my first trip to Germany since emigrating in 1939 and I was anxious to reconnect with family members who had remained there, including my sister and her family. I took my three children with me and left them with Rele near Stuttgart. Then, utterly exhausted, I joined the German teachers from Brazil in Munich.

I did not like what we were shown of the German school system. I made a point of looking at the history books they used and found very little about Hitler or the war. Nobody I encountered admitted to having been a Nazi or knowing anything about concentration camps. Our Munich landlady told me and the two Brazilian teachers who accompanied me "I had no idea about the existence of the [nearby] concentration camp in Dachau." And of course she had not been a party member.

Melita must have heard about my trip through Rele, and begged me to come see her. I don't remember how I got to Darmstadt but in April of 1963 — 30 years after we first met — I went. The two of us were alone and I spent most of a day and an entire night reading *Account Rendered* in manuscript.

To say our meeting did not go too well would be an understatement. I was utterly shocked by what I read in her memoir. I hadn't realized the extent of her activities during the war. I was confused, hurt, overwhelmed, and unable to talk about it. She cried when we said good-bye. I did not. In retrospect, I would say she behaved in a direct straightforward way and I did not. Although I stayed longer in Germany with my sister's family, I never saw her again.

I returned to Panama and we moved to La Jolla, California. In 1964, I became an Instructor of German at the University of California, San Diego and became active as a volunteer at the San Diego Museum of Man. I was the mother of three teenagers and disinclined to enter into the emotional turmoil of a relationship with Melita, even though she kept on writing to me from India where she became a follower of an Indian guru. I rejected her attempts to renew our relationship and, though I remained fond of my German relatives, I rejected Germany.

In December of 1964, after her memoir was published, Melita wrote me from a hospital where she was being treated for a gall bladder infection. She called herself a "Schreiberling" – a scribbler – who wrote many letters, kept a diary, and regarded her books as her literary children. We remained different in that regard as well.

I did not write about myself until 2006. I started work on an autobiography and was going through all my papers — my certificate of baptism, June 9, 1918; my confirmation certificate, March 3, 1934 (signed by Niemöller); the telegram of acceptance from Bryn Mawr College, November 5, 1939; my diploma from

Yale, June 16, 1945 — when I came upon Melita's letters. I typed up what interested me, then threw out the originals. I didn't think they would be of interest to anyone. I am now very sorry that I didn't keep at least one.

Marianne in 2008 (courtesy Marianne Schweitzer Burkenroad)

Thinking about it now, 80 years after we first met, I can say that Melita's betrayal and Hitler's destruction of what I valued in Germany are reasons why I do not think of myself as a German. I am impressed with the achievements of post-Hitler Germany but it is just another country in my mind now, like France or Spain.

As far as Melita is concerned, even though we never renewed our friendship I have to give her credit for having the courage to write and publish *Account Rendered* at the time she did. In 1963 nobody I met admitted to having been a Nazi and Melita's friends warned her not to publish such a book. She may have been the first German and certainly the first German woman who tried to face her past with honesty. No other book at that time said unequivocally "I was a Nazi and here's why." I respected her. I am certainly treated well in her memoir, with insight and respect. Melita eventually came to be horrified by Nazism and I believe she really meant the book as an apology.

Melita Maschmann (1918-2010) was born in Berlin and attended boarding school in Thuringia. She joined the BDM (Bund Deutscher Mädel, the Girls' Section of the Hitler Youth) secretly in 1933 against the wishes of her parents who were conservative and nationalist, but not national-socialist. She worked for the Labor Service in East Prussia (1936-37), then as a journalist for the press section of the BDM (1937-41) in Frankfurt-an-der-Oder and in the Wartheland (German-occupied Poland). She was in charge of women's Labor Service camps in Poland and Germany (1941-43) and responsible for the BDM's press and propaganda division in Berlin (1943-45). She did war work, including preparation for "Werewolf" (S.S. sabotage) activities (1945) before the US Army captured her in Austria in July 1945 with a clandestine group manufacturing false documents for "comrades". She was interned in the "Frauenlager 77" (internment camp for women) near Ludwigsburg, and later in Darmstadt until 1948. Denazification authorities considered her a "follower" ("indoctrinated" and too young to be fully responsible); Maschmann finally broke with National Socialism only in the 1950s. After her release, Maschmann wrote for the *Darmstädter Echo* and the *Frankfurter Rundschau*. She travelled to Afghanistan and India in 1962-63 and moved permanently to India shortly thereafter, becoming a follower of Guru Sri Anandamayi Ma. In India, Maschmann lived mainly in her ashrams, and after Sri Anandamayi Ma's death in 1982, worked in institutions for children. She returned to Darmstadt in 1998 due to Alzheimer's disease and died in a retirement home. She was never married and had no children.

Account Rendered was first published in 1963 as *Fazit: Kein Rechtfertigungsversuch* (No attempt at justification), translated into several languages, and republished seven times in Germany where it became a required high school text. Maschmann also wrote fiction (*Die Aschenspur, Der Dreizehnte, Das Wort Hiess Liebe*) and books about Sri Anandamayi Ma and India (*Der Tiger singt Kirtana, Indiras Schwestern, Eine ganz gewöhnliche Heilige*).

Helen Epstein (www.helenepstein.com) was born in Prague in 1947 and was educated in New York City and Jerusalem. A veteran journalist, she is the author of the books *Children of the Holocaust, Where She Came From: A Daughter's Search for Her Mother's History, Joe Papp* and *Music Talks,* editor of *Archivist on a Bicycle,* and translator from the Czech of Heda Kovály's *Under A Cruel Star: A Life in Prague, 1941-1968* and Vlasta Schönová's *Acting in Terezín.*

Plunkett Lake Press titles
available as eBooks

By **Lucie Aubrac**
Outwitting the Gestapo

By **Jean-Denis Bredin**
The Affair: The Case of Alfred Dreyfus

By **Lucy S. Dawidowicz**
From That Place and Time: A Memoir, 1938-1947

By **Inge Deutschkron**
Outcast: A Jewish Girl in Wartime Berlin

By **Alfred Döblin**
Destiny's Journey

By **Amos Elon**
Herzl

By **Helen Epstein**
Children of the Holocaust
Where She Came From: A Daughter's Search for Her Mother's
History

By **Charles Fenyvesi**
When The World Was Whole: Three Centuries of Memories

By **Sebastian Haffner**
Defying Hitler: A Memoir
Germany: Jekyll and Hyde
The Ailing Empire: Germany from Bismarck to Hitler
The Meaning of Hitler

By **Anthony Heilbut**
Exiled in Paradise: German Refugee Artists and Intellectuals in America from the 1930s to the Present

By **Eva Hoffman**
Lost in Translation

By **Heda Margolius Kovály**
Under A Cruel Star: A Life in Prague, 1941-1968

By **Peter Kurth**
American Cassandra: The Life of Dorothy Thompson

By **Jeffrey Mehlman**
Émigré New York: French Intellectuals in Wartime Manhattan, 1940-1944

By **Kurt Mendelssohn**
The World of Walther Nernst: The Rise and Fall of German Science 1864-1941

By **Vlasta Schönová**
Acting in Terezín

By **Dietrich Stoltzenberg**
Fritz Haber: Chemist, Nobel Laureate, German, Jew

By **Susan Rubin Suleiman**
Budapest Diary: In Search of the Motherbook

By **Dorothy Thompson**
Listen, Hans

By **Claudine Vegh**
I Didn't Say Goodbye

By **Richard Willstätter**
From My Life: The Memoirs of Richard Willstätter

By **Joseph Wechsberg**
The Vienna I Knew: Memories of a European Childhood

By **Chaim Weizmann**
Trial and Error: The Autobiography of Chaim Weizmann

By **Robert S. Wistrich**
The Jews of Vienna in the Age of Franz Joseph

By **Charlotte Wolff**
Hindsight: An Autobiography

By **Susan Zuccotti**
The Holocaust, the French, and the Jews

By **Stefan Zweig**
The World of Yesterday

For more information, visit
www.plunkettlakepress.com

9 780961 469641